WALKING
WITH THE
WISE II™

**70 Inspirational Mentors and Millionaires
Teach the Secrets of Prosperity in Business
and Life!**

Compiled by

Linda Forsythe

and

Lena Osborn

MENTORS Publishing House, Inc.
San Diego, California

Need Inspiration Information or Mentoring?

Visit our Web site!

www.mentorsmagazine.com

- **FREE** newsletters filled with guidance, from our nationally recognized mentors

- **FREE** online subscription to MENTORS magazine

- **FREE LIVE TELESEMINARS** by mentors and millionaires who interact and coach you toward success

- Connections with Mentors Worldwide

www.mentorsmagazine.com

www.mentorsmagazine.com

Dedication

Walking with the Wise II is dedicated
to anyone who has the desire
to be successful in business
and to experience a life
of prosperity with peace.

WALKING WITH THE WISE II ™

Copyright 2004 Mentors Publishing House, Inc.

ISBN 0-9729875-2-5

Printed in the United States of America

8 7 6 5 4 3 2 1 – 1 0 9

Published by MENTORS Publishing House, Inc.

This book is available at quantity discounts for bulk purchases and for branding by businesses and organizations. For further information, or to learn more about Mentors magazine™, mentorsmagazine.com™, Walking with the Wise™ *and other products and services of Mentors Publishing House, Inc, contact:*

MENTORS Publishing House, Inc.
11115 Affinity Court, Suite 6
San Diego, CA 92131
Telephone: (858) 549-9222
e-mail: publications@mentorsmagazine.com
Web: www.mentorsmagazine.com

Graphic Design, Art Direction by Bonnie Owen
Mentors Lighthouse Logo Design by Sam Defais
Illustrations by Kim Muslusky

The publisher would like to acknowledge the many publishers and individuals who granted us permission to reprint their cited material or have written specifically for this book.

Foreword

What if you KNEW you could do it?

By Linda Forsythe

I am going to divulge a secret that people who have obtained greatness all throughout history knew. This secret is the same for individuals who have made major scientific discoveries, overcome insurmountable obstacles, accomplished incredible feats of physical strength, become heroes against overwhelming odds or manifested miracles throughout our time here on earth. These people, many times, weren't blessed with what we would call superior intelligence or physical abilities. More often than not...it was quite the opposite. What was it that they had, that made them different? What was the secret for their accomplishments?

They KNEW...they absolutely KNEW...with unwavering faith that there was a way and an answer. They KNEW...they absolutely KNEW...that they were going to accomplish their goal. Sometimes they weren't sure HOW they were going to do it...they just knew it would happen. There was absolute conviction they were going to make it somehow. Failure was not an option. Temporary set backs were very temporary because the final goal was in site. Just like a man stranded in a desert without water for days...nothing will deter him from reaching his goal for survival when he can see the oasis with refreshing water in front of him. Focus is laser straight. Determination is absolute. Faith is unwavering.

What if I told you that YOU have that same power for greatness? I don't care what it is that you want to accomplish...you CAN do it. I want you to take a moment to visualize something. Think about one goal you would like to accomplish. Picture in your mind what it looks like. What does it feel like? Now...imagine or dream in your mind that someone is walking up to you who has a mystical air about them. You can see that this person has an inner light and somehow has an endless sight into the future. You can feel their power emanating and you suddenly feel at peace. Then this mystical person says to you, "I can see your destiny. You have been placed here on this earth to make a significant difference for good. You will accomplish _____. It is pre-ordained and it must happen. You may have difficulties on your journey, but fear not because you will be watched over and guided. "Resonate with this thought for while. How would you act if you KNEW....ABSOLUTELY KNEW with unwavering faith that there was a way to realize a worthy dream?

Here is something else for you to think about...Whenever a major discovery happened in history, the answer already existed for an eternity.

When man discovered the wheel, (I'm assuming it was a man), the answer was already floating out there in the universe somewhere...he just tapped into it and took the action to bring it into something tangible. What about discovery for space travel, radio waves, electricity, medical treatments or even feelings of peace? All these things or ideas already existed. When it was conceived of and acted upon...the idea manifested into our reality. The ability was there...it was just discovered and brought into being. This has been an on-going truth since man walked the earth.

Dear reader...you have the power right now to bring into being anything you want. I am not mystical...I just know. We all have the power but unfortunately most of us do not use it. We just don't seem to believe it. We don't seem to have the faith. But it's there...kind of floating around inside and all around you right now!!!

Looking back on the early days when the seed of a dream was planted in my mind to start Mentors magazine...I had spent a great deal of time trying to find encouragement and motivation to start. I was a single mom without any publishing background and zero ability to borrow money. The line of people who advised me to NOT start something of this magnitude were extensive and formidable. Yet...something inside kept urging me forward. I can't explain it. All I remember is that I KNEW I COULD DO IT. I couldn't shake it. It didn't make sense. It continued to plague me until I just couldn't stand it any longer. I knew there was a way to do this AND create a better life for myself and my children.

Ten years have passed since the beginning of that dream. Mistakes and set-backs happened – some that were quite severe – but failure never was an option. I didn't quit. My past history of homelessness, fear, exhaustion and constant worry, was not something I EVER wanted to experience again. I was aware that I could easily fall into that dark pit of despair again if allowed. This alone encouraged me to keep my mind on track and to keep looking forward. A valuable lesson learned, (albeit in hind-sight) is if I had ever taken the time to LISTEN to and learn from the many accomplished individuals who already traveled through the "school of hard-knocks" I wouldn't have had to nurse so many wounds.

Because of the nature of MENTORS magazine....I was blessed with a multitude of mentors who came into my life. Some of the advice given wasn't easy to hear. But it was the mentors who pointed me in the right direction. It was through the combination of unshakable faith, an inner knowing or "gut" feeling and the loving continual guidance of these mentors...that the world-wide empire of MENTORS International became a reality.

Through the trials and hard lessons...many truths came to fruition. It is my responsibility to pass these truths onto you. Please don't learn the hard way!!! The hard way hurts...believe me. If you have a passion, a dream, a genuine desire to make matters better...then seriously apply these truths to your to your inner being:

- **Don't ever give up!!!** Everything throughout history that has ever been discovered came because of persistence. Do what ever it takes to stay motivated. Read, listen to tapes, change your thinking, repeat affirmations, put reminders around you, meditate and pray.

- **If it isn't working...then try another path**. Keep in mind that persistence doesn't mean you keep doing the same things over and over again if they don't work. The Bible says: "But wisdom is shown to be truth by what results from it." (Matthew 11:19) So many people keep trying the same thing over and over again thinking they will get different results. If you do the same thing, you will get the same results. A seed will grow into what it was meant to be....PERIOD. Take serious notice of your surroundings and realize that the life or situation you are growing is like planting a garden. If you plant a seed...watch to see what grows. Dig up the weeds and nurture the seed that supplies good fruit. If the seeds you are planting aren't producing good fruit..plow them up and plant different seeds until you get the good fruit you want!

- **Find a loving mentor in the field of your dream.** Accomplished people all throughout history certainly had the faith, but they also had mentors. Every single one of them had someone somewhere who influenced them (even if it was subtle). Sometimes the voice of experience can see that the seed you have planted will grow into a weed before it does. The voice of experience can tell you when and where to plant. A good mentor can let you know what seeds you should nurture and which you should let die. They can guide you to plant something else and maybe in ground that is more fertile.

- **Follow your own "gut" feelings.** I am not talking about the whisperings of "fear" that might be destroying your dream. I'm talking about the "inner knowing" that whispers for you to move beyond fear. As long as you know that the seed you are going to plant is going to ultimately produce good fruit, find the courage to move forward.

- **Be charitable.** Know that it isn't the attainment of your goal that brings prosperity...it is the journey. Be kind. Help those in need when ever you can. Give money, but giving of yourself many times can mean more. If you care about the needs of your clients, family and friends...including taking the time to love yourself...prosperity WILL be yours in the end.

- **Truth will stand the test of time.** If you are moving forward with the right intentions for yourself and others...if ultimately what you want to do will bring peace....if you move forward with love and a life of balance...the final fruit will be good. The fruit of abundance.

But here-in is a word of warning: Money and power is not the key to prosperity. If all you want to do is accumulate as much money and/or power as possible – if your

7

goals are out of pure selfishness without caring who you hurt, – If you ignore your health, or family, or others in need, then I promise you one thing: you will fail. It may not be right away, but you will fail. You will be affected in ways that aren't expected. There are those who have a very large amount of money and live miserable, lonely lives. Some may eventually be sent to prison and lose everything. Money and a dead spirit do not equal prosperity.

History shows proof of those who spent all their time acquiring money while ignoring their health, and who ultimately spent all their money to get their health back. History shows proof of those who spent all their time acquiring money or position who ignored their family,and lost it all in divorce – money, possessions and family. I could go on for some time about the type of seeds planted and the fruit they produce...but I think you get the idea.

Therefore we bring you this second volume of Walking With the Wise. You will find many points of view inside of these pages; your responsibility will be to listen to what resonates best with you. We have tried to bring you individuals who have a proven history of success, experience and expertise in their particular niche. Because we want you to live a life of BALANCE...we have divided the book into sections. The idea is to teach about business strategies, but also to provide guidance in developing the right way to think. There is inspiration on how others over-came obstacles, advice about health, and suggestions for family. As you conduct research in reading these articles...you will find that most people who live in true prosperity also have strong spiritual beliefs. They also apply these spiritual principals to their daily actions. I encourage you to explore and develop your own spirituality as part of your path to prosperity. If you want to live a life of prosperity, walk with the wise... listen to what they say...and do what they do. When you walk with the wise...you will prosper.

Linda Forsythe is the founder of MENTORS International, MENTORS magazine, www.mentorsmagazine.com and the Walking With the Wise book series. She has dedicated her life to guide others toward a life of abundance. This has led her to create multiple forms of media that include wisdom from mentors around the globe. Linda is highly sought after to appear in print, television, radio and seminars. She encourages you to contact her and let her know how this book helped you. Linda@mentorsmagazine.com.

TABLE OF CONTENTS

SECTION II – HOW YOU THINK DETERMINES YOUR LIFE

"Prosperity Thinking, Belief and Spiritual Wisdom Produce Prosperity Results."

SECTION III – BUSINESS TIPS FOR SUCCESS

"Business Secrets From the Masters."

SECTION IV – KEEP YOUR HEALTH TO KEEP YOUR ABUNDANCE

"Nutrition, Exercise, Lifestyle and Health Management for Optimal Living."

SECTION V – REMEMBER YOUR FAMILY!

"Remembering Your Spouse, Children and Parents on Your Journey to Prosperity Will Help You Keep It When You Arrive."

SECTION VI – SURPRISE BONUS SECTION

"Rare Exclusive Interview With Brad Sugars."

Acknowledgements
And Many Thanks...

Lena Osborn - For my savvy French business partner who has provided both heart and brains to this company. Your business management, networking, legal and financial planning genius has helped MENTORS magazine spread its wings as a world wide conglomerate!

Cheri Hoffman – For being the Editor-In-Chief of the century!!! Thank you for working with every article contributor, (a huge task in itself). Thank you for making sure that what was written by each contributor was worthy to be printed in a book with high standards. It takes talent and patience to edit well known professionals!

Bonnie Owen – For being an incredible art director and graphic designer. It is because of you that our magazines and books are completed in record time and the finished products have a great look.

Scott F. Hickey, Paul Stokstad, Ted Nevels (MENTORS magazine webmasters) – For making MENTORS magazine *THE* leader in the industry by creating, engineering and maintaining MENTORS on the Internet. (www.mentorsmagazine.com) All of you have worked together as a "well oiled machine" to create our multi-million dollar site and bringing mentoring information to the world.

Tiffany Young – For being my executive assistant and the MENTORS teleseminar program director. Thank you for keeping everything in line by running smoothly. Your organizational and public relation skills are phenomenal! You are an asset to all of us at Mentors International.

Yvonne Stovall – For being my mother and first mentor. Thank you for your loving guidance and belief in me. You have made the ultimate difference in my life!

Jason Wright – For being the most wonderful son that a mom could ask for. I love your sense of humor and zest for life.

Nina Martinson – For being my life-long friend who I have always looked up to, even when we were only three years old. Thank you for being there for me when I needed you most. You're my soul sister and mentor.

Eric Lofholm – For having terrific confidence that we both were going to live our dreams and be an inspiration to many people. Thank you for helping me overcome the past and build a great future!

Dan Kennedy – For taking the time from your very busy schedule to support and guide me. You've taught me so much and are a constant source of inspiration. I will always cherish our friendship.

Our article contributors – For taking the time from your very busy schedules to provide words of wisdom that will change the lives of all who read them. You are all angels!

With Love and Gratitude,
Linda Forsythe

Whoever walks with the wise...

will become wise

Whoever walks with fools...

will suffer harm.

Proverbs 13:20

But Wisdom is shown to be truth

by what results from it.

Matthew 11:19

How To Overcome Obstacles on Your Journey to Prosperity

© 2004 Kim Muslusky

Money Has No Power of its Own

By Suze Orman

When I first started writing about money and talking about it on television, my mother was horrified. I wrote about my mom and dad, and the hard times we experienced financially when I was growing up. I wrote about the many times I messed up with money myself as I was finding my way as an adult. My mom would say, "Suze, I have spent my whole life hiding the truth from everyone and now you go on TV and tell the whole world."

In time, however, she stopped being upset with me, and even came to approve of what I was doing. People who ran into her would thank her for letting me tell the truth about our situation, because it had been their situation too, and their neighbors' and friends' situation. Few people talk openly about their finances or tell one another the same things they say behind closed doors. My mom learned that telling the truth about money can be liberating.

Today my mom is eighty-nine. She and I now spend more time talking about the years that she may or may not have left than we talk about money. Just a few months ago, I asked her during one of these conversations, "What is the most surprising thing that you have learned in your life?" Her answer shocked me. She said that finally, after all these years, she had come to realize that she was more powerful than her money. When I asked her what she meant by that, this is what she said.

SUZE'S MOM'S LESSON

True power does not reside in a bank account

"Suze, even though it is getting harder for me to live alone, at this point I can still cook for myself and for you and your brothers, I can drive myself to the grocery store to get what I need whenever I need it. And that, my dear Suze, is more than almost all my friends can do at this point in their lives – regardless of how much money they have. When your father died, I thought my biggest problem was going to be that I didn't have enough money to be okay for the rest of my life. Remember? That was before you had any money. Because I thought I didn't have money, I felt powerless. I'd inherited this condo and a small sum of money, but even so I had no idea what to do with them. Little by little, though, with your help, I learned how to make ends meet and work with what I had so that I could create what I now have today. So, today I do have enough. In fact, I have *more* than enough. But the money, to my surprise, is not what is making me feel powerful. Don't get me wrong...Thank goodness I have it. It give me great peace of mind to know that I can pay my bills, go to visit my sister in Florida, and go out to eat whenever I want.

However, all the money in the world would not be enough to enable me to do all that I do at my age on my own. I look at my friends, the few who are still alive, and now my greatest fear is that one day I will end up in a nursing home like many of them and not have the power to take care of myself. Money is not the solution to that problem for me, and that surprises me."

My mom is right.

Money is definitely a vital force in your life, but as my mom was saying, it is not your life force. Where many people tend to go wrong is that they somehow think, just as my mom did years ago, that money will make them powerful. I can't tell you the number of times I've been talking to someone who is in serious financial trouble and all of a sudden she looks up to the heavens and says, "God, I wish I had some more money." Money is never a permanent solution to any problem. Money can come in to your life but it can also go out. Look at all the people who have won millions in the lotteries – many of them have less today than they did even before they won.

You already know that wishing or praying for more money will not solve your problems, or you wouldn't be reading this book. Nonetheless, I want you to redefine money for yourself. Many people define their own self-worth by how much money they have. But it's you who give your money its energy, force, and direction. You give it potential, meaning, and life. When you do, your actions with money enable you to keep what you have and create what you deserve in your life.

I know this truth can be difficult to accept, because the world we live in does seem to define everything according to monetary standards. But this law was really brought home to me in another way.

SUZE'S LESSONS

A penny lost is a lesson learned

One hot summer day in New York City, I was taking my favorite walk along Third Avenue, past all the wonderful stores with their window displays offering everything under the sun – fancy furniture in one store and simple trinkets in the next. Summer is my favorite time of the year in New York, and I took this same walk every day, crossing Third Avenue at Fifty-ninth Street and continuing up the avenue past Bloomingdale's. I had turned this walk into a daily ritual, one that I loved.

An integral part of my ritual was bending down in the middle of Fifty-ninth and Third to try to retrieve two pennies that were embedded deep in the tar in the middle of that well-trafficked intersection. Both these pennies had been there for as long as I could remember. I usually used my bare hands to try to pry those pennies out (no tools allowed in my game), and more than once I drew smiles or puzzled looks from others crossing the street. My efforts were tied to the timing of the lights, and my little game ended each day when I had to stop to let the traffic move on. This had become quite an obsession with me. I remained convinced that one day I would set free at least one of those pennies.

On this particular day – the hottest I can remember in New York City, so hot in fact that steam was rising from the sidewalks – I was passing my penny pit, as I called it. I bent down, dug in a nail, and pulled on one of the pennies. The tar was soft, softer than it had ever been, and it seemed to me that the penny moved – for the first time ever. I continued digging and pulling on this one penny, ignoring the fact that I was utterly destroying my thirteen-dollar manicure. I could feel the penny moving, the tar yielding. With one more tug, to my amazement, it came up. I have to tell you, I felt as if I had just won the lottery. I was jubilant. I had set that penny free. I tried for a second to get the other one out, but the light was changing, the traffic was threatening, and I decided to let the other penny alone. I was as happy as I could be with my accomplishment.

And then this is what happened. While I was waiting at the next corner for the traffic light to change again, I started to flip this penny, throwing it in the air and having just a great time with it. I was already thinking, "What will I do with this penny that I've been trying to get for years, now that I finally have it?" At that moment, I accidentally dropped the penny. I watched as the penny – moving as if in slow motion – landed on its side, rolled a few inches, and went right down into the drainage grate. *Gone!* I could not believe it. It was like a bad joke. It had taken years to get that penny, and just a few minutes to lose it.

Money has no power of its own

This little adventure with a penny was a graphic lesson for me and a new way of looking at money. With my own eyes, I saw how money – or in this case, a penny – was unable to do anything on its own. The penny had been totally inert and would have stayed right where it was, forever and a day (just like the other penny, which is still there) until some other nut took a serious amount of time to pry it out of that tar and spend it, save it, or lose it, as I did.

What happens to that penny, or any penny, depends completely on a person's actions. Do you see that money has no power of its own? All its power flows through you.

People first, then money

Do what is right for you *before* you do what is right for your money. It's one thing to know what is right for you and your money and another to have the power to act on that knowledge.

So to personalize this law for you, please ask yourself these questions. If you have been taking actions with your money, and you still don't feel powerful in your life, why don't you? And if you have been using money as a substitute for power, why is that?

***

Suze Orman is a Certified Financial Planner® professional and a bestselling author of personal finance books, lecturer, host of both radio and television shows.

To book a speaking engagement with Suze contact:
International Creative Management
Lecture Division
Carol Bruckner
email: *cbruckner@icmtalent.com*
212.556.5602

Suze's Agent is:
Amanda Urban
International Creative Management
212.556.5600

Life Spinning?
Try Letting Go
By Neal Gray, MBA

One moment I was at peace, flying all by myself four thousand feet above the ground, practicing maneuvers in a single engine Cessna. The next moment I was out of control in a nose-dive spin, heading straight for the ground. My only thought was, "I can't crash – I haven't even told my mom I was taking flying lessons!" Have you ever felt that way in your life or in your business? What do you do? How do you recover? How you think can make the difference.

The flight had started out just like all the practice flights before. The day was beautiful, with a slight fall breeze and only a few clouds in the sky. There was just one difference between this and all the other flights. This was the first flight I would take solo, away from the airport traffic pattern. Just me – no instructor. Up until now when flying alone I was only allowed to take off, circle back, land and repeat the pattern. This time my instructor gave me the go ahead to leave the area of the airport and fly around over the countryside south of Dayton, Ohio. It was 1978, I was 23 years old, and I knew what I was doing.

It was a fantastic flight. I had been out flying and practicing for about 25 minutes when I decided to do one last stall maneuver. This is where you drop the engine speed down to idle and gently pull the nose of the plane up until it slows to the point where there is no longer any lift on the wings. I knew what I was doing. If you hold the wings level and the rudder peddles even, the nose of the plane drops. Then you gently give it the gas, gain speed and return to flying straight and level. Although I had done dozens of them in the weeks before, this time it was drastically different. This time my feet were not even on the rudder peddles. Because of that, I did not drop out of the stall evenly. I came out and flipped over into a nose-dive spin, which I had never been in (let alone gotten out of) before – not even with an instructor.

My reactions were instinctive. I knew what I was doing, and I did as any good driver knows to do – I turned into the spin. Wrong! In a plane, that just makes the spin tighter. The force of the spin laid me across the passenger seat. OK, maybe I didn't know what I was doing. I only remember 3 other things during that spin. First, I thought, "I can't crash yet ..." Second, I discovered that when people talk about "having your life flash before your eyes" they mean it! It is absolutely true. I swear I saw every detail of my life from infancy to that point in vivid color and sharp detail, all in an instant. Third, I realized that I had not crashed, but was now flying straight and level just about 500 feet above the ground. I had dropped over 3,500 feet in seconds. How I got to level I have absolutely no idea, but there I was. My heart was racing, my hands were sweating, and my eyes were slowly refocusing on the horizon and the instruments in front of me as my breathing slowed to slightly above normal. What the heck was I doing?

Letting go

When I've told this story to others, some have suggested that it was divine intervention. Others thought that I must have followed the instructions posted on the dashboard of the plane entitled "How to exit a spin." (Like I had time to read them!) Still others thought I must have just let go of everything and let the plane right itself. I don't know what happened. I've thought about that day many times since then and remember nothing more than what I've told you here. I tend to believe my instructor, who said that most likely I just let go of everything (a Cessna 152 is a forgiving aircraft).

I continued to fly straight and level after the spin for about 10-15 minutes before digging up the courage to turn the plane around and head back to the airport. I didn't want to make the wings leave the safety of being level, but my choices were get it back and land on my terms, or let it run out of gas and take my chances. Going back appeared to be the lesser of two evils at the time. I did land safely. I continued to fly for about a year after that, but it took months pushing myself through fear and panic each time I flew until I was able to fly with relative calm. It's like the old saying about getting back up on the horse…but this was a big horse (a flying horse!) and I was not about to let it beat me.

This is the first time I have ever written down these events. I have only told the story verbally all these years. I find that as I put these words to paper, I am discovering more lessons than I ever noticed before. I got the lesson about getting back up on the horse 25 years ago when it happened. Today, as I write this, I am finding a much deeper lesson. There are times in life when the issue is too big to handle by trying to wrestle it under control and pull out of the spin on your own. Sometimes, you just may need to let go of the controls and put your faith in something other than your own strength. For some, that's another person and for others, that's a higher power. Did I know that the plane would right itself? No. I had been told that it would, but had never witnessed it for myself. Would I have had the conscious faith to let go? I don't think so, because it made no logical sense. In fact, if I had to guess, I would say that letting go was either dumb luck or desperation. I don't remember anything about what I did. For all I know, I could have passed out momentarily.

This is a hard lesson for me, and a lesson I am still absorbing. You see, I grew up a strong-willed independent thinker who could take care of himself. I logically,

21

rationally, and systematically think through problems and issues to find the solution. I have never been a strongly spiritual person. In fact, in my youth and early adulthood I was at the far opposite end of the spectrum. I rejected religion and put my faith solely in the strength and goodness of people – mostly myself. I still believe in the goodness of people (especially family) and myself, but my life experiences suggest to me that I may be...well...wrong about the other. Although I am not devout in any spiritual beliefs, I am open to the input of others and the idea that I cannot control it all. Sometimes I have to let go of the wheel and the rudder peddles of my life and let other forces and other people help bring me back to straight and level.

Getting your business back to level

So, how does this profound lesson apply to business? As business owners, we often try to hold tight to the wheel and keep our own feet on the rudder peddles of our business, even when what we're doing isn't working. We may stay the course just because we see no other way. We may be acting instinctively to fix the business, and instead we're making the spin tighter and our control even less. For example, owners often say, "I need more customers; therefore, I need to advertise more." The truth is that most advertising doesn't work. If you do more of what isn't working, the spin tightens. Instead, if you learned how to advertise better for the same money (or less), you would reduce costs and increase sales, getting back to level. As a business coach, I am there to teach and mentor business owners through the turbulence, to talk them through the spin and back to level.

Most business owners won't ask for this help. Why? Maybe they don't know that they need it. Maybe it's pride, stubbornness, or...well...something else. The statistical reality is that most businesses will fail. The E-Myth Revisited by Michael Gerber states approximately 80 percent of all businesses will not make it to their fifth anniversary, and only 80 percent of those will make it to their tenth anniversary. That's a four percent chance of success. If you own a business in that statistical four percent you have jumped a significant hurdle, but you are never out of the woods.

I heard about another study that suggested that business owners who attend just three seminars on business can cut their chances of failure in half. Is the key going to the seminars? No. The key is the willingness to be open, to learn from others, to ask for help, and to accept help when it is given. We all need help from time to time. There is no shame in asking for help – only in quietly failing when help is within reach.

The many faces of help

There is a story I am reminded of that I heard years ago. A man lived in a small house near the Ohio River. One spring there were massive storms and heavy downpours of rain over several days. The river flooded its banks and began surrounding the man's house. A policeman knocked on the door and offered the man a ride to safety. "No," he said, "God will protect me." The river continued to rise. His porch was covered and the basement filled with water. A fireman in a rowboat came by to rescue the man, but the man said, "No thank you, God will protect me." The river was now up past the first floor windows. The man scurried up onto the roof. Soon a Coast Guard helicopter flew over and dropped a rescue worker down with a rope to pull the man to safety. Again the man replied, "No thank you, God will protect me." Hours later the house was swept down the river and the man drowned. Now the man stood at the gates of heaven at the feet of God. God asked the man, "Why are you here?" To this the man exclaimed, "I drowned because you didn't protect me!" God gently responded, "And who do you think sent the policeman, the fireman, and the Coast Guard to rescue you?"

Help doesn't often come in the form we think it will. If we don't let go of our clenched grip we may lose the chance to take what is given us and get out of the spin. The next time your business feels in a spin or you just want to prevent it from spinning, what do you do? How do you recover? Sometimes you just have to let go and let other people, other forces help. How much more can you gain with an open hand, rather than a tightened fist?

Make it a great day!!!

Neal Gray is president of The Anderson Gray Group, Inc. in southwest Ohio and is a writer, speaker, trainer, and licensed *Action International* business coach. To discuss letting go in your business to stop the spin, or to get your free copy of "17 Ways to Increase Your Business Profits" contact Neal today at 513.939.2145 or by email at *MyFavoriteCoach@aol.com*.

Big Obstacles

...Bigger Gifts

By Sue Erickson

Obstacles plague a majority of the population on a daily basis. This story is of my childhood bout with cancer, the amputation of my leg, a battle with addiction, my own child's brain tumor and my path from agnostic to Christ. It is my desire that you will gain the experience, strength and hope you need to conquer the obstacles in your path.

An early start

What was to become a life time of obstacles started very early for me. At age eleven, I was diagnosed with a cancerous bone tumor (Osteo Sarcoma) in my right knee. I was quickly admitted to Doernbecher Children's Hospital at the University of Oregon Medical School in Portland. You weren't placed at Doernbecher unless you were very ill. Mom had to leave every night so there I was, alone with strangers. Even though the nurses were helpful and kind, I'd never stayed alone without family before.

For three months I was treated with large doses of X-ray therapy and chemotherapy, which was very new in 1963. Nothing was killing the Cancer. About that time, a new girl was put in our room. She had an artificial leg that she put under the bed at night. I remember being very sad. I knew then, that's what "they" were going to do to me. I told no one about my feelings.

Amputation was the last resort with no guarantee that I would live – only a 1 in 20 chance! They amputated my leg. After the surgery I awoke and looked down towards the end of the bed, realizing there was only one long bump in the covers. How could my leg be gone? My brain was still sending the messages that my leg was still there. Overwhelming sadness and nausea consumed me. I told no one. Stuffing my emotions had become automatic. I was alone with this huge reality that part of me was gone forever. I wanted to cry, but I saw that as a sign of weakness. I thought that I had to be strong. It was hard to understand. It would be 25 years before I had any counseling about the emotions around the removal of my leg.

That first week out in Portland society as an amputee was a horrifying experience as a child. It never entered my mind that things would be different than before the surgery. People would gawk with their mouths open or whisper and point as I walked by. Why did they do that? We were in a department store once, looking at a rack of clothing. I happened to look down and there was a small boy looking up under my skirt. I was so embarrassed. His mother grabbed his arm and yanked him away. I looked to my mother for direction. We smiled at each other and laughed it off. Mom tried to ease the situation by saying, "He was just a curious little boy, honey." I was not laughing inside. I had to figure out how to protect myself from these unwanted experiences. On a lighter note, I didn't wear too many dresses after that!

We came home and resumed life as we knew it. I attended public school, took swimming lessons and played with neighborhood kids as usual. I was fitted with a prosthesis which I wore for six years at school only. It proved to be such a hindrance to me that I finally refused to wear it, preferring to use crutches. I had only worn it to make others feel better. When I thought I couldn't do something, my mother would say "Can't never did anything." As I learned later what Henry Ford said "If you think you can or you think you can't, you're right."

The limits of labels

As the years went by, I learned about words like cripple, disabled and handicapped. I hate these words because they are very limiting. When you label anything you automatically limit its reality. Do you drive a car, have you birthed two children, pushed a grocery cart, snow skied, written a book – how about taking a spin class at the gym? I am doing or have done all of these things…and more. I am a person with one leg. I am not crippled, not disabled, and most certainly not handicapped.

My goal has always been to defy these labels that society puts on people. My solution was to eliminate any traits that were associated with them from my persona. First impressions are crucial. Hair and clothes need to be stylish and fit well. The way I carry myself is paramount, straight posture, head up and making eye contact as I walk. It works. How do I know that? When I am wearing shorts and can walk up to a person and they ask how I broke my leg, I'd say I have accomplished my goal.

Life goes on

College was a whole new set of references and choices. I found alcohol, wrote off men, and learned to snow ski. Oh yes, education. Alcohol was fun, and fun was something I hadn't had much of to that point. The "fast lane" and "living on the edge" was very appealing to me. I became more entwined in it as the years went by. In the end it was a life of drama, insanity and pain. Don't go there!

All through these years I used only my crutches. Graduation came and what would I do now? It was clear that restaurants and retail stores wouldn't hire me because of the crutches. My dream was to be a Fashion Designer. I got a degree in clothing and textiles with a teaching certificate. I used both of these degrees in the following years, but all the time drugs and alcohol were part of my life. When I met my future husband, Mark, we "used" together until we came to the place where recovery was a necessity. After two years of sobriety, we were married.

Here we go, again

Could life be more perfect? Married, two children, house in the suburbs, clean and sober ten years. Here we go! My father dies, Mark is promoted to a new city, and my four year old child, Connor, is diagnosed with a brain tumor. "Not again!" flashed in front of me. I turned instantly into the survival mode I had learned years ago. We can do this! I can help him have a different experience than my own.

From the beginning, I gave him age-appropriate information. We talked about things before they happened so that there were no surprises. We prayed and asked others to pray. Right before Connor went into surgery, our pastor prayed with us. There was a total calmness about Connor. As he passed through the double doors to the Operating Room, my own experience flashed before my eyes. I cried. Why did my baby have to experience this? I often wondered what it was like for my parents. Now I knew. Heart wrenching! They had nowhere near the support we had.

When a family experiences a major illness of one of its members, all are affected. It is important to make sure everyone understands to the level of their ability. We took my other son, Bryce, who was two and one half years old, to see Connor at the hospital. Using the actual words "brain tumor" we showed him where it was located. Would he necessarily understand the term? No. But when you use a generic word like sick and then that child gets a cold, in their mind they are "sick." Would they have to be put in a hospital, too? We learned this with my younger brother. He lived in fear that if he got sick they would cut off his leg. My awareness now is that children need help learning how to verbalize what is going on in their lives. They have very literal minds and make assumptions that may not be true.

The breaking point

Connor had four operations that year. I could not abide another crisis. I was so depleted, I couldn't handle Connor's anger and frustration, which was being directed at me. We needed a break from each other. I enrolled him in day care for three days a week. It would be a huge struggle to even get him in the car seat. The teacher would have to come out and get him, or he would throw himself onto the floor and flail, but once I left he was fine. It was the last straw for me.

We started attending a church. I knew I needed something greater than myself and for me, that was Christ. After I asked Christ to come into my heart, I realized for the first time that every obstacle in my life was a challenge and a miracle. I had been given a second life. Yes, I am an amputee but there isn't much of anything I can't do.

By now we have sixteen years of sobriety, my child has absolutely no brain damage and best of all, I became a child of God. Every one of these miracles was essential to bring me to where I am today: willing to step out of the box and out into society to share my God-given miracles with you.

My biggest obstacles were my biggest gifts

Today is an incredible journey unfolding before my eyes. You can say my road has been far from easy. However, every twist and turn has brought me to my present place: a life filled with spiritual, emotional, physical and financial abundance. Life on the other side of fear is sweet! Remember "Can't never did anything." Know that you can and Go For It!

Sue Erickson has been a Cancer survivor for over 40 years, and as an amputee she knows first hand about overcoming obstacles. She is a consultant, speaker and author of the upcoming book *Big Obstacles...Bigger Gifts*.

Visit Sue at www.sue-erickson.com or send email to *sue@sue-erickson.com*.

Forget Your Ego –
Take Good Advice

By Zig Ziglar

My career – especially until I reached age 45 – has been a roller coaster. I had an extraordinarily difficult time getting started in the world of sales, but after P.C. Merrell inspired me, my career took off big-time. For the next four years, my success was unbelievable.

Then I stopped growing and started swelling. The results were catastrophic. In the following five years, I was in 17 different companies. Some of those companies were just slick new deals, but others represented real opportunities. However, my ego had reached the point where I actually believed that I had the answer to everything.

If the company I was working for didn't buy into my brilliant suggestions, I said, "I don't have to put up with this!" And off I went to a company that appreciated me. As I left, I predicted failure for that company, though it may have been in business for 50 years.

Seventeen deals in five years. Many of them were "get-rich-quick" deals, but after five years, not only had I not gotten rich quickly, but I hadn't gotten rich at all. As a matter of fact, I was getting deeper and deeper into debt. Finally, I decided to do something that I had vowed that I never would do: get back into the cookware business, where I had earlier enjoyed remarkable success.

The president of the Saladmaster Corporation in Dallas made me a significant loan, bailing me out of a really tight spot, and I was back in the cookware business. I was a franchise dealer in Columbia, South Carolina. Soon after I joined the team, the division supervisor came to visit with me and offer some suggestions. He had been a preacher all his life and had gotten into the cookware business to pay his daughter's medical bills.

To be honest, I thought that I knew more about the cookware business than this man did and that I should be the supervisor. Consequently, I didn't like the fact that he was my boss, and my ego and attitude stopped me from being in much of a listening mood. However, as he talked, I realized that in the last five years I had jumped from pillar to post and had less than nothing to show for it.

One of the man's statements made a great deal of sense. He said, "Zig, you are an excellent salesman – one of the best I've seen. But your ego makes you vulnerable to being manipulated. People brag on you, feed your ego, and lead you to believe that you can do things that simply are not doable. You've tried virtually everything that's come down the pike, and your results have not been very good." Then he said, "Now, Zig, I'm going to give you some advice. It's free... And as you know, most free advice is worth about what it costs, but let me offer a suggestion: You've set some records in this business. You've gained some national respect as a result. But, Zig, the next time one of these 'good deals' comes your way, why don't you put the blinders on. Tell the person that regardless of how attractive the offer is, you've made a commitment. You're going to stay in this business until you stabilize yourself from a financial point of view and rebuild your reputation as solid and dependable, instead of just flashy and always looking for a 'deal.' Zig, if those deals are all that good, they'll still be good a year from now. And if they're not good a year from now, they're not good now."

Though I hated to admit that I had an ego problem, I recognized the wisdom of what my supervisor was telling me. Things were tight for a number of months, but thanks to much hard work and that commitment to stabilize myself, I managed to finish fifth in the nation out of over 3,000 franchises that year. The following year, I was number one in personal sales in the United States.

Regardless of what you may think of the messenger, listen to the message. My supervisor gave me some of the best advice I've ever gotten, and over the years, we developed a genuine friendship. I would have missed a great deal had I not swallowed my ego, put my nose to the grindstone, and gotten back on sound financial ground.

I sincerely hope that you haven't missed great opportunities because of a swollen ego, and I sincerely hope that if you have, you recognized your ego as the culprit of your demise. Nothing knocks you down a notch quicker than an inflated opinion of yourself. Don't get me wrong; being proud of your accomplishments is good, but when you start thinking that you know more than the next person, watch out!

Zig Ziglar is an internationally known authority on high-level performance. He is chairman of the Zig Ziglar Corporation, which is committed to helping people more fully utilize their physical, mental and spiritual resources. His courses, lectures and best selling books have influenced millions of people worldwide.

Make Your Life A Masterpiece:

One Baby Step at a Time

By Jan Cooper "The Renaissance Man"

Do you want your life to be fun? Would you like it to be customized? Would you like to discover a trail or a road that is easy to follow? If this is the case, then you need to create your own map. Don't be foolish! Learn from other people's experiences. Michael Lynton stated, "One person, thinking differently, can turn conventional wisdom on its head."

Learning from babies – one step at a time

We entered the world first as babies. Let's look at what babies do: they crawl, they walk, they fall down…they learn from their experiences before they begin again. You too must crawl, walk, fall down, and learn from your experiences before you can acquire the results you desire.

By taking one baby step at a time, you can pave your way to HEAVEN on earth. It's time to psyche yourself up about your future! Don't mess around, wasting your talents and abilities. Your ideas are like glass – VERY FRAGILE. If you do not write your ideas down and put them into action, they will just waste away. Why? Because you were not willing to take the necessary baby steps to make your DREAMS a reality.

So what's new? You are changing. In fact, change and learning to live with change is everything. Yes, you are in control of your destiny. A new concept is born, to shorten your path with better answers so you can keep your sanity. Why? So you will not forget to learn and apply what you have learned, one little baby step at a time.

It is not what you say but how you say it to yourself that will express the real you. If you are willing to take one baby step at a time, learn from your experiences and make connections, YOU are going to have one fulfilled life. If you take these tiny little steps you are going to be flying, jumping, hopping and skipping to where you need to be. Hey! Love what you do and the fortunes, the successes, the money and the ultimate will arrive.

Your ideas are big and you do have a place to go – so listen up! Life is better when you have a short-cut to your goals. Influence yourself to be the best you can. Get psyched about your future. Double dare yourself to be the best you can be. Stop shooting in the dark and let people know you exist. Everything is one baby step at a time.

Preparation– physically, mentally, spiritually and financially

Yes, you really do know all the answers. But a simple little tool was created to shorten your path, one step at a time. It is an equation all can follow. If followed, PREPARE to add sizzle to your life. Prepare so you won't be just a face in the crowd. PREPARE! It is your words, your actions, and your decisions that give you POWER.

It is NEVER too late. I do not care how old you are. I do not care how sick you are. I do not care how handicapped you are. But, this I do want you to know: THIS IS YOUR YEAR! Stick to your resolutions and create. Grow rich physically, mentally, spiritually and financially.

Failure is no option. Hope is your weapon. You must always, continually, THINK physically, mentally, spiritually and financially. You must think as Napoleon Hill did to write Think and Grow Rich. You must think as Dottie Walters did to write Speak and Grow Rich. You must think as Dan Poynter did to write Write and Grow Rich. Now we have Create and Grow Rich. Use these books to go where you want to go. And…I just remembered there is another book out there called Pray and Grow Rich!

You are you, and you know where you have been. You know your successes and failures – or should I say, learning experiences. You know the steps you should have taken and didn't. You know you wanted instant gratification. You know you wanted to show your parents, neighbors or friends that you had what it takes to make it BIG TIME! But none of this will happen if you do not have balance in your life. Moderation in all things will one day make you a success. Your health is your most precious gift. Many multi-millionaires would gladly give you all their money, all their properties, all their investments, all of their heirlooms, if you would give them your health.

Prove to yourself that the reality of your life is only a tool kit away to your DREAMS. Play smart. Do what you need to do to gear yourself up to giving the best performance for an incredible value, again and again. This word of mouth advertising will have individuals, businesses and corporations coming to you again and again.

Start the REVOLUTION. Protect yourself like GOLD. Teach yourself to NETWORK. Reach out your hands to others and make the first move. You cannot change your past – you can only learn from it. But you can change and move on to improving your life. You must think physically, mentally, spiritually and financially. Make sure you get the maximum return on your personal investment.

You have the power you need

Throughout history, people have wanted POWER, trying to be number one and on top of the hill. Many people today could have this ingredient if they put their knowledge into action. It all starts with one baby step at a time. You have to move

31

slowly to prosper and harvest. All good things take much time to accomplish. Start planting the good seeds of prosperity and watch them grow.

The difficult part is figuring out how to take a person's dreams and turn them into reality. One must know why they want something. They must recognize their own weaknesses and strengths. This is why you must know what you really can do, what results you expect and the effort you are willing to put forth. Your must know yourself in order to have the POWER you need, when you need it.

You must make the hidden obvious. You must maximize your knowledge to bring out your fullest potential, one little step at a time. Tell your story by making your DREAM work for you. Knowledge, courage and direction are just a few steps away to your POWER. You must get the most out of your life if you want to feel satisfied. If you are going to be satisfied, you have to remember all those dreams – those things you always said you would do. This may be your last call! You may not be given another chance. You have no alternative. YOU have to prove to yourself while you are alive that you can have a LOVE affair with LIFE by doing what your heart tells you to do.

The key to a productive life

By failing, we learn. It is our failures that make us and take us to our highest potentials. By learning from our failures and combining that with action, you are on your way to success. The true secret, formula, or equation to SUCCESS – whether you are a businessman, artist, author, or scientist is that you have a sense of purpose and you live your dream. The people who live their dream have a happy and productive life. They also work on themselves daily and are continually striving for improvement in every aspect of their life. These habits are POWERFUL tools that were developed one baby step at a time! For you to use your power tools, you too will have to take the baby steps that lead to reaching your full potential.

Everything in life that is PRODUCTIVE starts with baby steps. In my youth, I was blessed with negative thinking, inferiority complexes, the label of a "slow learner," remedial classes and dyslexia – reversing my words, letters and numbers. I say I was "blessed" because I learned to eliminate these bad habits and replace them with positives. I am not perfect. I still have areas in my life I'm working on, just as we all will until the day we leave this wonderful world. The greatest secret – if there is a secret – is learning to use our time wisely and striving to overcome in all areas of life. As Lawrence Olivier said, "Use your weaknesses; aspire to strength."

Yes, POWER, SUCCESS, and FORTUNE can fall upon you if you are willing to take the baby steps necessary for fulfillment. You must find out what it is that most people want and find a way to help them get it. You must help them solve their problems by making their lives easier, simpler, and happier.

The journey to greatness

When you have conditioned yourself to take baby steps in every area of your life, soon you will be skipping, running, jumping, and playing with the energy of youth. Why? Because you will have rediscovered the way you were created to learn: one little small baby step at a time.

Baby steps will take you to heights that are far beyond your dreams. They will put you on a trail to GREATNESS. You can be a hero or villain on the stage of your life. It's all up to you. Self-knowledge is the key to your future, success, or GREATNESS. It's okay for you to act now on the way to a healthier, happier, more peaceful you. There are no accidents. We are here to help one another, so please learn to serve, give, change and help those who are need with purpose.

Do you love enough to provide a service to help others? Are you willing to spend years developing your skills and talents without pay? Are you willing to share your expertise for free until you are an expert? If so, you are well on your way to greatness. Turn your life into a masterpiece, one little baby step at a time. You are your own artist. You are your own brushes. You are your own colors. You are the star of your life. It's up to you to take the necessary baby steps to turn your life into a MASTERPIECE!

Jan Cooper is on your team! Should you stumble or fall as he has done, he's just a phone call away. You can reach him at *jc@masteryourlife.net* or find more information at www.masteryourlife.net.

How 7 Secrets of Loyalty Turned Around My Embarrassingly Broke Life...

And What These Secrets Can Do For You!

By Jeff Kaller

I was voted least likely to succeed – the class clown. I lived under the shadow of my college slogan – "Party 'til you puke!" Dead-end restaurant jobs followed one after another – **yet, underneath it all, throbbed a true passion for life.** Years later, I was the Founder of a company with yearly gross sales exceeding $8 million and recognized as the country's leading expert in buying and selling pre-foreclosure properties. I owe it all to a personal credo – a belief system which, in its purest form, can be easily written on the back of a napkin as follows:

LOYALTY

In itself, the word "loyalty" is just another word – but it's how I created unbelievable results in the face of adversity, why I did it, and how you can easily do the same. All of us are bound by a set way of being that comes from a "core" belief system. That belief system creates an outcome whether we want it to or not. I loved my previous life, although economically, I was a walking disaster. After my daughter Allie was born, this way of being was no longer any use to me. Now, at age 38, I've carefully held to my most powerful reasons that I am where I am today.

For you, I've clarified and distilled my personal credo into "7 Laws of Loyalty." I give them to you in hopes that they will be utilized on your life journey. Take them to improve the quality of your life. I promise you, just as for me, the money will flow.

Before I begin, it's important to understand that loyalty affects anyone's quality of life in this INTERRELATED MATRIX:

- The income you earn, and the lifestyle you live
- Interaction with partners and business associates
- Opportunities you create for employees
- A strong family "unit" with spouse and loved ones
- Interaction with your customers
- The mentors with whom you surround yourself
- Faith in people, faith in deals outside your comfort zone, spiritual balance

Each work in tandem, interwoven together. It's all right that you'll always be striving to balance these elements – that's what life and the journey is all about.

LAW #1: Be loyal to the income and quality of lifestyle you desire, and how you want to spend your free time.

You must choose and stay loyal to an income-producing vehicle that can economically support the lifestyle you want. You already know it's not about the money – it's about quality of life.

If running a petting zoo could pay me $50K per month, heck – I'd probably be doing that. Make sure your work turns you on - gets your heart beating and keeps you up thinking late at night. But be careful that what you love also supports the quality of life you desire. Owning goats and sheep for kids to pet and feed ain't gonna buy you an island in the Bahamas – which happens to be my ultimate goal. To make this goal achievable, I've stayed loyal to investing in pre-foreclosure properties. I'm clear about how I want to spend my time. When working on an important project, I shut off the cell phone and create productive "think time." TV, following the markets, and most news tends to discourage me – I stay away from that crap. Stay loyal and committed to how you spend your time. Stay focused and on track, and this will support the income you want.

LAW #2: Stay loyal to any business partners and associates with whom you have dealings.

I've seen fickle business people chase a dollar so hard they forget that one of the reasons successful companies exist is because of their ability to maintain stable relationships in today's market. No matter what your future plans are, look and stay strong in your work environment relationships. An old boss and/or co-worker may provide an opportunity in the future. In my teaching and real estate businesses, I never break off a relationship with harsh words. Unless someone steals, I've found that most relationships fall aside from LACK OF COMMUNICATION. Start business arrangements with upfront written agreements, communicate expectations clearly, and negotiate what works for both sides, instead of possibly destroying an already deteriorating business relationship altogether. As a side note: get the heck out of soured business very quickly – cut your losses and move on. I once had two business associates embezzle $180,000 – I cut ties, never looked back, and at best estimate was able to triple the income I lost in half the time.

LAW #3: A loyal leader builds loyal employees and a "Dream Team" to share and execute their personal vision.

If you don't have employees or even ONE person helping to implement your plan, there are only two reasons: 1) There is no need for an employee, or 2) You don't think you can afford one. In a multiple-company environment, I must have people to see that operations get done. As a general rule, one of the most important attributes to growing any company, in my opinion, is NOT knowing how to personally do all of your company's operational tasks. It's OK to understand how things work; I just

35

see too many brilliant entrepreneurs handling ALL the details, rather than being able to concentrate and focus on the overall vision.

Operational Managers should be able to keep business functions running smoothly. Get out of their way – stay out of the unnecessary details that suck your energy. Make sure employees understand the overall vision. I create trust by seeking my employees' opinions and trusting them. My people know how much the company makes in revenue. I also make it completely clear that without my sacrifices, there would not be a company. Praise, rewards, and bonuses create loyalty. If these rewards happen to create envy or greed, then it's time to get them out at all costs, and get someone else to support your vision. Be committed to a very specific income that supports your lifestyle, keeping the smallest, most productive "Dream Team" possible to make it happen. For some this may be only one Personal Assistant to keep you organized and on track.

LAW #4: A loyal husband and father/wife and mother create the blueprint for a successful business.

I believe alignment in this area of your life will help fix the broken parts. The purpose of any business is to support the creator, and to enhance the quality of life by the freedoms granted by self-employment. Schedule vacations one year in advance, with special pockets of time around these vacations. From the day I met my wife, Sofia, she and I have worked together. After sixteen years, we still haven't killed each other. We forget the business on personal time. I'm committed to take a call from my daughter during any meeting, any time, any place. I take a "Dad & Daughter Trip" with my eight year old, Allie, two weeks out of each year – just she and I. No cell phone – just an exotic getaway such as Costa Rica, Dominica, Nevis, St. Kitts, and this year Kenya and Botswana, Africa. After all, what do we do all of this for? Any person, man or woman, who has drifted from the family "unit" can easily regain love just by committing to spend more time enjoying those to whom he or she is connected by marriage or blood.

LAW #5: My customers get the best I can give them. I stay loyal to the reason they became my client in the first place.

In the pre-foreclosure business, sometimes we find people whose lives are a mess, financially and mentally. During this chaotic time, it's our goal to keep the bank from repossessing their home, and to save their credit. In most cases, we get paid handsomely to do so.

The lender doesn't get another liability on the books. This is an interesting "tug-of-war," but the goal is a win-win at all times. (For a dynamic FREE audio CD discussing a pre-foreclosure investor's conversation with a homeowner, call 1-800-646-2574, and ask for Alex.) As I teach others to negotiate debt and buy real estate with none of their own credit, money, or liability, my commitment to these customers is that I deliver the best, cutting-edge, underground strategies available in this country.

I'm known as "the kid who created the 'Ninety-Fiver Club™'". This is a conglomerate of people from all walks of life, some with no previous knowledge of real estate, to whom I have given the knowledge and ability to CASH A CHECK FOR $95,000 OR GREATER ON ONE DEAL!! (To see how to become a Member, go to www.mrpreforeclosure.com, and click on "The Ninety-Fiver Club™.") Not only do I understand the inner workings of buying pre-foreclosures, I thrive on giving these details to others to make a bundle on their own.

In whatever you do, remember that your customer gets value at all costs. Screw this up and you'll fail. Anytime you are able to outperform your competition and your customer hits a home run, GET A KILLER TESTIMONIAL LETTER FROM THEM. "The proof is in the pudding." Don't tell people what you can do – prove it to them. Here's an example:

"Hey, Jeff,

I wanted to give you an update on my successes since the August Boot camp in Nashville. Using the negotiation strategies we learned at the Boot camp from MR. X, I was able to negotiate a first mortgage down from $132,000 to $40,000. Your boot camp taught me how to present a short sale offer to the lenders in such a way that it made sense to cut their losses now, and accept my offer.

I met the appraiser at the property and I pointed out everything that was wrong with the house. Thankfully the house smelled like cats, and the 10-15 full litter boxes sure helped. I put the short sale package together, backing up all the information with estimates and pictures, just as we learned in the boot camp. I even showed them a side-by-side comparison of what the bank would get if they took the property back vs. selling it to me at a discount. The bank jumped at my offer.

Using none of my own money, I hired a contractor to do the minor repairs, put in new carpet and new paint for a total repair bill of just over $20,000. I had a contract to sell the property well before the repairs were even finished. I sold the house for $144,000.
It gets even better... The house was on a double lot. I sub-divided the lot, and sold that for $32,800 CASH. So I walked away with a profit of $116,415. NOW THAT IS WHAT I CALL A PAYDAY. I have had several successful short sales in the past, but nothing ever compared to this... and I owe to all to you, Mr. X and an appraiser who doesn't like cats.
Jeff, you promised me that you would change my life, and my entire family is in full agreement that you are truly a man that lives up to his word. THANK YOU!!!

Warmest regards,
Doug
N. Oshkosh, WI"

Here it's said in Doug's own words – more powerful than anything I could ever say. By the way, Doug is in "The Ninety-Fiver Club™". Check him out on our website (www.mrpreforeclosure.com).

LAW #6: Employ and stay loyal to a mentor and a carefully chosen group who is willing to support your belief system.

I started my real-estate investing journey when I bought the Carlton Sheets Course "No Money Down." Over fifty houses later I found myself struggling to manage cash-flow, and even lost one of my own houses to foreclosure. Ted Thomas first opened my eyes to debt negotiations. Ron LeGrand pushed me out of my "comfort zone" more than once. Dan Kennedy and Joe Polish have mentored me with marketing ideas worth millions. I seek out the best personal mentors such as these at all costs, paying as high as $10,000 to consult for just a few hours. The list is too long to go on. Was it worth it? You tell me. My goal is to buy a private island in the Bahamas this year. Many of my students and company affiliates will gain use and benefit from doing business with me. Some companies and investors are on their knees eaking out a living. Those around me are talking about creating a lifestyle most people only dream of. I wonder where they got the idea? I take credit for nothing, and I'm no better than anybody else. I will tell you this: I'm on a lifestyle mission, and I am willing to become a mentor to those ready for a change.

I feel so strongly about mentoring, I've seen to it that the Mr. Preforeclosure Organization provides a Coaching Program and high-level consulting, along with Membership Plans, showing people how to work less and make more. These same people are leaving dead-end jobs, and have changed their way of thinking. It's not about money – it's about finding loyal mentors to give you your goals on a silver platter.

LAW #7: None of this matters without unstoppable faith.

I believe in people. I think many people try to do the right thing, also understanding that desperate people do desperate things. My goal is to enable people to have dreams, and to avoid the "sheep" who think it's owed to them. I lost patience with that long ago. It's important to personally confide in those around you in an open way. It creates synergy and allows others to take part in their future. Guidance is all good people require. Have you seen Donald Trump's new TV show "The Apprentice"? One of Trump's loyal executives has been with him for over 20 years, and most likely controlled billions with his own decisions. Trump, without question, has faith in key people – this enables his own goals to come to fruition.

In casual observance over the past five years, I see that those who look for bigger deals not only have more confidence, but are in it less for the money and more for the chase. Thinking in the small, steady paycheck realm is all right, I suppose, but comes from not understanding what is on the other side of the fence. The last couple of years, I've spent much of my time teaching people how simple it is to close bigger deals. Buying and selling $400,000 to multi-million dollar properties is just as easy as a $35,000 house. It takes no money and a lot of faith.

I've seen people traveling down two paths – some folks have faith and a belief system in a Maker in whom they confide in prayer; others don't. As an observer, I see that both parties usually enjoy very similar levels of monetary success. But without a doubt, I see those who are spiritually balanced have a more productive lifestyle, and truly enjoy the journey more than those without spiritual faith.

"Trust God's Authority – not Man's Majority."
~Author Unknown~

These are the 7 Loyal Credos that drive me each day, whether working or not. Stop at nothing in your conquest – understand that someone has always figured it out before you. All you have to do is find that person or organization, and employ them to give you what they have. As my special gift to anyone who has picked up this copy of the Mentors Book, I will give you a special deal on our one-time year-end bash where we will have Donald Trump and many other phenomenal personalities in an event destined to effect your lifestyle transformation! Call student services at 800.646.2578. You'll get a very special gift **just for registering!**

Stay loyal to yourself! To your explosive success…

Jeff Kaller, a.k.a. "Mr. Preforeclosure," is the Founder and President of the Mr. Preforeclosure "How to Leave Your Job in 90 Days" Organization. This company dedicates its resources to making new real estate entrepreneurs outrageously successful through proprietary Seminar Events, Home Study Systems, Mentoring, and Deal Splits – all conducted around the little-known niche of pre-foreclosure properties

39

Breaking Bones, Bricks, Barriers
...and Just Being Broke At Times

By Reggie Cochran

How do you go from being born prematurely, weighing barely three pounds, being expected to die, and living with physical hardships, to become a three-time World Champion martial arts fighter? From a poor formal education to coaching and consulting others? From a broken, dysfunctional family that could easily be featured on daytime TV talk shows, to being happily married 26 years and raising two great kids? From bankruptcy to running a successful business and living very well? The answer is: "By your choices."

Life is full of choices. Those who become successful are the ones who learn how to make more right choices than wrong ones. Realize that where you start does not have to determine where you will finish. Know that what you have done or not done in the past does not have to determine what you do or don't do in the future…unless you let it!

I personally chose not to let where I started keep me down. I worked very hard to overcome the problems of my past and not to dwell on them. However, you must first have a glimpse of where I started in life to fully understand how far I have come. So let's take a very brief look at some major barriers I have had to break down in order to move forward toward my goals. Maybe the lessons I learned will help you.

Obstacles in my way

At birth, physical problems were present that would continue to plague me most of my life. My mom divorced my dad when I was two. She eventually remarried when I was seven. Their marriage was rocky from the start, creating a constant tension in the home. Money was always tight, which only added stress. My mom used food to attempt to reduce her stress and gained a lot of weight. Since I did not have many friends in my early years, and physical activities were tough, I would spend time eating with my mom. I too began putting on extra pounds. By the time I was twelve, my official nickname was "fat man."

My mom threatened suicide on a regular basis most of my life. When I was fifteen, my step-dad actually did kill himself. I ended up dropping out of school. My mom quickly found a boyfriend to move in with us. He was still married and there were constant fights with his family. Not a great childhood by most standards.

As an adult I have had my share of ups and downs, too. I have had several business ventures fail. I have had to file bankruptcy. I experienced marital problems due to financial stress, compounded by problems with my mother and step-brother. In my late thirties, I finally had to totally sever my relationship with my mother and brother, because they constantly put my wife and kids' lives in jeopardy. I still struggled with physical problems. My twenties and thirties are what I call my "breaking bones, bricks, barriers and just being broke at times" years. Thankfully, I broke more bricks and barriers than I did bones.

So you see, I was not born with a silver spoon in my mouth and my life was not supervised by awesome parents. I had more than my fair share of barriers to overcome. It was hard living through the bad times. And it was not easy overcoming all the problems.

Success no one could have imagined

But, praise God, I did break down most of my barriers and have enjoyed many successes in all areas of my life. I literally met and married the girl next door while still in our teens. We just celebrated our twenty-sixth wedding anniversary and have raised two great kids to adulthood. I developed a close spiritual walk with my Lord and Savior Jesus Christ.

I have been blessed as an athlete. I currently have a 7th degree Black Belt from Chuck Norris and act as a Regional Chairman and Advisor to his and his brother Aaron's martial arts organization. I recently retired from martial arts competition with several honors, including three World Champion titles. Although I am retired from competition, I still train and occasionally teach seminars.

Business has never been better. I have run several successful businesses, including martial arts studios and network marketing ventures. I have an exploding Life Coach practice with several internationally known clients. I am constantly asked to be a motivational speaker and seminar trainer. I also have a great business partnership with my close friend, "The Million Dollar Man, Ted DiBiase." Ted and I have several projects in the works. If you want to stay informed of what we are doing together, simply visit Ted's site at www.milliondollarman.com. We will be posting regular updates there.

I did not list my accomplishments to brag, only to complete the picture of how far I have come in spite of everything that was against me. Now let me share some of the things I put into practice that helped turn my life around.

Making your way past the obstacles

As I mentioned earlier, you must decide to make changes. You need to write down the changes you want to make in your life. Then write down why you want to make them. In other words, set a goal and list why you want to accomplish that goal.

Next, write down everything you need to do in order to accomplish your goals. You must be willing to literally sacrifice blood, sweat, tears, time and money to successfully do the things on your list. There are many great goal setting programs on the market that provide fill-in-the-blank type forms for each step of the process. *www.wealthtacticsclub.info* provides an awesome goal making program to their Gold members. I use it myself.

"See it, say it, be it," is a mantra I live by. Use the power of visualization and affirmations to speed up your goal-making process. Two of the most powerful success tools available to mankind are positive visualizations and positive affirmations. And unlike many tools, they are absolutely free to the user. These are two things you can't do without if you are serious about being the best you can be in life. This is one topic that I speak and train on regularly.

Find a Life Coach

Find a Life Coach and role models with proven success records. Your role models should be people who have already accomplished what you are wanting to accomplish. You should also respect the way they achieved their accomplishments. Unlike a Coach, a person chosen as a role model does not have to be living. Thanks to books, audio and video products, you can learn a great deal from successful people who have passed away.

A Coach should be someone you trust and feel confident can help you stay on track with your goals. Over the years, I have had many Coaches and role models. Some are even in this book you are reading. One I will mention and give thanks to is my wife, Terry. Yes, even a family member can be a Coach or role model.

No matter what you may have been told, success in life is hard work and does not come without sacrifice. So prepare yourself for the hard work ahead. You will make wrong choices and experience setbacks. Some will be minor, some may be substantial. But that's OK. Just because you lose a few battles, does not mean you have to lose the war. Very rarely did I win a fight without taking some great shots from my opponent in the process.

Spend so much time on self-improvement that you don't have time to pick at the imperfections of those around you. Finding the flaws in others only wastes time you need to strengthen your own weaknesses. As a fighter I learned that I could only control my actions and reactions. I could influence my opponent's actions, but could not actually control them. So, I spent my time improving my own strengths and weaknesses. I let my opponent worry about his.

Treat everyone exactly how you want to be treated. One of the strongest natural laws of this world is that of sowing and reaping. You get what you give. Or to use a very common phrase, "what goes around, comes around." If you want respect, give respect. If you need money, give money. If you want love, give love. If you need more energy, burn more energy. If you give hate, you will receive hate.

"Trying" is not an action or a result. You either DO or DON'T DO something. You either decide to change your life or you don't. You either complete your goals or you don't. You either win your fight or you don't. Totally eliminate the word "try" from your vocabulary.

In closing, I urge you to read this book cover to cover. The lessons and information within can be priceless to those that properly apply them. God Bless!

Reggie Cochran is an internationally known peak performance coach, speaker, author and entrepreneur. Reggie is currently available for key note speeches and teleseminar training. For more information, visit www.blackbeltsuccess.com.

Wrestling With Failure

By The Million Dollar Man, Ted DiBiase
(Celebrity Wrestling Champion)

The private jet lands and my personal valet, Virgil, escorts me to my private stretch limo. I am whisked away to the Presidential Suite of the best hotel in town to get freshened up before going to work. When I arrive, every eye is on me and the hotel staff is tripping over each other to take care of my every need and desire. After I sign several autographs, I make it up to my suite where Virgil orders me the most expensive items on the room service menu. I may or may not eat any of it, but I order it just because I can.

It is now time to go to work. Virgil escorts me to my stretch limo to be taken to the local auditorium where I will first conduct several television and magazine interviews. Then after I honor all the lowlifes with my time, I am escorted to my private dressing room where I will physically and mentally prepare for battle. In a short while, I will step into the ring to face one of the toughest men on earth in front of millions of viewers on a live televised pay per view event.

I am not concerned for my safety because I know if I can't defeat him with my physical and mental skills, or with the help of Virgil, I will buy him with my money. I can do this because I live by the Golden Rule...He who has the gold, makes the rules. I am Ted DiBiase, the Million Dollar Man. People know I am loaded because they have seen me on Lifestyles of the Rich and Famous. They have seen me pay people hundreds of dollars to kiss my sweaty feet on national television.

The Million Dollar Man

I am the Million Dollar Man and my motto is "everybody's got a price." I buy people's dignity for fun – just because I can. I even bought the World Heavyweight Wrestling title from legendary Andre The Giant. There is no limit to my money and there is no limit to my abuse of people with my money. Men envy and fear me. Women desire me. I am large and in charge.

Ladies and Gentlemen, yes, I am Ted DiBiase and yes, I did all the above as the Million Dollar Man. However, it was acting and entertainment. It was an illusion. The Million Dollar Man was a fictional character created to make money from wrestling fans around the world. The illusion was sold through one of the strongest identity-branding marketing campaigns ever launched.

The real truth of the matter is that I was not born with a silver spoon in my mouth. I was not even born with a tin spoon in my mouth. My money supply is not unlimited and the jets, limos and valet were not paid by me. In fact, the house I was interviewed at on Lifestyles of the Rich and Famous was not even mine. It belonged to the owner of the wrestling organization I worked for.

I was not even born Ted DiBiase. My biological dad's name is Ted Wills. My mom divorced Ted while I was still a baby and spent most of her time working traveling jobs, leaving my older brother and I to be raised by my grandmother in Willcox, Arizona. At that time, Willcox was a very small town of a few hundred people.

While on the road, my mom changed careers to that of a pro wrestler. This is how my mom met another pro wrestler, Iron Mike DiBiase. Soon after my mom met Mike, they married. Then Mike legally changed my name from Wills to DiBiase. I was only five at the time. Mike rescued us from Willcox. We actually moved several times during my youth due to Mike's job as a wrestler.

It is Mike DiBiase that I consider to be my father. It was from Mike DiBiase that I learned how to be a man. It was Mike who I looked up to and wanted to be like. It was Mike who started me on the road to becoming a successful athlete. Before becoming a pro wrestler, Mike lettered in football and was also a national collegiate wresting champion.

Iron Mike died in the wrestling ring of a heart attack when I was only 15. It hit all of us very hard in many ways. Mike died without life insurance, even though he sold it at one time. My mom had a drinking problem before Mike died, but it got worse after. I quickly found myself back in Willcox with my mom on a path of self destruction – a path that I did not want to follow.

Setting goals

Fortunately, my father had taught me that if I wanted my life to change, it was up to me. He also taught me the importance of setting goals, committing to those goals and having a strong enough work ethic to accomplish my goals. While my mom wallowed in self pity, I started setting goals to become a success and get out of Willcox.

Wanting to follow in Mike's footsteps, I wanted to be a pro athlete, maybe even a wrestler. Both Mike and my mom did not want me to become a pro wrestler due to the many hardships of the industry and the lifestyle that goes along with it. So I set out to become a successful football player and kept the idea of being a pro wrestler as my backup plan. I followed the advice my dad gave me and eventually won a college scholarship to play football. But as fate would have it, I was not good enough for the pros.

When I saw that plan A was going to fail, I started working on plan B, a career in pro wrestling. Through the help of long-time friends of the family, Dory and Terry Funk, I quickly found myself living the life my parents wanted me to avoid. Space will not let me share with you all of the hardships of becoming a success in the wrestling industry. Just let me say that it is a very tough life – one that I do not want any of my three boys to experience. Wow! I really did grow up to be like my dad. I feel exactly like he did about me.

Remembering the basic success formulas I learned from Mike, I reset my goals and got back to work. With the help of people in the wrestling industry like the Funk brothers, Harley Race, Dick Murdock, Bill Watts, Vince McMahan and others, I overcame all of the hardships to become a pro wrestling superstar. I went from being overworked and underpaid regional wrestling star Ted DiBiase, to the internationally known Million Dollar Man. Still overworked, but much better paid!

Because of personal problems I was experiencing, I eventually retired the Million Dollar Man character. Shortly after, due to major injuries, I was forced to quit wrestling totally. Just like before, I went back to the basics of success to start over. This time my new occupations are not based on my athletic performance.

A new life by changing my thinking

Through a series of life altering events, I turned my life over to Jesus and felt lead to enter into Christian Ministry, peak performance training, coaching and speaking. Today I spend my time spreading the Gospel of Jesus Christ and helping people become more successful in all areas of their life. This is much more satisfying than paying people to embarrass themselves in public.

As a wrestler I had many tag team partners. We even wore a few tag team title belts along the way. Today my main partner is my wife Melanie, to whom I owe more than words can say. Together we wear rings around our fingers that mean more to me than any belt I ever wore around my waist. I could not be the man, husband and father I am today if it were not for her love, prayers and support.

I also surround myself with mentors who are experts in financial planning, marketing, sales training and self improvement. One of them, Reggie Cochran, is also featured in this book. Together, we have several books and audio series about to be released. The first will be *Wrestling With Finances*, coauthored with internationally known insurance manager and financial expert Terry Cochran, CLU, CLF. That will be followed shortly by *Wrestling With Forgiveness* and *Wrestling with Failure*. For updates on release dates, visit www.milliondollarman.com and www.blackbeltsuccess.com on a regular basis.

The Million Dollar Man said "Everybody's got a price." Ted DiBiase says "success has a price." However, it is a price most people can afford. I challenge you to pay the price of success to improve your life and of those around you. The price you will pay for success is much less than the price you will pay for failure. God Bless.

Ted DiBiase is available for Corporate and Christian speaking events as a keynote speaker and trainer. Ted is also available for teleseminars, fundraisers and autograph sessions. For more information visit www.milliondollarman.com

Notes

How You Think

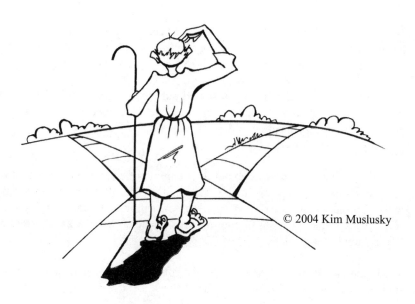

© 2004 Kim Muslusky

Determines Your Life

You Don't Have
TIME
to Feel Down

By Somers White

Every professional will go through periods of time when he or she is down. When we are down, we don't present ourselves as effectively as we could. When we're down, people don't pick up on our enthusiasm, and we do not function as well. Nobody is going to be up all the time and, perhaps, there's a time to be happy and a time to be sad.

What we are talking about is the time when you are in the doldrums. It may be because of a problem with a spouse, one of your children has you worried, a friend isn't feeling well physically or it may be business hasn't been going too great.

On the other hand, maybe you started out feeling rather well when you walked into the office but were greeted by the following situation: the computer is down, your secretary calls in sick, it's Monday and you are dreading the pile of papers you left on your desk Friday.

A weak professional will go out for a cup of coffee to buy time. The strong will bring in temporary help for the day, revamp the plan of action and tackle the most dreaded project first. The rest of us are somewhere in between. We bring our cup of coffee back to the desk, shuffle our papers in general, make a half-hearted attempt. We feel the Monday blues.

Remember there is always one person you can count on and that is you. Here are some suggestions to pull you out of those blues.

1. Take a check-up from the neck up. How are you reacting to these particular situations? Are you allowing these inconveniences to influence you negatively? Is there anything you can do to change the fact that your secretary is ill? No. How can you set up a substitute? Another person?

2. How can you learn from this experience to prepare for a future similar situation?

3. William James wrote, "We can alter our lives by altering our attitude." Most of us forget that this particular technique can and should be used by the day

and by the hour. It's not the situation as much as the attitude toward the situation that has us depressed.

4. Get control of your attitude and your circumstance. Find your best solution. Apply it immediately. Don't waste time worrying about the details.

5. Choose to be around 'Up' people. We tend to fall into the category of "monkey see – monkey do." When we see others handling their situations in a positive way, we can learn by watching. Choose to be around 'Up' people. Get rid of the Neggies – that's how I refer to negative people.

6. Do the things you dread the most first. This takes a burden off your attitude.

7. Give yourself time allotments. Stick to them even if you have to use a 60-minute timer. Procrastination never feels good.

8. Last but not least, I have found a secret to getting yourself up. It is simply to remember what Abraham Lincoln said: "People are as happy as they make their minds up to be." I say, "We are as up as we make up our minds to be."

Get and keep yourself up: you're the only one who can, and there are big rewards for doing so. Remember, victory is more fun than surrender. Don't fail by blaming everyone else. Take responsibility for your actions. It is your responsibility to get started and get yourself up.

We all have failures, but the real failure comes in surrendering to negative thoughts.

Somers H. White is President of Somers H. White Company, a management consulting firm in Phoenix, AZ. He is a former Arizona State Senator and at one time was the youngest bank president in America. He has spoken professionally in all fifty states and six continents.

Prosperity

By Louise Hay

"I deserve the best, and 1 accept the best, now."

If you want the above affirmation to be true for you, then you DO NOT want to believe any of the following statements:

Money doesn't grow on trees.
Money is filthy and dirty.
Money is evil.
I am poor, but clean (or good).
Rich people are crooks.
1 don't want to have money and be stuck up.
1 will never get a good job.
I will never make any money.
Money goes out faster than it comes in.
I am always in debt.
Poor people can never get out from under.
My parents were poor, and I will be poor.
Artists have to struggle.
Only people who cheat have money.
Everyone else comes first.
Oh, I couldn't charge that much.
I don't deserve.
I'm not good enough to make money.
Never tell anyone what I have in the bank.
Never lend money.
A penny saved is a penny earned.
Save for a rainy day.
A Depression could come at any moment.
I resent others having money.
Money only comes from hard work.

How many of these beliefs belong to you? Do you really think that believing any of them will bring you prosperity?

It is old, limited thinking. Perhaps it was what your family believed about money, because family beliefs stay with us unless we consciously release them. Wherever it came from, it must leave your consciousness if you want to prosper.

To me, true prosperity begins with feeling good about yourself. It is also the freedom to do what you want to do, when you want to do it. It is never an amount of money; it is a state of mind. Prosperity or lack of it is an outer expression of the ideas in your head.

Deserving

If we do not accept the idea that we "deserve" to prosper, then even when abundance falls in our laps, we will refuse it somehow. Look at this example:

A student in one of my classes was working to increase his prosperity. He came to class one night so excited, for he had just won $500. He kept saying, "I don't believe it! I never win anything." We knew it was a reflection of his changing consciousness. He still felt he did not really deserve it. Next week he could not come to class, as he had broken his leg. The doctor bills came to $500.

He had been frightened to "move forward" in a new "prosperous direction" and felt undeserving, so he punished himself in this way. Whatever we concentrate on increases, so don't concentrate on your bills. If you concentrate on lack and debt, then you will create more lack and debt.

There is an inexhaustible supply in the Universe. Begin to be aware of it. Take the time to count the stars on a clear evening, or the grains of sand in one handful, the leaves on one branch of a tree, the raindrops on a windowpane, the seeds in one tomato. Each seed is capable of producing a whole vine with unlimited tomatoes on it. Be grateful for what you do have, and you will find that it increases. I like to bless with love all that is in my life now – my home, the heat, water, light, telephone, furniture, plumbing, appliances, clothing, transportation, jobs – the money I do have, friends, my ability to see and feel and taste and touch and walk and to enjoy this incredible planet.

Our own belief in lack and limitation is the only thing that is limiting us. What belief is limiting you?

Do you want to have money only to help others? Then you are saying you are worthless.

Be sure you are not rejecting prosperity now. If a friend invites you to lunch or dinner, accept with joy and pleasure. Don't feel you are just "trading" with people. If you get a gift, accept it graciously; If you can't use the gift, pass it on to someone else.

www.mentorsmagazine.com

Keep the flow of things moving through you. Just smile and say "Thank you." In this way you let the Universe know you are ready to receive your good.

Make room for the new

Make room for the new. Clean out your refrigerator; get rid of all those little bits of stuff wrapped in foil. Clean out your closets; get rid of all the stuff you have not used in the last six months or so. If you haven't used it in a year, definitely get it out of your home. Sell it, trade it, give it away, or bum it.

Cluttered closets mean a cluttered mind. As you clean the closet, say to yourself, "I am cleaning out the closets of my mind." The Universe loves symbolic gestures. The first time I heard the concept, "The abundance of the Universe is available to everyone," I thought it was ridiculous. "Look at all the poor people," I said to myself.

"Look at my own seemingly hopeless poverty." To hear, "Your poverty is only a belief in your consciousness" only made me angry. It took me many years to realize and accept that I was the only person responsible for my lack of prosperity. It was my belief that I was "unworthy" and "not deserving," that "money is difficult to come by," and that "I do not have talents and abilities" that kept me stuck in a mental system of "not having."

MONEY IS THE EASIEST THING TO DEMONSTRATE! How do you react to this statement? Do you believe it? Are you angry? Are you indifferent? Are you ready to throw this book across the room? If you have any of these reactions, GOOD! I have touched something deep inside you, that very point of resistance to truth. This is the area to work on. It is time to open yourself to the potential of receiving the flow of money and all good.

Love your bills

It is essential that we stop worrying about money and stop resenting our bills. Many people treat bills as punishments to be avoided if possible. A bill is an acknowledgment of our ability to pay. The creditor assumes you are affluent enough and gives you the service or the product first. I bless with love each and every bill that comes into my home. I bless with love and stamp a small kiss on each and every check I write. If you pay with resentment, money has a hard time coming back to you. If you pay with love and joy, you open the free-flowing channel of abundance. Treat your money as a friend, not as something you wad up and crush into your pocket.

Your security is not your job, or your bank account, or your investments, or your spouse or parents. Your security is your ability to connect with the cosmic power that creates all things. I like to think that the power within me that breathes in my body is the same power that provides all that I need, and just as easily and simply. The Universe is lavish and abundant, and it is our birthright to be supplied with everything We need, unless we choose to believe it to the contrary.

54

I bless my telephone with love each time I use it, and I affirm often that it brings me only prosperity and expressions of love. I do the same with my mail box, and each day it is filled to overflowing with money and love letters of all kinds from friends and clients and far-off readers of my book. The bills that come in I rejoice over, thanking the companies for trusting me to pay. I bless my doorbell and the front door, knowing that only good comes into my home. I expect my life to be good and joyous, and it is.

Rejoice in others' good fortune

Don't delay your own prosperity by being resentful or jealous that someone else has more than you. Don't criticize the way they choose to spend their money. It is none of your business. Each person is under the law of his or her own consciousness. Just take care of your own thoughts. Bless another's good fortune, and know there is plenty for all.

Are you a stingy tipper? Do you stiff washroom attendants with some self-righteous statement? Do you ignore the porters in your office or apartment building at Christmas time? Do you pinch pennies when you don't need to, buying day-old vegetables or bread? Do you do your shopping in a thrift shop, or do you always order the cheapest thing on the menu? There is a law of "demand and supply." Demand comes first. Money has a way of coming to where it is needed. The poorest family can almost always gather together the money for a funeral.

Visualization – ocean of abundance

Your prosperity consciousness is not dependent on money; your flow of money is dependent upon your prosperity consciousness.

As you can conceive of more, more will come into your life.

I love the visualization of standing at the seashore looking out at the vast ocean and knowing that this ocean is the abundance that is available to me. Look down at your hands and see what sort of container you are holding. Is it a teaspoon, a thimble with a hole in it, a paper cup, a glass, a tumbler, a pitcher, a bucket, a wash tub, or perhaps you have a pipeline connected to this ocean of abundance? Look around you and notice that no matter how many people there are and no matter what kind of container they have, there is plenty for everyone. You cannot rob another, and they cannot rob you. And in no way can you drain the ocean dry. Your container is your consciousness, and it can always be exchanged for a larger container. Do this exercise often, to get the feelings of expansion and unlimited supply.

Open your arms

I sit at least once a day with my arms stretched out to the side and say, "I am open and receptive to all the good and abundance in the Universe." It gives me a feeling of expansion.

The Universe can only distribute to me what I have in my consciousness, and I can ALWAYS create more in my consciousness. It is like a cosmic bank. I make mental deposits by increasing my awareness of my own abilities to create. Meditation, treatments, and affirmations are mental deposits. Let's make a habit of making daily deposits.

Just having more money is not enough. We want to enjoy the money. Do you allow yourself to have pleasure with money? If not, why not? A portion of everything you take in can go to pure pleasure. Did you have any fun with your money last week? Why not? What old belief is stopping you? Let it go.

Money does not have to be a serious subject in your life. Put it into perspective. Money is a means of exchange. That's all it is. What would you do and what would you have if you didn't need money?

We need to shake up our money concepts. I have found it is easier to teach a seminar on sexuality than it is one on money. People get very angry when their money beliefs are being challenged. Even people who come to a seminar wanting desperately to create more money in their lives will go crazy when I try to change their limiting beliefs.

"I am willing to change." "I am willing to release old negative beliefs." Sometimes we have to work with these two affirmations a lot in order to open the space to begin creating prosperity.

We want to release the "fixed income" mentality. Do not limit the Universe by insisting that you have "ONLY" a certain salary or income. That salary or income is a CHANNEL; IT IS NOT YOUR SOURCE. Your supply comes from one source, the Universe itself.

There are an infinite number of channels. We must open ourselves to them. We must accept in consciousness that supply can come from anywhere and everywhere. Then when we walk down the street and find a penny or a dime, we say "Thank you!" to the source. It may be small, but new channels are beginning to open.

"I am open and receptive to new avenues of income."

"I now receive my good from expected and unexpected sources."

"I am an unlimited being accepting from an unlimited source in an unlimited way."

Rejoice in the small, new beginnings

When we work for increasing prosperity; we always gain in accordance with our beliefs about what we deserve. A writer was working to increase her income. One of her affirmations was, "I am making good money being a writer." Three days later, she went to a coffee shop where she often had breakfast. She settled into a booth and spread out some paper she was working on. The manager came over to her and asked, "You are a writer, aren't you? Will you do some writing for me?"

He then brought over several little blank tent signs and asked if she would write, "TURKEY LUNCHEON SPECIAL, $3.95," on each card. He offered her a free breakfast in return.

This small event showed the beginning of her change in consciousness, and she went on to sell her own work.

Recognize prosperity

Begin to recognize prosperity everywhere, and rejoice in it. Reverend Ike, the well-known evangelist from New York City, remembered that as a poor preacher he used to walk by good restaurants and homes and automobiles and clothing establishments and say out loud, "That's for me, that's for me." Allow fancy homes and banks and fine stores and showrooms of all sorts – and yachts – to give you pleasure. Recognize that all this is part of YOUR abundance, and you are increasing your consciousness to partake of these things if you desire. If you see well-dressed people, think, "Isn't it wonderful that they have so much abundance? There is plenty for all of us."

We don't want someone else's good. We want to have our *own* good.

And yet we do not own anything. We only use possessions for a period of time until they pass on to someone else. Sometimes a possession may stay in a family for a few generations, but eventually it will pass on. There is a natural rhythm and flow of life. Things come, and things go. I believe that when something goes, it is only to make room for something new and better.

Accept compliments

So many people want to be rich, and yet they won't accept a compliment. I have known many budding actors and actresses who want to be "stars," and yet they cringe when they're paid a compliment.

Compliments are gifts of prosperity. Learn to accept them graciously. My mother

taught me early to smile and say, "Thank you" when I received a compliment or a gift. This advice has been an asset all my life.

It is even better to accept the compliment and return it so the giver feels as though he or she has received a gift. It is a way of keeping the flow of good going.

Rejoice in the abundance of being able to awaken each morning and experience a new day. Be glad to be alive, to be healthy, to have friends, to be creative, to be a living example of the joy of living. Live to your highest awareness. Enjoy your transformational process.

Louise Hay is a metaphysical lecturer and teacher and the best selling author of numerous books. Since beginning her career as a Science of Mind minister in 1981, Louise has assisted millions of people in discovering and using the full potential of their own creative powers for personal growth and self-healing.

Visit her web site at: www.LouiseHay.com.

If You Could Use a "Financial Breakthrough,"
Here Are Five Places to Get One

By Dan S. Kennedy

Recently, I participated in a fairly typical late-in-the-year conference call with members of one of my coaching groups. Here are a few of the actual results reported: one member's company sales were up 72% over the prior year; another had doubled by mid-year, then increased by 40% per month since then; another was up 28%. Another one not only doubled his income, but started taking two days off per week. Now, here is what is striking about these reports – not one could point to any significant 'mechanical' or 'process' changes in their businesses to explain their robust improvements. Instead, these otherwise rather hard-nosed, tough-minded, very pragmatic business owners admitted, somewhat reluctantly, that the only explanation for the growth was in the intangibles. There were significant changes in their own thinking – about money, about time, and about themselves.

I am brutally pragmatic. I make my living predominately by teaching, writing about, speaking about, and consulting on very practical, procedural methodologies such as direct-response advertising and marketing. I tend to attract clients, coaching group members, and Kennedy Inner Circle Members who are much in my own mold. But those with whom I have long and in-depth relationships, long after methods are mastered, are always working on the less tangible aspects of the game – the mental or psychological factors.

In working closely and hands-on with literally hundreds of private clients, individual entrepreneurs who have skyrocketed their incomes and wealth in short time frames, I have catalogued five breakthrough changes in their thinking. I believe these mental shifts account for the rapid and dramatic changes in their fortunes. Here they are:

1. Thinking about Price

2. Thinking about Time

3. Thinking about Money

4. Thinking about Marketing

5. Thinking about Adverse Events

I have created hundreds of hours and thousands of pages of information about these five opportunities for breakthrough. My newest program, *The Renegade Millionaire System* (www.renegademillionaire.com) focuses on them. It is a daunting task to summarize them in enforced brevity in this single chapter, but I will try.

Breakthrough #1: Removal of all limits and pre-conceived ideas about price

These entrepreneurs have set aside all industry norms, competitive norms, and personal beliefs about price, and focused on presentation of value and targeting those buyers for whom price is not the prime means of making decisions. Consequently, for example, a millionaire martial arts school owner in a small market, is whipping nine different competing schools all within a stone's throw of his, yet he charges 200% to 500% more! Then there is the cosmetic dentist who increased his average case fee from $25,000 to over $40,000 to become the highest priced in his entire market – yet he attracted more patients than ever. I could cite at least 30 more examples that are intimately familiar to me.

Discovering how remarkably elastic price is and learning to design, market and command premium prices is a huge breakthrough for numerous reasons, including needing fewer transactions and/or customers to hit a sales objective, and having more to invest in acquiring each new customer. I have an entire arsenal of strategies and tactics for marketing successfully at prices substantially higher than competitors' or industry norms, but frankly, the person's attitude about this is even more important, and it is harder to alter that than to teach and implement the strategies.

Breakthrough #2: Very tough-minded investing and safeguarding of time

One of my clients imposed a new discipline this past year: to take on no new business project unless it would realistically promise at least $100,000 net in the first 12 months. Another's minimum is one million dollars in 36 months. This is one of many different types of what I teach as "Numbers to Live By." In many cases, the "Numbers to Live By" mandate strict rules about how you protect and invest your time.

I'll give you some personal insight. I am never interrupted by an unscheduled incoming phone call because I do not accept any. I am not distracted by mail or faxes, because they go to a distant office and are routed to me – urgent ones next day, the rest once a week. I use neither e-mail or cell phone. Because I work free of interruption, I get ten times more done in one-tenth the time. People in my business insist you cannot make yourself so inaccessible without it costing you a ton of business. They're wrong. And others who have copied me in other businesses have discovered the same surprising results. Sure, you may still insist my modus operandi is far too extreme for you, and you may or may not be right. But I'll wager the biggest steak in Texas you are much farther toward the opposite extreme than need be, letting others control your time.

My friend and client Tracy Tolleson, a top mortgage broker earning over $400,000 a year, got 72% of his business this year referred by a select group of real estate agents with whom he works. Real estate agents show houses and run open houses evenings and weekends – but Tracy turns his phone off at 6:00 PM and leaves it off all weekend. Every other mortgage broker I tell this to swears it can't be done. They are at the mercy of their clients 24-7, talking on the cell phone even while in the men's room! Friend, if you can't even pee in peace, your life is way out of whack!

I have gotten even tougher and more rigid about all this since I first wrote my book *No B.S. Time Management* in 1997. The new edition being released by Entrepreneur Press in August 2004 will reflect the recent discoveries, success stories, and the even tougher approach. (If you're reading this before 8/04 and would like a preview, go to www.dankennedy.com/nobsbooks, or www.nobsbooks.com.)

Breakthrough #3: Thinking about money

Most people think about money in terms of 'lack,' 'difficulty' and having to 'make' it. We think in terms of unlimited abundance, ease and attraction. This is more than a cute semantics exercise.

Here's the blunt and simple truth about the movement of money in our society: everybody finds the money to buy what they really want. If you doubt it, go find the worst, saddest, poorest trailer park, and take note of the satellite dishes. How many have TV's? Cable? There's never a shortage of money. For the entrepreneur, it's never a money problem: it's always, only, a marketing problem. Since you are not a tree rooted in the ground, you are free to move: to move geographically, to change demographically, to market to different people in different places, to market differently, to market something different for which an enormous desire can be created. Therefore, for you, there's never a shortage of money. And there's no legitimate excuse for not taking in as much as you'd like.

Breakthrough #4: Accepting marketing as job one

Most entrepreneurs get into their chosen businesses for the wrong reasons, and once there, invest their time in doing the wrong jobs. For 29 years, I've been correctly teaching that the biggest, fastest quantum leap in income is the mental shift from being a "doer" of your thing to a "marketer" of your thing.

Several years ago, I was doing a considerable amount of consulting as well as advertising copywriting for a big, brand name company, the subsidiary of a Fortune 500. At one point, its President took me into his office to broach discussion about – probably with the hope of re-negotiating – my fees and royalties, which had hit a major benchmark. He said that he'd calculated the company was paying me more per hour than it was paying him. I responded that there was good reason: he knew far, far more than me about every aspect of that business except one. The one he was clueless about, I was adept at: getting customers. I then reassured him that the

61

discrepancy in our pay and the reason for it would remain our private secret! Yes, it was a fun moment, and it's an entertaining anecdote, but more than that, it contains the actual secret of maximum income few entrepreneurs ever grasp. The highest paid, most indispensable, least delegate-able role is marketing. It's far easier to find a bean counter than a bean getter.

Breakthrough #5: All news is good news

This is a statement I teach in my *Wealth Attraction for Entrepreneurs* and *Renegade Millionaires* programs. It is very, very hard to swallow on the surface, yet proven at over 30 different key pivot points in my own life. It's known to all hugely successful, resilient entrepreneurs. Again, this is not Pollyanna-ish, but practical, because without this understanding, you fail to uncover and act on the opportunities presented in every single initially apparently adverse event.

Just as an example, I have a client who worked tirelessly for three years to reach a point where she could sell her business, in which she was tired of toiling and which was frustrating her. Shortly after the sale designed to put her on "Easy Street," the entire deal came apart like a cheap suit in a hurricane. The buyer failed to honor his obligations, did untold damage to the business, and months later she had no option but to take it back. When this first occurred, she was horrified, angry, and depressed. But because she understands that all news is good news, and is therefore exceptionally resilient and opportunity-oriented, she determined to totally transform the business in a new way that pleased her and suited all her other lifestyle preferences. That tragedy, only 2 years later, now pays her more per year than its total selling price – and she works only part-time!

Several times as a speaker, I appeared at events with George Foreman. I met him, liked him, and started paying a lot of attention to his career, past and present. In his first boxing career, George achieved the heavyweight championship – but admits to wasting all opportunity that came with it. He did not present or cultivate a likeable persona, was not media-friendly, and ultimately used up all his money. Instead of being a bitter and broke ex-boxer (and there are plenty of those), he staged a comeback in the ring that ultimately shocked a skeptical sports world. The bigger objective was making himself into a likeable, popular, beloved and eminently marketable celebrity. He accomplished that, which led to his role as a TV infomercial star and spokesperson for the Salton Company and its product, a fat-reducing grill, re-named the George Foreman Grill. Doing so made George a multi-millionaire. I believe he sold his royalty interest for over 130 million dollars. In all probability, had he not squandered his first shot at celebrity, he never would have achieved the far greater celebrity from his comeback as the oldest boxer ever to re-take the title, nor fully grasped the need to become and stay a wholesome, popular, marketable personality.

The biggest secret is behavior

So far, I've been talking about how I and the entrepreneurs I work with think differently in five key areas. However, the truth is, you cannot just "think and grow rich." Way too much has been written about "thinking" without making the connection to "behavior." Thinking alone is best reserved for a safe, secure academic environment, for students supported by their parents or tenured professors supported by taxpayers and donors. In the real world, it is what you do, are doing, and get done that matters. Behaviors, not thoughts. Behaviors, not ideas. Your breakthrough will come from a change in behavior.

Dan S. Kennedy is a highly-paid direct-response copywriter, consultant, coach and advisor to thousands of his 'Inner Circle Members' worldwide, and a confidante to over 100 first-generation, from-scratch millionaire and multi-millionaire entrepreneurs. He is the author of nine books, including the *No B.S.* series of books published by Entrepreneur Press. Information about Dan is available at *www.dankennedy.com*.

Becoming Aware of Your Highest Self

By Wayne Dyer

Within you is a divine capacity to manifest and attract all that you need or desire. This is such a powerful statement that I suggest you reread and savor it before you begin this journey.

Most of what we are taught to believe about our reality conflicts with this statement. However, I know it to be so true and valuable that I encourage you to surrender any hesitation and let this thought enter your consciousness: *I have a divine ability to manifest and attract what I need or desire!*

Becoming aware of your highest self does not happen through physical effort, nor can one rely upon supernatural techniques such as invoking angels to do this heavenly work for you. What is essential is that you learn that you are both a physical body in a material world, and a non-physical being who can gain access to a higher level. That higher level is within you and is reached through the stages of adult development.

The developmental stages of infancy through adolescence have been explored by many writers, but very little has been written about the developmental stages of adulthood. There are four stages that each of us seem to traverse once we reach adulthood. These stages of our lives represent a way of thinking, although they are not necessarily associated with age or experience. Some of us proceed rapidly through these stages, learning at a young age that we are both a physical self and a higher self. Others remain in one of the earliest stages for a lifetime.

Carl Jung, writing in *Modern Man in Search of a Soul*, provided some critical insight into the developmental tasks of adulthood. He believed that an awareness of a higher self is a developmental task of adulthood. In the next section I am offering my interpretation of Dr. Jung's stages of adult development.

The four stages of adult development

The Athlete

The word "athlete" is not meant to disparage athletes or athletic behavior. It is intended as a description of the time in our adult lives when our *primary identification* is with our physical body and how it functions in our everyday world.

This is the time when we measure our worth and our happiness by our physical appearance and abilities.

Those abilities are multitudinous and uniquely personal. they can include such things as how fast we run, how far we throw a ball, how high we can jump and the size of our muscles. We judge the worthiness of our physical appearance by the standard of attractiveness based on the shape, size, color and texture of body parts, hair and complexion. In a consumer culture like ours, judgement even extends to the appearance of our automobiles, houses and clothes.

These are the concerns one has when he or she is in the earliest stage of adult development. This is the time when life seems impossible without a mirror and a steady stream of approval to make us feel secure. The stage of the athlete is the time in our adult development when we are almost completely identified with our performance, attractiveness and achievements.

Many people outgrow the stage of the athlete and make other considerations more significant. Some of us, depending on our personal circumstances, move in and out of this stage. A few stay in the athlete stage for their entire lives.

Whether or not you have moved beyond the athlete stage is determined by how fixated you are on your body as your primary source of self-identification. Obviously, it is healthy to take good care of your body by treating it kindly and exercising and nourishing it in the best way your circumstances allow. Having pride in your physical appearance and enjoying compliments does not mean you are body-fixated. However, if your daily activities revolve around a predetermined standard of performance and appearance, you are in the stage that I am calling "the athlete."

This is not a stage in which you can practice the art of manifesting. To reach the ability to know and use your divine inner energy, you must move beyond your identification as being exclusively a physical body.

The Warrior

When we leave the athlete stage behind, we generally enter the stage of the warrior. This is the time when the ego dominates our lives and we feel compelled to conquer the world to demonstrate our superiority. My definition of ego is the idea that we have of ourselves as important and separate from everyone else. This can be a acronym for Earth Guide Only, since ego represents our exclusive identification with our physical selves in our material world.

The ego-driven warrior objective is to subdue and defeat others in a race for the number-one spot. During this stage we are busy with goals and achievements in competition with others. This ego-dominated stage is full of anxiety and endless comparison of our success. Trophies, awards, titles and accumulation of material

www.mentorsmagazine.com

objects record our achievements. The warrior is intensely concerned with the future and who might be in his way or interfere with his status. He is motivated with slogans such as: "If you don't know where you're going, how will you know when you get there?" "Time is money. and money is everything," "Winning isn't everything, it's the only thing," "Life is a struggle," "If I don't get mine, someone else will."

In the warrior state, status and position in life are obsessions. Convincing others of our superiority is the theme of this other-centered time of life in which the ego is the director. This is the time when we are attempting to do what warriors do, conquer and claim the spoils of our battles for ourselves.

The test of whether you have left this stage is to examine what it is that is the driving force in our life. If the answer is conquering, defeating, acquiring, comparing and winning at all costs, then it is clear that you are still in the warrior stage. You can probably regularly shift in and out of the warrior stage as a way of effectively functioning in the marketplace. Only you can determine how intensely that attitude dominates your existence and drives your life. If you do live primarily at this level, you will be unable to become a manifester in the sense that I am describing.

The Statesperson

The statesperson stage of life is the time when we have tamed our ego and shifted our awareness. In this stage we want to know what is important to the other person. Rather than obsessing over our quotas, we can ask what *your* quotas are with genuine interest. We have begun to know that our primary purpose is to give rather than to get. The statesperson is still an achiever and quite often athletic. However, the inner drive is to serve others.

Authentic freedom cannot be experienced until one learns to tame the ego and move out of self-absorption. When you find yourself upset, anxious or feeling off purpose, ask yourself how much of your emotional state has to do with your assessment of how you are being treated and perceived. When you can let go of your own thoughts about yourself and not think of yourself for a long period of time, that is when you are free.

Shifting out of the warrior stage and into the statesperson stage of life was an extremely freeing experience for me. Before I made the shift, I had to consider all of my ego needs when I gave a public lecture. This meant worrisome thought about how I would be received and reviewed, whether people would want to purchase my books and tapes, or fears about losing my place and becoming embarrassed.

Then came a time when, without any concerted effort, I began to mediate before my lectures. During my meditation I would silently recite a mantra asking how I might serve. My speaking improved significantly when I shifted away from my ego and entered the stage of statesperson.

The statesperson stage of adulthood is about service and gratefulness for all that shows up in your life. At this level you are very close to your highest self. The primary force in your life is no longer the desire to be the most powerful and attractive or to dominate and conquer. You have entered the realm of inner peace. It is always in the service of others, regardless of what you do or what your interests are, that you find the bliss you are seeking.

One of the most touching stories I have ever heard is of Mother Teresa, who even in her eighties ministered to the downtrodden in the streets of Calcutta. A friend of mine in Phoenix was scheduled to do a radio interview with her. As they spoke before the interview, Pat said to her, "Mother Teresa, is there anything I can do to help you with your cause? Could I help you raise money or give you some publicity?"

Mother Teresa replied, "No, Pat, there is nothing that you need do. My cause is not about publicity, and it is not about money. It is about something much higher than that."

Pat persisted, saying,"Isn't there anything I can do for you? I feel so helpless."

Mother Teresa's response was, "If you really want to do something, Pat, tomorrow morning get up at four A.M. and go out on the streets of Phoenix. Find someone living there who believes that he is alone, and convince him that he is not. That is what you can do." This is a true statesperson, giving of herself each and every day.

When we help others to know that they are not alone, that they too have a divine spirit within them regardless of the circumstance of their lives, we move to a higher self that provides us with a sense of peace and purpose unavailable in the athlete and warrior experiences. It is here that we might recall the words of Mother Teresa: "I see Jesus Christ every day in all of his distressing disguises."

There is one stage even higher that the statesperson. The fourth stage is where I have been carefully leading you on this journey of awareness development.

The Spirit

When you enter this stage of life, regardless of your age or position, you recognize your truest essence, the highest self. When you know your highest self, you are on your way to becoming a co-creator of your entire world, learning to manage the circumstances of your life and participating with assurance in the act of creation. You literally become a manifester.

The spirit stage of life is characterized by an awareness that this place called earth is not your home. You know that you are not an athlete, a warrior, or even a statesperson, but that you are an infinite, limitless, immortal, universal and eternal energy that is constantly changing.

As a soul with a body you are passionately drawn to your inner world. You leave fears behind and start to experience a kind of detachment from this physical plane. You become an observer of your world and you move into other dimensions of consciousness. This inner infinite energy is not just in you, it is in all things and all people who are alive now and have ever lived. You begin to know this intimately.

In order to evolve beyond the earth plane, you need to learn to leave it at will by finding the source of this infinite energy that is responsible for filling your lungs, beating your heart, growing your hair and making it possible for you to read the words on this page. You the physical being are not growing your hair, your nature is doing that for you. The energy that is you is handling all of the details. That spirit that is you is not contained by the physical domain at all. It has no boundaries, no form, no limits to its outer edges. You are aware of the real source of your life, even though you have been conditioned to believe otherwise.

When you reach this level, you are in the space I think of as *being in this world but not of this of world*.

This energy that is you, call it what you will – spirit, soul – can never die and has never died in the past. Most people think of the spiritual world as a future occurrence that they will know after death. Most of us have been taught that the highest self is something that you cannot know as long as you are trapped in a body on this planet. However, the spirit is now. It is in you in this moment, and the energy is not something that you will ultimately come to know but is what you are here and now.

The unseen energy that was once in Shakespeare or Picasso or Galileo, or any human form, is also available to all of us. That is because the spirit energy does not die, it simply changes form.

Even though our rational left-brain mind has been trained to believe that when a person dies his spirit is gone, the truth is that you cannot destroy energy. Your highest self is the spirit presently within you. The energy that was Picasso was not his body, nor was the energy that was Shakespeare his body. It was the inner feelings and creative genius that took the form of a body and a creation on canvas or paper. That has never died. It can't die because it has no boundaries, no beginning, no end, no physical characteristics that we call form.

That energy is within you. If you want to know it, you can tune into it, and when you do, you leave the limitations of this earth plane and enter a dimension of limitlessness that allows you to create and attract to you whatever it is that you want or need on this journey.

At this level you loosen your emotional attachment to what you view as your reality. This detachment is followed by a knowing that the observer within you who is always noticing your surroundings and your thought is in reality the source of your physical world. This awareness, along with your willingness to enter this domain, is the beginning of learning to attract to yourself that which you desire and need while you are in a physical body.

Up to this point, you probably have been unable to loosen your attachment to the material world. You may believe that there is no other world. If so, you have actually abandoned your divine capability, which is the cause of the sensory world you so assiduously embrace. Gaining the awareness that you have a higher self that is universal and eternal will lead you to gaining access to that world more freely and to participating in the act of manifesting your heart's desire.

The seen and the unseen

Consider for a moment the world of form that you see around you including your body. What is the cause of all that you observe? Contemplate who it is that observes and notices all of the "stuff." Who is that invisible "I" inside all of the tubes, bones, arteries and skin that are your physical form? To know yourself authentically, you must understand that everything that you notice around you was and is caused by something in the world of the unseen. That something is the world of spirit.

When you look at a giant oak tree, ask yourself what caused that tree to become what it is. It started from a tiny acorn, a seedling that grew into a mighty tree. Your logical, rational mind says that there must be something resembling the "treeness" within that acorn. But when you open the acorn you find nothing resembling a tree. All you find is a mass of brown stuff, quiet dust. If you further examine the brown stuff that makes up the acorn, you will find smaller shreds of brown stuff, until ultimately you discover distinctly"acornish" molecules. then you find atoms, then electrons, then subatomic particles, until you finally go as small as is possible with a microscope at full magnification. Here you will find that there are no particles, but waves of energy that mysteriously come and go.

Your conclusion will be that the acorn and the tree itself have a creator that is unseen, immeasurable and called by those of us who need to classify such things the spirit or soul. The source of all therefore is no-thing, since it is not in the dimension of the measurable.

The unseen world that is the source of the world of the seen is also the cause of you. Observe yourself scientifically and you will discover that you are not your creation. If you did not create yourself, what was it that created you?

We can go back to conception and explain creation as one drop of human protoplasm colliding with another, resulting in our appearance in the form of a tiny speck that grew into the body that is you today. But, if you delve further into those drops of human protoplasm, and turn up the magnification on the microscope, and if you do the same with the speck that was your first experience of form, you discover the same truth that described the acorn. In the beginning is energy, energy that has no dimensions, energy that is not in the visible world. This is our original self. It is a potentiality, not an object. A"future pull," if you will, that is a potential to become a something and no-thin more.

The general concept of soul or spirit is that you have one, but it is not that important to daily life. It may become really significant, though, after your body dies. I am taking a different position here, and it is the core of this first principle of manifesting. It will lead you to your highest self, and then on to the ability to live a miraculous life of co-creating with God your ideal state of being. Furthermore, this spirit is permanent and incapable of being lost or removed.

Your destiny is to become a co-creator with God and to treasure the sanctity of all that comes into this world of form that we call home, but which is only a transitory stopping place.

Your creative ability originates in the unseen mind. It begins in the unseen world of waves and energy. So, too, do the planets, the stars, the flowers, the animals, the rocks, you, your possessions, your creations – all of it, no exception. Examine everything and anything and you find that at the core there is no form, only an unseen quality that brings it from the world of the unseen to the world of the observable.

It is this world of the unseen that I would like you to consider as you read these words. Imagine that there are two worlds in which you co-exist at all times. Look around you now at the world of form. Then look within and realize that it began in the unseen dimension that we are not even close to comprehending.

Then, make the big leap to the awareness that you are both of these worlds simultaneously. You are not separate from the world of the unseen any more than you could be separate from the world of the seen. You are a combination of both at all moments of your life, even if you have come to believe that you reside exclusively in the world of the seen, and that the unseen is something other than you. It is you, all of it. Right now!

The problem that faces most of us in becoming manifesters and learning to manage the circumstances of our lives is that we have forfeited our ability to oscillate between the world of form and the unseen world. Imagine that there is a line down the middle of the room that you are in at this moment. Pretend that everything to the right of the line represents the world of the seen. To the left of the line is everything that is the cause of everything on the right. The unseen world is on the left, the seen world is on the right.

Now, question your belief that you (the whole you) cannot enter the world to the left of the imaginary line. If you were to cross that line every now and then, you would be entering the world of the creator. Have you been taught that the creator is something outside yourself? (I will deal with this more thoroughly in the second principle.) If so, your inner world (the world of the unseen) is full of notions that prohibit you from participating in the creative process.

There are dogmas that represent participating in the creative process as blasphemy, or foolishness, or thinking too highly of yourself. But go back to the opening sentence of this first principle and reread it until it resonates within you: *Within you is a divine capacity to manifest and attract all that you need or desire.*

It is more than within you. It is you, and you must overcome our conditioning and give yourself permission to enter this world. Cross the line that separates the physical you from the you that is just as real, but unseen. When you overcome the obstacles of your mind that prevent you from crossing the line, your unseen self will be your ticket to creation in your life.

Transcending your conditioning

Like it or not, all of us have been conditioned to think and act in ways that have become automatic. We need to figure out how to get past this conditioning if we want to gain access to our highest self. You can be sure the ego will not take well to this kind of effort.

Asking the ego to help diminish its own significance so that you might have access to your higher self is akin to attempting to stand on your own shoulders. Ego is as unable to move aside in deference to spirit as your eye is able to see itself or the tip of your tongue able to tough the tip of your tongue!

Your task thus becomes a quagmire of paradoxes. If you rely upon your ego to get past the influences of the ego, it will only strengthen its hold on you. You must figure out how to emancipate consciousness from the limitation of your mind and body.

In the ego state you generally experience yourself as a separate entity. To move past this conditioning you want to begin to see yourself as humanity itself rather than as a separate form in a body. Very simply put, if you feel that you are disconnected from the rest of humanity and truly a separate entity needing to prove yourself and compete with others, you will be unable to manifest your heart's desire.

Manifesting is not about getting things that are not here. It is about attracting what is already here and is a part of you on a spiritual level. If you remain separate, that which you wish to manifest will be forever unavailable to you. If you shift that awareness around and are able to see yourself as a part of what you desire, you will have transcended the conditioning of your ego and of all the other egos who have contributed to this process in our life.

With the realization of God within yourself, you not only dissolve your ego's identification as separate from God, but you leave behind the old ways of seeing yourself. As you awaken to your highest self, your conditioning as a separate being will be overcome with practice.

Below are a few of the conditioned thoughts that will keep your ego in charge of your life and prevent you from materializing what you desire and what desires you.

1. *I am not in charge of my life. That force is outside me.* This kind of conditioned response to the circumstances of your life puts the responsibility on something outside you and becomes a handy excuse when your life is not going as you would like it to. You can change this perception in any given moment, and begin to trust that the vital force of the universe is exactly what you are. Entertain this notion every day by noticing the life force flowing through you. Turn your attention away from the ego-dominated thoughts about the circumstances of your life to the present moment by consciously noticing your breath, the sounds, textures, smells and scenes that the life force is experiencing through you. Practice stepping away from the thoughts about your life in any given moment, and step into the experience of the life energy flowing through your senses.

2. *People cannot manifest, it is all a function of the cosmic throw of the dice.* This is a very popular idea, particularly for those who are in less than propitious circumstances. Blaming luck or some external, invisible force that controls the universe is a habit of conditioning that leads to disempowerment and ultimately defeat. You will have to rid yourself of this hallucination that you are a powerless to attract what you desire. Keep in mind that you are not playing magic when you learn to manifest, you are simply manifesting a new aspect of yourself that has been hidden.

   You are the universe. It is not something outside you. You are that force which is in everything, even the things that have previously failed to show up in your life. Remember, as you think, so shall you be. If you think you can't, you are right, and that is precisely what you will see showing up in your life. The results of "I can't" lead to the next conditioned response.

3. *I have tried before and it has never worked for me.* Here, the conditioned response is believing that once having tried and failed further efforts will yield the same results. A key word in this thought is "try." Trying means struggling, working at it, giving it a lot of effort, setting goals and so forth.

   Just for a moment, stop and try to pick up a pencil from the table. Just try to pick it up. You will find that there is no such thing as trying. You either pick it up or you don't. Period. What you call trying to pick it up is simply not picking up the pencil.

Let go of your obsession with the past and with trying, and instead remain relaxed and casual and in the moment, noticing your life force minus your judgements and explanations. You will see good multiply as needed, when you come to know that you are not powerless to make it happen. The universe is rich with abundance that will be provided to you when you let go of reasoning that says your past must be your present.

The reason that you have been unsuccessful in manifesting what you want is because you are attached to an idea that is erroneous. Your past is an illusion. It is the trail left behind you, and a trail behind you cannot drive you today, regardless of what you choose to believe. All you have is now and you have never tried anything. You have simply not done it yet. You can now shift that reasoning right out of your inner world.

4. *Only highly evolved beings can manifest.* This is the ego saying that you are separate and distinct from your spiritual teachers and others who live at the highest levels. Even though every spiritual practice encourages you to see the divine within yourself, to know you have in you the same mind as your master, and to discover the kingdom of heaven within yourself, your ego cannot buy it. It is sold on separateness, and convinces you that you are less than those highly evolved beings you've heard about. Relinquish those thoughts and replace them with seeing yourself as connected to everyone by that unseen life force that is your divine essence. Refuse to put others either above or below you, but instead see them as you. It is necessary to grasp this idea firmly before you can experience true manifestation.

These are a few of the thoughts that swirl around in your head whenever you contemplate the idea of having what you want and need want and need you.

This first spiritual principle directs you to overcome your conditioning. It requires you to adopt a new attitude about yourself, and then to put this attitude into daily practice. I am encouraging you to know the highest self rather than read about it. To know it in the deepest reaches of your being, and then to never again doubt it.

Having a philosophy is useless if it is simply an awareness of rituals and the teachings of experts. To make your philosophy work for you it must become an energy pattern that you use in your daily life. It must have both an eternal truth to it as well as a utilitarian quality that makes you feel, yes, I know this to be true because I apply it and it works.

You do have a highest self. You can know this highest self in both the seen and the unseen dimensions of your life. Once you are convinced of this, the belief that the ego is the dominant motivating force in your life will lose its power.

I encourage you to follow these suggestions for developing this first principle as a permanent part of your total awareness. This plan of action worked for me. If I encounter doubt, I return to this four-point plan. It always reacquaints me with the highest self.

How to know your highest Self without any doubt

1. *Here is a great definition of enlightenment: to be immersed in and surrounded by peace.*

    Your highest self only wants you to be at peace. It does not judge, compare or demand that you defeat anyone, or be better than anyone. It only wants you to be at peace. Whenever you are about to act, ask yourself this question: "Is what I am about to say or do going to bring me peace?" If the answer is yes, then go with it and you will be allowing yourself the wisdom of your highest self. If the answer is no, then remind yourself that it is your ego at work.

    The ego promotes turmoil because it wants to substantiate your separateness from everyone, including God. It will push you in the direction of judgment and comparison, and cause you to insist on being right and best. You know your highest self by listening to the voice that only wants you to be at peace.

2. *Go beyond the restriction of the physical plane.*

    The purpose of the highest self is to assist you in this effort. You do this by creating an inner sanctuary that is yours and yours alone. Go to this silent inner retreat as often as you can, and let go of all attachments to the external world of the ego.

    As you go to this sanctuary, a light will be born within you that you will come to know and respect. This light is your connection to the energy of manifestation. It is like taking a bath in pure light; you will feel this energy as you go silently within. This light is not of the earth plane. It will help you go beyond the physical world. Remember, you cannot go beyond the earth plane if you are still in it. The real you, the unseen you, can attract the energy of the sun, the wind and all that is celestial.

3. *Refuse to defend yourself to anyone or anything on the earth plane.*

    You must learn to stay within your higher energy pattern regardless of what goes before you in the material world. This means that you become like an unknown sage who refuses to lock horns with anything on this physical plane.

    This is the challenge of the highest self. It is beyond the reality system that you identify as material and as form. Use your inner light for your alignment and allow those who disagree with that perspective to have their own points of view. You are at peace. You never explain, and you refuse to flaunt your energy. You know it, and that is enough for you.

4. *Finally, surrender and trust in the wisdom that created you.*

You are developing a faith that transcends the beliefs and teachings of others. This trust is your corner of freedom, and it will always be yours.

Your highest self is not just an idea that sounds lofty and spiritual. It is a way of being. It is the very first principle that you must come to understand and embrace as you move toward attracting to you that which you want and need for this parenthesis in eternity that you know as your life.

Wayne Dyer, Ph.D, is a psychotherapist, best-selling author and internationally recognized lecturer,and is one of the foremost inspirational speakers of our time in the field of spiritual growth and personal development. Dr. Dyer received his doctorate in counseling psychology from Wayne State University and the University of Michigan. He can be seen and heard regularly on radio and television. Over a dozen of his books have helped move this generation to a higher awareness of their inner potential These include *Your Erroneous Zones, Pulling Your Own Strings, The Sky's the Limit, What Do You Really Want for Your Children, Gifts from Eykis, You'll See It When You Believe It, Real Magic, Everyday Wisdom, A Promise Is a Promise, Your Sacred Self and Manifest Your Destiny, Staying on the Path, Wisdom of the Ages* and most recently *There's a Spiritual Solution to Every Problem.* Dyer's tapes include *How to Be a No-Limit Person, The Awakened Life, Choosing Your Own Greatness, Your Life Begins Now* and *Voice of the Feminine Spirit.*

His essential and urgent message is that as spiritual beings we possess unlimited power to recreate our lives, and ultimately the world.

Visit the Wayne Dyer website at: www.drwaynedyer.com.

Assembling your Toolbox for Life

By Susan Gilbert

"The truth is that our finest moments are most likely to occur when we are feeling deeply uncomfortable, unhappy, or unfulfilled. For it is only in such moments, propelled by our discomfort, that we are likely to step out of our ruts and start searching for different ways or truer answers."

– M. Scott Peck

Anyone who has repaired or built something knows that it's much easier when you have the right tool. We all have a toolbox that we have assembled on our journey through life. We always have a choice what tools we will use as we focus on the design of our lives, just like we have a choice of what tools we use if we are going to build a new home.

Some of these tools serve us well, get easier and easier to use over time, and become precious treasures. Others were needed at one time in life, but we have now outgrown the need for it – yet, out of habit, we retrieve that tool and use it where it is no longer appropriate.

What if we assembled a new toolbox?

One that would fix the stickiest problems?

Tools that would make whatever job we are facing seem easy as 1-2-3?

Teaching ourselves to create what we desire

The first part of teaching ourselves to create what we desire with clarity and focus is understanding how to use the best tools to create the space in front of our face. The second part is understanding that what comes to us presented itself from the place of what we believe to be true. Choosing what we desire in life and then using the tools to create it is a part of our evolution. In fact, we as individuals are the human physical aspect, or tool, for part of that evolution.

Many of us have desires that we pay attention to. Others of us choose not to pay attention, at least not yet. What is the difference between the two?

It's the difference between reaching into our toolbox of our thoughts and saying 'Yes!" to what we are presented with as we live our days, which opens up many more things to say yes to. However when we continually say 'No," or add judgment to events and people, then that again presents us with the difference between being open to life and saying no to it. It's the difference between being thankful for what enters our life because we have designed it to be there, or grumbling and complaining about that which we have created, which is constricting and limiting to our possibilities.

Paying attention

What would make us choose the latter, which stops any creative flow? Not paying attention to the information flowing our way from everywhere as to how things REALLY work!

Have you been paying attention to what you are constantly being shown?

And if you are, are you then taking the next step and honoring (without question) WHAT is showing up for you?

If life isn't going as well as you'd like it to, chances are you are focused on the 'why is the happening to me' or 'I'll never find my way out of this problem' syndrome. It's natural. Most people do it. So don't beat yourself up.

Just know that those thoughts (or tools) will NOT get you the results you desire.

Can I share with you the tools that I have in my toolbox?

Gratitude

The first tool in my toolbox is "Gratitude."

Oh right! you may be thinking. You want me to be grateful for this mess I'm in?

YES!

Somewhere, someday, you will look back at what is happening right now, and say something like, "Gee, last year when I lost my job, I thought it was the worst thing in the world. I thought life couldn't get any worse. Now I look back and can see it was the best thing that ever happened to me. I HATED that job. I was just afraid to make a change. It took a few months, but now I'm doing work that is entirely different, is paying me more, and I LOVE IT! I never would have left my old job if I hadn't been fired."

This first tool, "gratitude", is unconditional acceptance of what appears in your life TODAY, knowing that there is no good or bad.

Like attracts like. It's your choice. When you are grateful, you are in an open and receiving place where more good can come into your life right now – without wasting moan and groan energy. It's a tool that will revolutionize the way you will look at what shows up in your life. It's a tool that lays a solid foundation for the life you are building.

The "I Can Mindset"

Once we are in the proper mindset, we can begin to focus – or get very clear about what we want to create in our lives. What goals we want to achieve. What life we want to live.

I am not talking about busy, exhausting activities, done out of habit, that lead nowhere. I'm talking about focused steps towards what matters to you.

Use the power of focus.

Focus is where you place your attention. It is awareness. It is clarity of purpose. When action follows this focus, you will create your desired results.

Now it's time to use a tool called the "I Can Mindset." The first half of this mindset includes using intention, imagination and intuition.

I use Intention first, and begin with these three easy steps.

1. The first step is always to state a clear intention about what you are wanting for your life.

2. The second step is to PAY ATTENTION to what shows up. Something will show up.

3. The third and most important step is to "Honor" what you have been shown. I know, it might be uncomfortable to step out of the rut you're in. But trust me.

Follow through on the idea, the inspiration, which often times we dismiss, thinking that the next step has to show up in a physical event or person. The next step can very well show up in an event or person, but just as real and valid are the ideas and inspirations that gently flow into our minds.

This is how we all walk on water. The rocks come up before us to step on, and in our new understanding, we know beforehand that the rocks will show. This is not about having faith that the rocks will show for us to walk on water. It is the KNOWING that as we intend/choose/decide, we are placing those rocks out in front of us on purpose.

We purposely design our lives with this focus and create the path of the rocks on which to walk. Teach yourself those three steps. And watch the magic of your life unfold.

Are you focused…or fretful, or frazzled? Focus is everything! It is the big difference between accomplishing your dreams and sitting around wishing they would come true. **Susan Gilbert** is America's Focus Expert, helping you to focus on what matters in order to create the results you desire. Quoted in *Entrepreneur, Inc, USA Today* (and many more) as well as a sought after radio and TV personality, Susan can motivate you to attain your goals, achieve balance in life, and create great tomorrows. Visit her website at: www.susangilbert.com and sign up for her free report: *How to Train your Mind to be Laser Sharp.*

The $177 Million Dollar Secret

By Bob Scheinfeld

We all have different wants, needs and challenges. We have unique backgrounds, personalities, and environments. Yet we have one major thing in common. We all have "gaps" we must bridge on a daily basis.

Successful individuals have goals. For instance as a business person you might want to increase sales and profits, reduce expenses, increase your income, attract and retain top talent, create a new product or service, solve a problem, outfox a competitor, etc. What you're not always clear on is the best way to get from where you are now to where you want to be – the quickest and best way for you as a unique individual to achieve your unique goals.

When you know where you are, and you know where you want to go, but you don't know the quickest or best way to connect the two locations, a gap forms.

The process of becoming successful and continuously enhancing your success consists of bridging a constant stream of gaps. Why? Because the minute you bridge one gap to reach a new destination, you choose another goal or destination. Another gap forms, and the process of gap formation and bridging then repeats itself endlessly.

In all the success stories I've participated in, I began without knowing how to produce the results I ultimately achieved. I began without always having the contacts, ideas, skills, knowledge, and resources I needed and would eventually use to succeed. But I always began with the absolute confidence that I could apply a special system I call "The 11th Element" to bridge the gaps necessary, find what I needed, and produce extraordinary results. To maximize the results you produce, you need a proven system for bridging your own gaps on a daily basis – for finding the people, ideas, resources, techniques, strategies and help you need to succeed.

I'm now going to introduce you to The 11th Element System. Let me begin by giving you two reasons why you might want to pay extra careful attention to what follows:

1. The System was originally passed to me by my grandfather, who used it to turn a simple idea into a Fortune 500 multi-billion dollar powerhouse (Manpower, Inc., the world's largest temporary help service), to amass a vast personal fortune, and live a lifestyle most only dream about.

2. I used the System to build a string of successful businesses and create wealth for myself and others. Most recently, I transformed a tiny company doing $1.27 million in sales into a $44.2-million "shining star" in just four years. The company was named to INC. Magazine's "500" list three years in a row. Then we sold it for $177 million!

Larger and more powerful than the Internet . . .

Logging on to the Internet is just about as amazing as making a phone call. We rely on it to communicate, research, sell, buy, and find recreation. But as amazing as the Internet appears, it has serious limitations. However, there's another network you can access to get the help you need to succeed. It's much larger and older than the Internet, infinitely more powerful, and doesn't require a computer. I call it "the invisible network." Within it lies the heart and soul of The 11th Element.

The Internet connects us at the conscious level. The invisible network connects everyone on the planet together at the unconscious level and stores information on what we're all doing. Once considered "new age" or "way out," today international scientists, including those at Harvard University, Stanford Research Institute and other private institutions, have documented the existence of the invisible network.

You've already connected . . .

Have you ever known something was going to happen before it happened? Or picked up the phone knowing who was on the other end? Perhaps you've known what someone else was going to say before they said it. You've certainly had hunches that proved to be accurate. Where do you think this knowledge came from?

Rob Strasser, once a top executive with Nike, had a hunch, a feeling that the company should invest major resources in the new "Nike Air" line of shoes. Without any hard data backup, he pushed the project forward despite tremendous resistance from the management team. Nike Air ended up being one of the most successful product launches the company ever made. Where do think Strasser's "feeling" came from?

Stare at anyone through car window glass at a stoplight or in a crowded mall or sitting several seats in front of you in a theater. Often the person will turn to look directly at you because they "felt" you staring at them. How did they know not only that someone was looking at them, but where that person is?

Why do you think you have an instant attraction to or dislike of someone you've met for the first time? Why do you feel you can trust them or that they make you feel uncomfortable? What information are you accessing and how did you access it?

All these unexplainable experiences are examples of how we constantly log on to the invisible network without conscious intention. The real question is not: "Is there really an invisible network connecting us all together?" The real question is: "How can I use the invisible network to help me build my business and wealth?"

The invisible network serves two purposes. It's an information storehouse and a communications "switchboard.

1. Information Storehouse

On the Internet, "search engines" store huge collections of information you can access to research virtually any subject. The invisible network also has search engines, but their functionality is much larger and more complex than their limited Internet counterparts.

The invisible network automatically receives information about everything and everyone in the world and stores that information in its search engines. For example, if someone is working on a cure for cancer in Japan, developing an invention in Australia, has a special skill and lives in South Africa, offers a unique product or service in the United States, or develops and applies new strategies in England, the details are automatically sent into the network where you can access them for your benefit. Even more amazing, the information in the invisible network is continuously updated on a real-time, moment-to-moment basis.

No matter what result you want to produce, or problem you want to solve, the perfect solution is stored within the invisible network. You can find it – if you know how! That's why tapping into the invisible network helps you produce extraordinary results, and provides access to raw power that goes so far beyond our conscious capabilities.

2. Communication "Switchboard"

Messages flow 24/7 through the invisible network at the unconscious level. Every second, people are sending messages asking for help in achieving goals and specifying the kind of help they're willing to offer others. And just like in the "surface world," we discuss, negotiate, make decisions, and make agreements at the unconscious level: "I'll do this for you if you'll do that for me." The excitement comes when we see "on the surface" the positive result of our "unconscious requests."

If the Internet excites you, imagine magnifying its available resources and possibilities billions of times, and you have a slight idea of what's possible when you start tapping into the invisible network. No matter what's going on in your business or financial life right now—with sales, profits, income, operations, employees, net worth, investments, and so on—it's all being shaped in powerful and amazing ways by information and messages previously sent into the invisible network.

Asking for help through the Invisible Network

If you send out 20 e-mails with a question, you'll get answers back – but you can't expect answers to questions you don't ask. The invisible network works the same way. You must ask for the help you want and need!

It may not always seem so, but at the unconscious level, everyone on the planet wants to help everyone else fulfill their life purposes and complete their missions.

And just like on the Internet, other people will help you if you ask them properly. You just have to know how to find the right people and how to ask them for help so you get the positive response you desire.

The 11th Element System allows you to access the invisible network in the most effective way by working with what I call your "Inner CEO" (an inner intelligence that goes way beyond what's usually called "the subconscious mind"). Your Inner CEO helps you attain your goals based on their relevance to your mission and purpose. And you can begin as I did, without having the contacts, ideas, skills, knowledge, and resources you will ultimately need to succeed. Begin by asking for help and letting your "Inner CEO" be your guide.

Bob Scheinfeld helps entrepreneurs start and build businesses, and use them as springboards to live "The Ultimate Lifestyle." His speeches, seminars, books, audios, and other learning resources have helped hundreds of thousands of people in 160+ countries produce extraordinary results, in less time, with less effort and much more fun.

To contact Bob, visit:

http://www.bobscheinfeld.com

http://www.11thelement.com

http://www.ultimatelifestyleacademy.com

Or call 434-220-3440.

Mind, Body, Money:
Programming your Subconscious Mind

By Glenn Wilbor

Programming your subconscious mind is a concept that is often misunderstood or relegated to new age mystic status, but it is a concept vital to your success in any area of life. Programming your subconscious mind sounds difficult. Some have said, "I have a hard enough time programming my conscious mind, so why would I want to program my subconscious mind?" The answer is, either you program it or your environment does it for you. Which do you think is better?

The need for strong references

Programming your subconscious mind can happen as quickly and easily as someone saying that you look like you're getting sick. If you do not have strong enough references for wellness and health, then this can enter your subconscious mind, and your subconscious then creates symptoms. Some of you may think, "Yeah, right!" But if you have ever been on a boat and watched people get seasick, you can see that it's true. The simple suggestion of getting sick can actually cause some people to get sick. They don't have strong enough references for not getting sick on a boat. Now, if you tell the Captain he looks like he is going to get seasick, he will laugh out loud. His subconscious mind has so many references for not getting sick that it literally rejects the information as an impossible joke.

Now, some of you may be thinking that is one just unusual situation, and one has to get used to the sea before they can overcome seasickness. Here's the truth: everyone in the above example has the potential for seasickness, but everyone also has the potential for not being seasick. Everyone has the potential for programming their subconscious mind for whatever results they are looking for. Need proof? Every single accepted medical experiment has a control group that does not take the drug but takes a placebo. Doctors know that a certain percentage of any control group will physically get better just on the belief that that the pill they took worked. Their subconscious mind took over and actually made them better without anything but a sugar pill! Once you understand this concept you understand the power of your subconscious mind. Then you can understand the need to program it.

The "how to" of programming your subconscious mind

So how do you program your subconscious mind? I am sure all of you have heard of affirmations and visualization. Some may have thought of these as new age mystic

BS, but think about it a little more. How did the captain literally reject the suggestion to get sick? He had references that told him he does not get sick on boats. Maybe he has been on a boat 500 times before. Each one of those memories and experiences creates a reference for not getting sick. He has literally taught his body that he does not get sick.

People learn in three ways: visually, auditory, and kinesthetically. In other words we see it, hear it and feel it. Our memories are nothing more than pictures, sounds and feelings. If the captain has 500 references or memories that tell him he is not going to get sick, then he's not going to get sick. Then is it possible that we could create strong enough references to be at the same level as the captain? Obviously, the answer is yes. We could all go out on a boat 500 times and focus on techniques he used for not getting sick when he first started going on a boat, such as staying above deck, watching the horizons, eating right, maybe even taking Dramamine the first couple of times. Whatever he did when he was first learning not to be seasick, we could model. In other words, if we copy his beliefs and actions, we will get the same results. After 500 times, we would have just as strong a reference as him for not getting sick. We now would have those experiences and memories in pictures, sounds and feelings of not getting sick.

Could we model just those experiences without actually going out on a boat? Well, we know that he has learned from experience that he does not get seasick. So, if we visualize those same experiences and affirm that we don't get seasick, and if we ask questions about why we don't get seasick (providing two of three ways that you learn), we now have strong references imprinted in our subconscious minds. Through strong enough visualizations, we can even experience the feelings. When you sleep, doesn't your subconscious mind work so well that in every dream you experience things just as strongly as in reality? If you don't think so, think about the time you had dream about someone you loved and they betrayed you. You woke up and knew it was just a dream, but you still had bad feelings toward them. Sometimes we actually need to talk to that person to make things right – that's getting new references!

Programming for success

Now that you realize that your subconscious mind can be programmed, how can it be programmed for success? It involves the same techniques: affirmations, visualizations and questions. Affirming "I am wealthy" or "I am successful" will build strong references. At first it will feel almost idiotic. You will think, "How is this affecting anything in my life?" But think about this for a moment: if someone told you one thousand times you are ugly, don't you think you might start to think you're ugly? Now reverse the process: if someone says you are good looking or "hot" a thousand times, do you think that would start affecting your image of yourself?

Does that actually change how you look? Well, let's analyze that. Confidence is attractive. Your posture will definitely improve, you probably will smile more and you might pay more attention to wardrobe, maybe even start working out. People will perceive you as more attractive. If people tell you are ugly, then maybe food becomes your friend or you stop grooming, your posture gets worse, you stop smiling and altogether stop trying. You let yourself go, drop out of the game, give up. We have all seen these types of people.

Now think about success. What is affirmed becomes reality. Once you build reference in reality, it is just affirming what is already taking place. What if you just said these things to yourself a thousand times (even a thousand times a day!). This is what I do in the shower almost every morning. I say an affirmation ten times quickly, and count that as one. Then ten more counts as two, and doing that I count to one hundred. You may think that is a lot, but it only takes about ten minutes. Do you have ten minutes a day to program your life for success?

Most people don't – and most people "live quiet lives of desperation" (thanks Thoreau). You ask them what they have been doing and they say "same old, same old" – and it is true. They just live their boring little lives. How fun is that? If you want to be different from the boring average person (the typical masses), then you need to do things differently from them. Most people think it is strange, but I think if you are reading this book, you're different. You are trying to gain insight, but is up to you to take action. Remember that 90% of our country is overweight. Do you want to eat and exercise like everybody else? Well, only if you want to get fat! The rich are a small minority in this society, and believe me, we do things differently than everybody else.

By visualizing what being successful is to you, this again will build references in your subconscious mind. It might feel like a childish dream to you, but all successful people have been visualizing their success (what they would look like or be like) since childhood or at least early adulthood. If you haven't been doing this, then you have a lot of catching up to do. This is why the kid that was always day dreaming and using his imagination ended up creating companies. The kids that always did as they were instructed end up working for them – following more instructions for the rest of their lives.

The last thing you need to do to program your subconscious mind for success is to ask yourself empowering questions that reaffirm why you are successful. These are questions such as: Why am I successful? What do I have in abundance? What is working well in my life? What am I thankful for? How can I feel successful today? How can I achieve "whatever"? If you ask your subconscious a question, then it will find an answer. If you ask yourself, "Why am a loser?" Or "Why does nothing ever work out for me?" the subconscious mind will find an answer to those questions. That is completely disempowering. It is very important to ask empowering questions. Watch the questions you ask yourself. Ask like an attorney would – know the answer you're looking for before you ask yourself any questions.

Without practice, all of these things are difficult and awkward to do, so you need to do these daily. What do I visualize? The answer is anything and everything I want to have or experience.

Cognitive dissonance

What this does is create cognitive dissonance, or tension when your interior world does not match up with the exterior. Something will have to give if you keep the interior world stronger than the exterior world. Things will change. If you affirm you are millionaire a thousand times a day, then when you make $20,000 you are going to spend or use it in quite a different way then someone else. By programming your subconscious mind, you can program in your goals through affirmations, visualization, and power questions. When you create cognitive dissonance you will create motivation. It is opposite of willpower. Motivation is a subconscious yearning to do something. We all have been motivated at some time in our lives, whether to eat when we are hungry or to have sex. These are all just subconscious yearnings.

If you told yourself you're an athlete a thousand times a day, at some point your subconscious mind will buy into it and you will want to do something athletic. If you don't believe me, try it. If you're out shape, then the more you affirm this, the more cognitive dissonance you build and hence motivation. Eventually you might feel disgusted with yourself and take action to join a gym. If your mind thinks you are athletic and then you look in the mirror at reality, if your inner world is stronger than your outer world you will have to take action. Your subconscious will drive you.

It works the same for money. If you wake up and tell yourself you're a millionaire then show up to manage a McDonalds each day, eventually you start taking actions that lead to becoming a millionaire. They will be much different from everyone else. You might get a job where your income is unlimited, such as in sales. Then while everyone else focused on the little deals, you focus on the big deal. When you make the money, what you do with it would be entirely different – you might try to leverage it as much as possible while investing for the highest return. How would you know how to do that? If woke up every morning and told yourself, "I am a millionaire," then surely you would have been motivated to read some books on investing. All this from only ten minutes a day spent programming your subconscious.

This is getting to sound like an infomercial…just buy my tapes and come to my seminar and you too can be a millionaire! But I have given you a logical explanation of why this works. Again, your affirmations, visualizations, and empowering questions create an inner world that is different from your outer world. That creates a tension in your mind called cognitive dissonance, which creates motivation, and that compels you to take action to make your outer world match your inner world.

Seems very reasonable and logical…but now I will get to the good part. "When things start to happen, don't worry, don't stir, just go right along. You will soon be happening, too" (thanks Dr. Seuss). Things will come your way. Something else aligns and people will come into your life who will help you dramatically. Things that you thought were going to take a lot of hard work fall into your lap. It seems incredible, but isn't so much of life? There are many things that we don't understand, but are true. If you want to see, try this for ten days. Something will happen without you doing anything, and it will lead you toward whatever you were affirming and visualizing.

At this point, you are probably wondering what new age mystic is giving all this advice. Maybe he is an artist, or a writer or a speaker where these touchy-feely ideas work, but not in the real world of business. Well, I am a finance geek. I own a mortgage banking company in San Diego. I deal with accrued interest, basis points, proformas, spreadsheets and secondary markets for mortgages all day long. I know these concepts work in the most black and white of businesses. I know they work in sports – I am also a triathlete who competes at least four times a year and trains continuously. Once you understand the importance of your subconscious mind, you will want to train your mind just like your body.

Glenn Wilbor is an entrepreneur and real estate developer. He is the founder and president of California Equities, a mortgage banking firm, which lends direct to the public as well as providing loan products to other mortgage brokerage companies. Glenn is currently developing two residential condominium projects in downtown San Diego near the new ballpark. Glenn enjoys working with others to develop and encourage entrepreneurship. He can be reached at *Glenn@californiaequities.com*.

Change the Way You Think...

By Warwick Beauchamp

Business should be better than this...Why am I working such long hours? Why aren't I getting the return I should be? Great questions – and for many business owners, very real ones too! If you know there's something more, if you're frustrated with your lack of achievement, or if your dreams still linger, just out of reach, consider this: "How does your thinking need to change?" To think well fuels your actions with purpose and clarity.

In 1998, I was teaching school to 12 year olds, earning $36,000 per annum, running a small boat hire business part time, and driving a pretty rough 1972 Toyota Crown which I had previously re-powered with a Holden engine. You see, I was good with my hands. Right from the time I was a small boy, I'd pulled things to bits – and put them back together again! I had learned that if I wanted something, I needed to make it myself or fix someone else's – for I believed what I'd been told: "We don't have the money."

Now as a grown man, with a wife and two daughters, I was living in a house that needed fixing, with a business that used mechanical things that often needed fixing. Our rusty old Toyota Crown had just failed its 'WOF' inspection, and it required at least $1,000 to fix it. Of course – you guessed it – we had NO MONEY!

What would you do? My old thinking automatically kicked in. I starting thinking, "Who do I know with a gas welding set that I could borrow?" Having previously trained as a Mechanic, I knew I could fix it! Of course it would take many hours of hard work. But wait...new thoughts were emerging...foreign thoughts, thoughts that didn't come naturally, thoughts that were both exciting and frightening...

One of my more redeeming passions is that I love learning, and recently I'd been listening to Business and Personal Development cassettes. From that inspiration I decided I'd try a new approach. "Honey," I announced as I arrived home, "We've got an OPPORTUNITY! The car's just failed its WOF, and I can't see how we've got the time or the money to fix it."

There just had to be another solution. All I could think of was my familiar method of solving problems – invest my time at the expense of my family and do the job myself. Sound familiar? Hey, I guess the girls could learn how gas welding works - and they might even help with sanding!

Fortunately, new thoughts prevailed. Trish, my wife, and I sat down and thought, then we prayed, then we thought some more. We started to ask ourselves questions. How much more will the Toyota be worth if we fix it? How much is it costing us to run? How much would we get for it if we sold it as is? How much would it cost for another car? Where could we get money from? Who might be able to help us? Then we asked a key question: "What would a wealthy person do?" That sparked a memory of a piece of advice I'd heard from one of my friends who grew up in a wealthy family. Neville's Dad said to him, "You either pay interest or you pay repairs. Interest you can budget for, repairs you can only guess. They often come at inconvenient times, and usually cost more!" WOW – what a thought…

Could we change? This was scary!!! Would anyone lend to us? We kept asking questions. We did budgets. A plan evolved. Six weeks later we were ecstatic! Driving our freshly imported Nissan Laurel diesel made us feel like royalty. Interest and diesel cost us less than petrol and repairs on the Toyota. We'd bought it directly from Japan, well below market value, thanks to a parent of one of my students. What's more, we were able to borrow the full amount. Why hadn't we done this years ago? All it took was to change the way we were thinking…

In the last six years my thinking has changed enormously. I now own an Action International Business Coaching Franchise, a Toyota/Holden Dealership, a Joinery Factory, Student Accommodation, three rental houses, and part of a commercial re-development. Most of this I've done using little or none of my own money! I've recently bought and sold a small subdivision that netted me in profit more than twice my old teaching salary! Plus, I now spend more quality time with my family, go on more school trips with my girls, and we holiday overseas each year! I say this not to impress you, but to impress upon you the importance of changing the way you think! For the way you think is where it all starts. If you think great thoughts and then take action, you'll get great results and it can happen quickly! It has for me. Your speed of change is up to you…

Looking back on that story I recognise there are 8 key things I've learned along the way…

Take time to think

To be honest, I didn't spend much quality time thinking. Some of the best thinking I did was when I was forced to think by a crisis, or I was sick in bed with nothing else to do but think! What a sad reflection on my priorities! If you're anything like me, your life would be a whole lot better and your goals more quickly achieved if you proactively took time out of your day to THINK! I now know how important it is to schedule time during each day to just sit and think. Quite often I'll turn off the educational CDs in the car, just to think.

Take responsibility

I'm sure a lot of the reason why I didn't think proactively was that in some way, I didn't want to be responsible! If I stopped and thought about the car we were driving, it would reflect on my inability to provide well for my family. Ouch! Challenge is, whether I thought about it or not the facts remained the same. I now know I'm not powerless. I'd much rather see the Profit & Loss Statement and know exactly what's happening – good or bad. For when I take responsibility and think, I have the opportunity and the power to bring change!

Don't do something just because you can

I was good with my hands – and it cost me dearly! I'd already re-powered the car once, and I nearly fell into that trap again! Like many a technician in business, I'm good at doing technical things. I can build computer systems, I can do the accounts, I've even tried to fix the photocopier! How insane! Why choose the technical jobs that you can pay someone $50 an hour or less to do, when there are much better paying leadership jobs to do! The leverage gained from a productive team member will return a greater gain. A well executed sales or marketing campaign can easily return many times more!

Invest in education

It was education that triggered my new response. Looking back, you could call me an education addict! I listened to tapes or CDs in the car on my walkman when exercising. I read books, attended seminars and asked questions of successful people – and I still do! Much of my education cost me very little – books are free in the library, there are many free seminars, I even had other people notice my thirst for learning and give or lend me their material. Still, I recently added up what I've spent on my education in the last 6 years and it came to over $120,000. So don't be afraid to invest in education – it has sure paid off for me! As Brad Sugars, founder of Action International says, "If you think education is expensive – try ignorance!"

Change your vocabulary

To say, "Honey, we've got an OPPORTUNITY!" felt totally unnatural to me. I had to force those words out, when everything within me felt like saying, "Honey we're in deep doo-doo!"

As Robert Kiyosaki says in his book, *Retire Young, Retire Rich*, "A big difference between a rich person and a poor person is simply the quality of their words." I've since learned that words are powerful tools – and to choose them carefully! Observe the words that come out of your mouth – they are a reflection of your subconscious state and you can use them wittingly or unwittingly to program your own thinking!

Rather than say, "I can't afford it," say, "How can I make this happen?"

Ask Questions

To ask questions is to open your brain to new information. Sometimes that information comes from other people, and sometimes it will come from within yourself. A powerful strategy I've learned is to ask myself a question and leave it for my subconscious to work on. If you're not sure where to start, try this one: "What questions do I need to be asking today?"

Ask yourself questions about everything. Why am I doing this? To whom could I delegate? How else can I free up more time? How can I gain more leverage? Who could help me with this? With which contacts do I need to be in touch? Who needs encouragement? Who needs pressure? Who needs checking up on? What am I doing that I haven't recently examined?

I've discovered that questions are the essence of sales, key in negotiating, powerful in management and, when used well, the oil of relationship. As Alan Pease said in the title of one of his books, 'Questions are the Answer.'

Build a network

It was through building relationships with the parents of my pupils that I met someone who had the experience to import a car from Japan. Today my database is probably my most power tool. Here's a recent example:

A person on my database let me know about a commercial building that he had acquired an option to buy at a discount, based on it coming vacant. I contacted a money partner on my database and between the three of us, we forged a plan. I emailed my database at 4:00 pm on a Friday offering $10,000 cash to any person who could lead me to someone who would want to lease the building. I offered a good lease with 3 months rent free to entice a tenant quickly. By 5:00 pm I had a verbal yes from a contact in Australia who knew a business that wanted a premises in New Zealand. By Monday afternoon I had 7 more leads plus another contact from my database with an investor who wanted to buy the property with a new tenant in place. He too had a database of contacts. Should the deal have come together, the three of us would have made $100,000 profit each. Unfortunately we didn't make it in time – I need to build my database some more!

Decide

Probably the scariest part was making a decision! It was especially frightening when that decision was to do something new and different from what I'd done in the past. Even after doing the thinking, I could have procrastinated, stayed crippled from fear of the "What ifs" and resorted to old habits. What I wouldn't have recognized at the time was, that would have been a decision - a decision to choose the comfort of the known and the limitations that come with it. How glad I am that I made a decision to change – to face my fears and chart a new course! So many people live

93

the same, day after day, year after year – that's not for you or me. As Malcolm S. Forbes wrote, "Thinking well is to be wise; planning well, wiser; doing well, wisest and best of all." So be sure to follow your thinking through with ACTION!

Life is an awesome opportunity. There's so much fun to be had, money to be made, contributions to make, and relationships to enjoy…

Decide today that you'll live it to the fullest!

Warwick Beauchamp is a successful Business Owner, Educator, Business Coach and Presenter. He currently owns three businesses, one in manufacturing, an Automotive Dealership and an ACTION International franchise in which he was awarded "2002 Coach of the Year Australasia" Email him for your next event; warwickbeauchamp@action-international.com.

Visit his website at *www.warwickbeauchamp.com.*

Building Your Wealth Cycles

The Ultimate Wealth Technology

By Loral Langemeier

"First comes thought, then organization of that thought into ideas and plans. Then transformation of those plans into reality." –Napoleon Hill

Take a moment now to picture the financial life you want. Can you see it in your mind? Are you ready to take the steps in order to live that life? Do you want to know the step-by-step process that made me a millionaire by the time I was thirty-four? The same step-by-step process that I continue to use today? The same process that has created millionaire status in three to five years for many of my clients?

You'll be glad to know that it is well within your reach. Most people and programs teach you conceptually and theoretically how you can be successful financially. I will take you beyond the conceptual learning and show you how to reach your desired level of financial success, step-by-step. I will show you not only how to think, live, and breathe as if you were already financially successful, but also how to lead and take action so that you can accelerate your financial success materially and spiritually.

Get ready to embark on a journey where you will soon experience powerful changes in your life. Your self-esteem, resourcefulness, personal power and the control you have over all financial concerns will grow exponentially – practically overnight!!!

It can be very difficult to know exactly where to begin. Many people today are buried in debt, barely meeting their financial needs, and can see no end in sight. I am here to tell you that it doesn't matter if you're a 21-year-old college student knee-deep in debt or a 57-year-old forced to take early retirement. It doesn't matter if you're a 32-year-old divorced mother of two struggling to live on child support and alimony, or a happily married 73-year-old grandfather of four. No matter who or where you are, the program I will be sharing with you has proven, step-by-step procedures that will take you from the depths of debt to the heights of financial freedom.

Ready? Let's go!

Just as you follow a recipe to cook your favorite meal, there are specific steps, ingredients and measurements required to become financially successful. You build and grow upon a solid foundation by following the proven methods of those who have already accomplished that which you seek. We call this recipe our Wealth Technology.

There are three components to our Wealth Technology:

- Financial Conditioning
- Financial Foundation
- Wealth Acceleration

Financial Conditioning

Your financial conditioning is the way you think about money. The way you think will always impact your decision-making process.

Very few of us had any degree of financial education growing up. What most of us had was an education based on messages like "we can not afford it, don't ask for anything, you do not deserve it, rich people are bad, or you have to work hard for your money." If this is what you heard growing up, most likely, you still believe it at a cellular level and are making all of your financial decisions based on these old messages.

These messages have also created the thought that talking about money and financial success is inherently wrong or bad. What this has created is a world where very FEW people are having the real conversations about money and financial success that are necessary to succeed.

I say, "so what, now what?" LIVE OUT LOUD. Have the conversations about money, success, wealth, finance, investing and LIFE that you need to have in order to achieve the life that you want for you, for your family, for your wealth.

The first thing you must do is reverse your financial conditioning, or reset your mind and psychology to reinforce what it is you do want, instead of supporting the very thing you would like to move away from. To do this you must identify your sabotaging beliefs. These are the thoughts and attitudes that you have that limit your results. Once you have identified them you must change them to the positive present tense and then repeat, repeat, repeat!

Example of a sabotaging belief about money
Money is hard to earn and even harder to keep.

Example of a positive re-statement of a sabotaging belief
Money comes freely to me! Money is easy to keep and multiply!

This may seem like a relatively simple exercise, but let me assure you it is not. To really drill down and find the core sabotaging thoughts that are holding you back and restate them positively will make every cell in your body revolt against you. There are a wide range of responses you may have, from simply thinking to yourself that this is stupid, to becoming physically ill. Face each of these challenges as reinforcement that what you are doing is right. Put your positive restatements on flash cards in your pocket, post-its on your computer, and flip chart paper around your house. Look at them and say them out loud every chance you get. You will be amazed at how quickly your thinking and your results change.

Financial Foundation

Your financial foundation is the framework that you build your success on and around. Just like your house or a city skyscraper, without a solid foundation, the building will crumble and fall with the slightest provocation. In other words, you need to know the reality of where you are TODAY, have a solid idea of where you want to go in the FUTURE and a plan to get from your TODAY to your FUTURE.

There are four steps to building a rock solid financial foundation. The first step is creating your financial baseline. This is your financial fingerprint. This is where you are TODAY. This includes all of your income (earned and passive), your expenses, your assets and your liabilities. You need to know your net worth and your cash flow per month.

This step is often a wake up call for many people. Either they are much further in debt than they ever imagined or they have more assets than they knew about. It is essential that you are 100% honest with yourself when doing this step. If you leave anything out, or try to make anything look better than it is, you will end up failing in the long run.

The second step is to determine your financial freedom day. This is where you want to be in the FUTURE. This is the day that you will live your "want-to life" versus your "have-to life." The want-to life is the one where you want to go to Tahiti and can because you are financially free, versus wanting to go to Tahiti and can't because you have to work.

So, choose a date, whether it is one year from now or ten years from now, as the day you will be able to declare you are financially free. What is that date? What is your monthly income? What is your yearly income? Is this earned, passive or aggressive? Design this day as specifically as you can, knowing that you can make adjustments as you grow.

The third step is managing your lifestyle cycle. This is where you take a close look at your lifestyle and how it impacts your financial success. Where and how do you spend your money? Are you living above your means and sinking into consumer debt just to portray a certain image to the world? Are you living below your means and hoarding your money, worried about a rainy day?

Once you look at it honestly you can begin to make informed decisions to change. Maybe you don't need that latte every morning. Maybe you should take the money out of your mattress and invest it. No matter where you are, I guarantee you will find a significant amount of money and resources that are being wasted in some way or another. Re-channeling these resources is the next step in this process.

The fourth step is to build a wealth cycle. This is where you structure your plan and frame your actions so that your core needs are handled automatically, while at the same time future-pacing the achievement of your long term goals, all with the money that you currently earn. Sound impossible? Sound crazy? When you successfully complete the first three steps of your financial foundation, this part is easy. You do this by purposely spending every single penny that you earn. This results in rent and bills being paid, college tuition being taken care of, retirement money being saved, and insurance needs being met.

Acceleration of wealth

The acceleration of your wealth is to leverage your current assets to generate even more wealth. You do this through owning businesses, utilizing investment strategies like real estate, stock market and gas wells, taking advantage of tax saving plans like IRA's and educational benefits, and using entity structuring techniques such as forming LLC's or Corporations.

Did that last sentence just overwhelm you? Don't worry! One of my favorite sayings is "You have to lead it; you do not have to do it." What this means is that it's your job to take a pro-active leadership role in your financial success; however, you do not have to have all the specialized knowledge, talent or expertise yourself. No one I know has ever become financially successful doing it alone. Every one of them, including me, has done it through the use of teams. I call mine My Wealth Team.

Leading a team requires a significant amount of skill. You must be an effective communicator, a dynamite task master, and a persuasive negotiator, not to mention a keen observer. All of these are skills that will take time and effort to acquire. This is why wealth acceleration is the most often ignored step in building financial success. It is also the ONLY step that will take you beyond where you are to where you want to be.

I trust if you are reading this book, you are at a cross roads in your life, and are looking for your next steps. I have just laid out for you step by step how I transformed myself into a millionaire by the time I was thirty-four. I diligently worked on and through my financial conditioning. I clearly established my financial foundation. To this day I actively lead my wealth team to accelerate my wealth. Whether you are fourteen, forty-four or ninety four, the same is possible for you.

I highly encourage you to start these steps today. Don't hesitate any longer. Seize your success…choose your destiny…LIVE OUT LOUD.

Through the years, **Loral** has emerged as one of the most inspirational, motivational and uniquely hands on speakers in the area of business and financial success.

To find out how Loral can change your life, contact us at 888-262-2402, *info@liveoutloud.com* or www.liveoutloud.com.

An Innovative Culture To Ignite Your Team's Creative Engine

By Kathleen Meyer

What is innovation?

Innovation covers a wide range of creative problem solutions. It can include new products or services, technical inventions that aid research or manufacturing, medical discoveries, practical solutions to common everyday problems, and creative alternatives to highly complex social/political dilemmas. These new solutions can be revolutionary and unique approaches, improvements on prior ideas, concepts and products, or creative variations of previous solutions. The list is virtually infinite and limited only by our imagination.

Regardless of the business you are in, innovation is a key determinant of whether your company grows and flourishes, or if it spirals into commercial obscurity and ultimately becomes yet another dismal statistic of a failed business.

Where does innovation come from?

Innovation can come from as many sources as there are ways to define it. When considering who can supply your next great idea, look first within your company. Innovations can emerge from the business' established research and development area, if you are lucky enough to already have one. If your company cannot afford the overhead of permanent, dedicated staff, you can assemble a virtual think tank group where members rotate on a continual basis. Collaboration is a critical element. Cutting across multiple functional work groups spawns new products and services that take into account more than one perspective of the development and implementation process.

Do not underestimate external innovation sources, such as your competition and alliance partners. They can be particularly valuable, especially if you are a supplier in a vertical market. But perhaps one of the most important determinants of successful innovation is how connected it is to the consumer's preferences and demands. Few sources are more powerful and can produce more successful results than those ideas we solicit from our customers and suppliers.

Particularly in a small business, where one's livelihood depends on the capture and retention of a small customer base, we must be constantly attuned to the wants, needs and emerging desires of our consumers. Taking the pulse of our consumers on a regular and consistent basis, formally and informally, will help secure our customers' loyalty, promote sustainable relationships that are built on trust and respect, and demonstrate our focus on creating new products and services that are in direct response to our customers' needs. This externally-initiated creative process has the power to transform new or improved ideas from our employees into demand-driven innovations that have been designed for the customer and sometimes even by the consumer.

How can business leaders create an innovative environment?

There are several key ways that business leaders can develop and nurture an environment that promotes innovation. Look into leveraging more than one source for the most successful breakthroughs.

1. Commit to creating an environment that empowers its workers to do what they do best. This means for example, that the shipping and receiving clerk in your company is considered the expert in that department. He or she probably knows better than anyone else in the company what works and what doesn't in the shipping department. Having that first hand knowledge, he/she is a valuable source for contributing innovative approaches, processes or techniques to improve an internal function which ultimately impacts customer service.

2. Develop your capacity to tolerate failures. Realize that not all ideas will develop into innovative breakthroughs, assuring profits that will reach the sky or put your company on the map overnight as an industry leader. Instead, consider where most of those ground breaking innovations that we admire today would be if their creators had not been allowed to conduct many iterations of trial and error.

Develop an environment for your employees to courageously – yet prudently – make mistakes along the path to innovation. Making mistakes is part of the learning process. Allow your employees to make them without fear of reprisal. To promote this open and trusting culture, first make sure that you are not promoting the myth that everyone must be infallible. Establish an open exchange of ideas, concepts and technical solutions with your customers, suppliers and peers. Do not harshly judge your employees when they do make mistakes. Mistakes can be capitalized on the next time they encounter a similar situation. Ask your teams to make a list of the approaches and techniques that did and did not work, and note in what instances and under what circumstances they did or did not succeed. Share this process, as well as the results, so that everyone can learn from them.

As the knowledge base grows, your team will be able to make correlations to other events with similar characteristics. It will be easier to predict and recognize recurring patterns. And, you may even be able to drive totally new solutions into the process. Lastly, in reporting progress, ask your team to include how the innovation being tried can or cannot respond to all requirements. In reality, we avoid future cost by uncovering problems caused by misconceptions about anything. There is a win in these mistakes. These discoveries can highlight what the costs might have been and also present opportunities to uncover better ways of tackling a problem the next time around.

Making mistakes is not a sin unless it is the same mistake committed repeatedly or worse yet, never corrected. Likewise, never making mistakes probably means we have not stretched enough to try something totally new. But remember, those who do and are free from anxiety about always being right can realize the largest and fastest payback on investments in innovation.

3. Develop processes and systems that become ingrained within the company's culture. Innovation should not merely be the result of an accidental discovery or a last minute decision in response to a crisis. Clarified procedures and guidelines will enable and support innovation as a process.

4. Develop the strategy that will be the glue to hold the innovative culture together. This is up to you as the leader. The company's culture must be flexible enough so that employee roles and responsibilities can quickly adapt and adjust to change. It should defy the silos of a hierarchical reporting structure and be sufficiently open, flat enough to allow cross-pollination of ideas between all employees. Of particular importance is a tightly networked environment that effectively links all team members, including customers and suppliers. The objective here should be to shorten the distance as much as possible between those developing the innovation and the customer.

5. Celebrate team successes in order to sustain an ongoing innovative climate in your company. Offer appropriate incentives and rewards to everyone, regardless of their rank or position. These incentives need not be limited to monetary compensation. Money can be a prime motivator for high performance, especially if it is directly tied to an innovative idea that increases revenue or profit margin, or reduces expenses. But there are many other effective incentives to inspire your team to innovate. These motivating factors can include something as simple as public recognition in a company newsletter, gift certificates, time off with pay, or free company merchandise that reflects the received company benefit of the implemented innovation.

6. Don't limit your sights. Innovation does not just apply to big-ticket items such as a totally new product or service. Innovation should be encouraged regardless of how large or small the benefit to the company. When successfully ingrained in the company culture, the spirit of innovation permeates the organization, producing positive energy and excitement and sparking healthy internal competition. Convey the message that innovation is

a core value of your company's identity. Everyone should always be looking for ways to improve the way the organization conducts its business.

7. Promote the concept of innovation teams. It is a well-known organizational tenet that a team effort can produce stellar results that could not have been achieved in a vacuum. Assemble innovation teams with a cross functional mix of talent, seniority and skill expertise. Consider extending your company team to include your customers and suppliers.

Lead with creativity as a core value in your company's culture

Fortunately, small business are usually not nearly as encumbered with deeply embedded bureaucracy and formality, so innovation should be easier for these nimble, fluid and agile organizations. But even small businesses, as they grow, can succumb to the rigidity and over-segmented functional silos of their bigger corporate brothers. As your business expands and matures, carefully assess your needs for process and structure. Resist the temptation to impose rigid processes for the sake of short-term efficiency gains without assessing their longer-term impact on the organization's effectiveness. Test and measure new processes and guidelines before you officially implement them to ensure they are meeting planned objectives. Revise them when and where they are not meeting their expected benefits. Develop short chains of command that will promote timely decision-making and permit knowledge sharing and the free exchange of information and ideas.

Leaders committed to establishing innovation within their organizations lead with creativity as a fundamental value of their business culture. They provide a safe and trusting environment for their teams to nurture and create new ideas, and from those new ideas spawn innovation in a continuous cycle of invention. This repeatable innovation process will improve upon the merits of previous ideas to fertilize the ground for the birth of new ones.

Wise business leaders and their followers reap the benefits of a culture that rewards teaming for innovation to sustain the company's competitive growth and longevity.

Kathleen Meyer, a Business Coach and Licensee of Action International of Colorado, mentors her business owner clients to achieve higher profits while spending less time and effort. As a business leader and executive consultant for over 20 years, Ms. Meyer has led large global consulting practices and guided Fortune 500 senior executives on technological and organizational strategies. Ms. Meyer is a lecturer and published writer on team building, organizational development, marketing strategies, and innovative technology solutions. For business coaching that gets positive results contact Kathleen at: 719-540-3661 or via email at: *kathleenmeyer@action-international.com.*

"First in Mind"

Making Sure Your Business Aligns With Your Strategy

By Claude Beaudry

- **How do you want to be perceived by your clients and prospects?**
- **And – how are you ACTUALLY seen by them?**

If those two aspects of your business are in perfect harmony, you're doing a great job of executing your corporate strategy. But if not, your dreams of growing your company can become elusive.

When I begin coaching new clients to develop a business strategy, this is the first assignment I give them: think long and hard about how you want to be perceived, and write it down for me.

First in mind

Your goal should be to make your company "first in mind" in whatever category you choose. We're all familiar with the concept of a unique selling proposition. "First in mind" is similar to the USP. It's the reason your product or service is the first thing customers think of when they're in the market for whatever you provide.

When I ask where you shop for low-cost groceries and household goods, you probably think, "Wal-Mart." If you're asked to name an upscale New York City jeweler, "Tiffany & Co." probably comes to mind.

So, what about your company? When a potential customer thinks about your product or service, is your product, service, corporate slogan or company name the first thing that comes into their mind?

Establishing how you want to be perceived is the first – and most important – step in building a business strategy. How you answer this question drives everything else in your company – not just marketing, but hiring practices, training procedures, quality initiatives and accounting policies. It determines everything related to how you deliver your products and services.

Remember: your idea of how you're being perceived may not be the same as what your clients actually see. You don't want to spend a tremendous amount of time working on your strategy, thinking everything possible has been done – then find out that the prospects don't perceive your firm the way you want them to see it. You can't assume your message is being perceived correctly. Talk to your clients. You may even want to assemble a group of current and/or prospective clients in a focus group setting to find out how they actually think of you.

The "Map of Attack"

Once you know how you want to be "first in mind," everything else is built on this foundation. You can't be perceived as the company with the highest quality of widgets if you produce a shoddy product. You won't be seen as a high-quality consultant if your representatives don't answer the telephone properly.

The first step is to define your vision for your company. Figure 1 (above) shows how to build your map of attack and put "first in mind" at the center of your planning process. Once you know where you're going, you use the "first in mind" principle to determine how to tackle your other departmental challenges, such as:

- Marketing
- Competition
- Sales
- Personnel
- Product or services

These various departments have strategies at their own sublevels that need to be aligned with the company strategy. Each department has their own mini-version of your broader strategy. You need to make sure everything in each area is aligned with the overall goals and objectives.

Figure 1:
Map of Attack

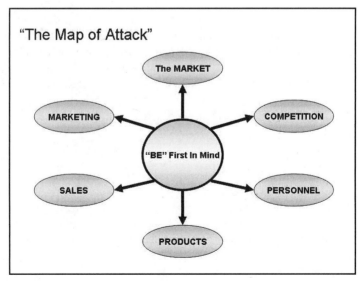

105

I see this problem in corporations of all sizes, but it's particularly common in small businesses. You simply can't have sales going one way and production another. To achieve your goals, they've all got to be on the same wavelength.

For example, I have a client whose salesmen are doing a great job of selling. The problem is that what they're selling does not always fit into the company's new priorities. Sometimes they overpromise something to a client that the production department is not sure it can deliver. Accounts Receivable is another area where the sales force is telling clients they can do things that are not consistent with company policies and strategies.

Departments that are not aligned generally contain people who decided over the course of time to do something that they felt was right. It may have been – but they've got to communicate with the other groups to make sure everybody is on the same page. Otherwise, someone may do something that will make the company look bad. If everyone's not aligned, and one department doesn't perform consistently with your perception, it's a problem for everyone. And it can be detrimental to your company. So make sure everyone's strategy points towards how you want to be "first in mind" for your clients and customers.

Keeping a balanced scorecard

"First in mind" is also the basis for developing your Balanced Scorecard, as shown in Figure 2 (below). The concept was developed by Dr. Robert S. Kaplan and Dr. David P. Norton, co-creators of the Balanced Scorecard. It provides us with a visual approach to building a strategy. The hierarchy shows how you break your vision down into more and more detailed plans as you work deeper into your organization. Ultimately, we use this model to build a precise strategy to implement your corporate vision.

Every person in your company needs to understand your strategy – and how it relates to them personally. Each team member has to be able to identify their job with that strategy. Your associates need to understand that the strategy governs how they answer the phone, how they perform on a service call, or how they make a sales presentation. Once they realize that how they perform needs to synchronize with your vision, they can see how their actions will lead to the greater good of company, as well as to their own personal success.

The power of a leader

All my clients have team issues, even the mature companies. Unfortunately, one of the major roles not played in many companies is "leader." It's not enough to come up with a vision: you've got to build it, explain it to everyone else, sell them on it. Communicating your vision includes deciding, then sharing:

- Core values. What does this company stand for?
- Vision. Where do we want to go?
- Marketing strategy. How are we going to get there?
- Point of attack. This plan reflects the first three points.

Again, you need to communicate the strategies and tactics across the company. Some clients tell me, "That stuff is all in my head." But that won't work until you share your vision with everyone else – then work to make sure it's part of their daily life.

The whole company needs to come together around this shared vision. If I have 13 people in my company, everyone should have a clear vision of what the company's about and where they fit into it. If 12 people are on board and one is not, he or she becomes the weak link in your chain. If that person's actions aren't consistent with how you want to be perceived by your customers, the person can undermine everyone else's hard work and success.

While you want your strategies to be complete, they should not be complex. The simpler it is, the easier for everyone to understand and retain. A complicated strategy will confuse your team, while a simple one will achieve clarity.

Figure 2:
Balanced Scorecard

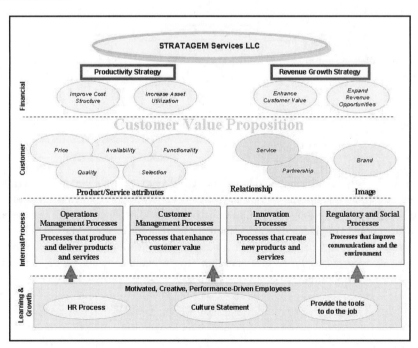

How do you know if your strategy is simple? Ask your employees to describe it in their own words, and then have them tell you how they relate their job to your strategy. How well did they do?

Also, while it can take months to develop a strategy, it doesn't have to be perfect. It's enough to have a good, solid message at the beginning, and then refine it as we go along. I have some clients who keep waiting for everything to be perfect. That's a noble goal, but it will never happen. If you wait for it to become perfect, you'll never get the job done. If you procrastinate, you'll never get there – and you may be missing opportunities in the meantime.

Once you establish a strategy, you can refine it over time, but don't change it. Of course, if the business undergoes radical change – say, you buy a new division and produce a new product – then it will need modification. But the simpler and more consistent you keep your vision, the easier it will be to meet your goal of becoming "first in mind" with your clients.

After all, that's the ultimate goal – aligning your business operations with your corporate strategy to the "first in mind." When your prospects' and clients' perceptions match your vision of how you want to be seen, you'll be the one they call every time they're in the market for your goods and services.

Claude Beaudry is a business coach. For over 30 years he has leveraged his skills in strategic business solutions and organizational transformation, to maximize profits and cash flow, and improve operating effectiveness and productivity. He teaches and coaches companies and individuals about how to produce their Map of Attack to generate the results for their businesses. You can reach him at *claudebeaudry@action-international.com* to schedule your FREE business assessment consultation.

The Gift of a Quiet Mind

By Carrie Hart

Do you have a special place you go when you need to think things through? For me it is my garden. I sit on a wonderful stone bench embraced by a white azalea bush, looking out over my roses: Abracadabra, Double Delight and Peace. I wiggle my bare toes in cool baby tears, breathe in the fresh air, and let the birds advise me.

About eight years ago, I sat on this bench to try something new. I wanted to expand my intuition, to go beyond what my rational mind could easily explain. Little did I know then that these fledgling experiments were the first steps of a wonderful adventure, a journey in which I learned to use my intuition to solve very real problems in all areas of my life, beginning with my most immediate need—my business!

I read about and tried various meditation techniques, such as mentally tracing a little blue light very, very slowly around the perimeter of my body. I experimented with intuitive exercises, such as analyzing mental journeys involving symbols like keys and water. Finally, taking the best of what I read and adding techniques of my own, I came up with some simple yet powerful tools, which I will share with you now.

Relaxation

It all begins with relaxation. Intuition is like a wild animal in the forest: chase it and it will run away and hide. You must sit quietly in the clearing and let it come to you. I began a practice of going to my garden bench each morning and doing just that. You will want to go to your own peaceful spot each day: a comfortable chair in your office, a bench in a park, perhaps your own garden.

Since I had no time or patience for lengthy meditation, I settled on this simple 5-minute relaxation technique. Sit quietly, close your eyes and breathe deeply but comfortably, counting silently from ten down to one. Breathe in: ten, ten, ten, ten, ten. Then out: ten, ten, ten, ten, ten. Then in: nine, nine, nine, nine, nine. And out: nine, nine, nine, nine, nine. Continue in this way until you reach one. If you are still tense, begin again at ten. Then, when you reach one, breathe in deeply once again and picture a tranquil lake with a bird gliding gently overhead. Now you are ready to tap into the great sea of information that Carl Jung called our collective unconscious, a place where you can access knowledge beyond your rational grasp.

Ask questions

A good beginning exercise is to ask, "What is my word for today?" An answer, a word or a phrase, will pop into your head. Jot down the words quickly before your rational mind has time to analyze or reject them. Then take the paper with you as you go about your day, marveling at how you were told "Prepare carefully" on the day the client grilled you, and "Relax and listen" on the day he just wanted to talk.

Over time, I found I no longer needed to count down; just breathing would do. I also learned I could ask more complex questions, anywhere quiet at any time of the day. Soon I began using this technique to help me prepare for all important meetings, even with people I had never met.

One of the first and most critical of such events was my meeting with Barbara. She had resigned and I was being brought in as a consultant to manage a multi-million dollar system implementation. I had just one meeting to learn what I needed to know.

I arrived early and sat in my car. I breathed myself down to a peaceful state and then asked, "How shall I approach this meeting?" The answer was definite: "Don't let her get away with anything!" I jotted this down and went to the meeting.

Barbara was personable and friendly. She handed me the latest project plan, went over it quickly and then moved on to the Unresolved Issues Log.

I glanced down at the project plan and then touched the note in my pocket: "Don't let her get away with anything!" A project plan is the key to success for a major system implementation. Why had she gone over it so quickly?

While she talked about other things, I looked again at the plan. Then I saw it.

"Where are the staff hour estimates?" I asked.

"I just didn't have time to key them into the plan," she said.

"May I see the estimates?"

She hesitated. "They're not actually written down anywhere."

That was enough for me. We spent the rest of the time probing into the project plan. By the end of the meeting, I knew I had a project which had been badly underestimated and was now in deep trouble. The dates showed when they wanted things to happen, not when the tasks would actually complete. No wonder she had resigned!

In the first days of the project I validated my intuition and then gave my client a quick assessment of the situation. I was able to begin the project with a new estimate, rather than wasting time attempting to manage to a flawed plan and becoming tainted with its failure.

After this experience, I always "checked in" before an important meeting. I was getting solid practical advice, and that was enough justification for me. As with light bulbs, television and airplanes, I am willing to make use of things I don't completely understand.

The greater gift

But now, let me share with you the greater gift I received.

One day, about 3 years ago, I went to my garden bench, but this time it was no game; I was trying to make peace with my father's death. I closed my eyes, felt a gentle breeze brush my cheek and caught the perfume of the roses on the air. I breathed in deeply and listened for the silence under the wings of the birds.

And then a picture began to form in my mind's eye, a picture not of my making, but one presented to me. I saw people walking about in a shadowy world, a world I understood to be this physical existence. Each person had a cord which extended up to a higher level. Some cords were glowing with a golden light and these people appeared vital and joyous. Some cords were twisted and only flickered here and there with light, and these people were less full of joy. Some cords were completely tangled, with barely any light flowing within them. These people were unhappy, tormented and lost.

On the level above I saw the source of the golden glow. Each person in the shadow world, our world, was connected to a ball of golden energy above. I understood this glowing golden ball to be the eternal self, the true self of each of us, and it consisted of love, peace and joy. I was a golden ball of energy and everyone in my life now, everyone I had ever known or would ever know, was there glowing beside me.

Then I saw the next level up beyond this, one infinite glowing ball of energy and love, with all of the individual, unique balls of energy subsumed within it. You may name this as you will, call it God or the godhead, the All or the One, this place of ultimate light and power.

And then I knew why my little intuitive experiments had worked. I understood that I could listen to the unexpressed and unarticulated feelings and thoughts of others, sense their desires and their fears, and anticipate their actions by connecting with them energy-to-energy on the level above. From living with this picture in my mind, I have now learned so much more.

I have learned how to bring myself to joy, no matter what is happening in my life. For now I know that I am joy, that it exists within me, and all I have to do is open up

111

the cord which reaches up from my physical body. I now do this every morning. I close my eyes and breathe deeply. I then picture a cord of golden energy reaching up from the top of my head, up and up until it reaches the source, the golden ball of energy which is me. And then I just let it flow down and fill me. I let it flow until the joy makes me smile.

I have learned how to diminish fear, for now I see that fear and doubt exist only as shadows, and if we shine brightly with who we truly are, they must withdraw. I have learned perspective, how to pursue goals with energy and vitality but not to suffer great disappointment when I fall short, for I understand now that there is only one goal that truly matters. That goal is to make myself ever more myself by letting the flow of love and energy pour down.

And I have learned how to bear loss, for nothing is lost; everyone is with us, always. If I sit quietly on my bench in the garden and reach upwards through my golden glowing cord of love, I can feel my father there.

A former CIO and Vice President of a Fortune 50 company, **Carrie Hart** is now an independent management consultant, author and energy healer.

- Visit *www.systematique.org* for information on Carrie's management consulting practice
- Visit *www.carriehart.com* for information about her healing practice and to read a daily inspirational message• Contact Carrie Hart at *carriehart@msn*.com.

RICHuals™: The Path of Powerful Living

By Michael Cody

I have had the privilege of spending the last fifteen years studying the lives and personal habits of successful people. In my research, a common pattern appeared that I have come to call **RICHuals™**. These **RICHuals™** are not merely confined to financial success, but rather apply to every aspect of life from emotional intelligence, relationships, and spiritual connection, to physical well-being, and professional fulfillment.

RICHuals™ is a path for creating lasting change. This path for change starts with the internal identity and then moves to external actions, behaviors and results. This article can be the beginning of your journey into developing new, empowering **RICHuals™** that produce for you the exact quality of life you are most committed to having.

RICHuals™ can be defined as the critical, automatic and conditioned responses that are necessary to develop breakthrough power in your life and the lives of those around you. **RICHuals™** are the habits that determine your destiny. They are guaranteed to foster self-confidence and success when applied with consistency and passion.

Quality of Life: Creating Your Ideal Life

RICHual™ 1: Connecting with Truth

Why seek to improve our situations, relationships, financial position, or physical health? Each of us, whether aware of it or not, has an imprinted "quality of life" that we desire at our deepest core. It functions like a map or compass leading us towards a destination that we must reach, or risk forever feeling disconnected from our truest self.

Some would call this "destiny." Others label it a "calling," and still others simply define it as their "purpose for living." Is this "compass" something preordained, or can it be influenced? Is our drive to accomplish a "quality of life" set in stone and fixed, or is it malleable, able to be shaped to our choosing? The answer to all these questions is simply, "Yes!" It is a question of "actual truth" versus "self-truth." The difference in actual truth and self-truth is the difference between that which is true for all, and that which is true for the individual.

The connection with truth (actual and self) is the foundational RICHual, required to connect with your own identity. If you do not have an honest relationship with yourself you can never hope to have one with others.

RICHual™ 2: Building an Identity on Purpose™:

Do we have the power to shape our own identity? Can we build it on purpose? Again, the answer is …yes! Identity is the bedrock upon which we found every decision we make and action we take as individuals.

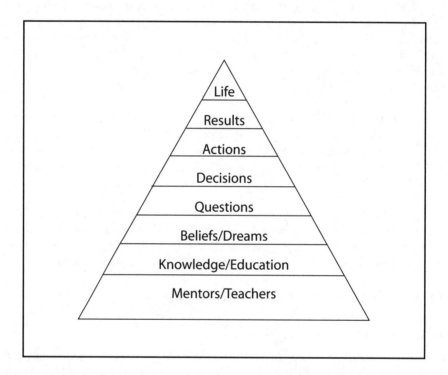

Sarah's Story

"I don't believe I can do this! I need to go home NOW," said Sarah, as she bear-hugged her binder to herself. I could see her whole body shaking as she dug her nails into the white vinyl binder and her heels into the floor.

Sarah was one of many participants in a public speaking workshop for an organization called The InterBIZ Business School for Entrepreneurs™ founded by two visionaries, Casey Combden and Brad Doyle. I had partnered with InterBIZ to help them create a training system designed to teach the most coveted of all entrepreneurial skills…emotional intelligence, or understanding the importance of **RICHuals™.**

We challenged them to not only face the public-speaking dragon, but pick a fight with it and knock its lights out. Initially for Sarah, it felt like the dragon was winning. Sarah's self-truth said that she was incapable of speaking in front of a group of three or more people. The actual truth is that speaking in public is simply a set of skills which anyone can master, given time and coaching.

I asked Sarah if I could be her coach…and she hesitantly said yes. That one decision on her part – the decision to open up, to allow new input – was likely one of the most powerful, life-changing decisions she will ever make.

She was looking for a mentor, coach, and a guide. Sarah made the decision to take ownership of her identity, rather than being owned by her identity. That put her on the verge of having a positive breakthrough that would change her life. She came to this course seeking to develop new habits and beliefs. What she discovered was that those beliefs she had previously accepted were actually disempowering self-truths, counter to her deepest desires and capabilities. She developed new **RICHuals**™ that reinforced the change she was committed to making in her life.

Sarah completed the course and mastered the skills of public speaking. Her breakthrough continues to this day, and her business is taking off like a rocket. She attributes this change to developing powerful new RICHuals™ in her life that connect her with new, empowering self-truth.

The purpose for building your identity with specific intent is to direct you towards the quality of life you deeply desire, and to provide you a clear path for change. By no means is this process perfect or exhaustive, but it works…if you work it. Yes, **RICHuals**™ can be learned, taught and updated to meet your needs, rather than leaving you enslaved to self-defeating habits, behaviors, and identity.

RICHual™ 3: Change the Quality of Mentors/Teachers

Part of defining our existing identity requires defining who and what we allow to influence us. Who is it that influences our beliefs about ourselves, family, relationships, sex, money, politics, and every other aspect of our lives? Part of taking control of our identity is to find where we have rooted our identity and who feeds our belief systems.

RICHual™ 4: Change the Quality of Your Knowledge/Education

Changing who you allow to feed into your life and identity has a corresponding effect on the quality of your knowledge and education. The fact remains that we can change the quality of our knowledge and education at any time. There is a flood of information available to us at any moment. I write this as my new cell phone receives e-mails, accesses the internet 24/7 and keeps me connected to breaking news at all times. If all we need is content, then we have more than necessary to accomplish any endeavor in life. The fact is that we must have context for use of the content.

By context we mean the application of knowledge versus the mere acquisition of knowledge. This is where the value of understanding your mentors/teachers and their impact on your identity, knowledge and its application becomes apparent.

RICHual™ 5: Change the Quality of Your Beliefs/Dreams

Improving the quality of your beliefs and dreams is directly proportional to the clarity of your objectives, knowledge and education related to your focus. People only move towards that about which they are clear. If you are having difficulty moving in a desired direction, then that challenge is often related to some lack of clarity.

RICHual™ 6: Quality of Questions

A change in the previous areas naturally begins to produce a change in the quality of questions that we ask ourselves. A few key distinctions stand out in the thinking processes of those who rise above or sink into anonymity:

Handling Conflict and Failure

Conflict and failure are invariably part of the human experience, and in many ways are the defining elements that highlight the character of a person. The common trend is to interpret failure through a process called Internalizing and Globalizing. Internalizing is the process of taking a conflict or failure and making it deeply personal, driven by the inadequacy of the individual. "Why do I always do that? Why does this always happen to me?" You are internalizing if you take ownership of an isolated situation/failure and make it a hallmark of your own inadequacy. Globalizing is where the individual takes the experience and applies it as a point of reference for all future experiences. Thus, a failure in one area automatically means a failure in everything this person does.

There is an alternative approach called Externalizing and Minimizing. Externalizing is when an individual takes the experience for what it truly is – a limited event. If there is a failure, acknowledge it and learn from it, but never incorporate it into your identity, thus labeling yourself as a failure. Minimizing is refusing to take an experience and apply it as a rule of thumb for everything going on in our lives. Rather, isolate the issue and use it as a learning experience. We must refuse to apply the failure as a lens through which we interpret the remainder of our lives.

Identity plays a significant role in the questions we ask ourselves. In the questioning process, the way in which you ask questions is more important than the questions themselves. Your subconscious mind will find answers regardless of whether the question is positive or negative. Change the nature of the questions you ask yourself and the manner in which you ask them to change the quality of the answers.

www.mentorsmagazine.com

RICHual™ 7: Changing the Quality of Your Decisions

When we change the quality of our questions, we get better answers. Those answers lead us to make new and different decisions based on the information we've gathered. Up to this point, all of the changes have been internal in their focus and nearly impossible to measure by external means.

Consistency is the glue that binds together this whole model for change. Decisions are not decisions if they are not backed by action and consistency. Without those two key factors, beliefs and dreams are merely fantasies, knowledge and education is fruitless, and mentors go unheeded.

RICHual™ 8: Change the Quality of Your Actions

The power is in the doing! If there is to ever be a change in results, there must be a commitment to action. Massive action yields massive results, but moderate action yields no results. Great breakthroughs in personal experience require a massive build up and release of energy, sustained over the long haul. To create a change in your identity and the quality of your life you must be willing to take off all the restraints and limiting beliefs, and succeed in spite of yourself.

What are your rules? What is keeping you from taking massive action? What are you going to do differently when you throw out the rule books and succeed in spite of yourself?

RICHual™ 9: Change the Quality of Your Results

Creating a change in results is one of the key focuses of **RICHuals™**. It is critical that throughout this process, you are measuring the results you get against the results you intended. Results are the outcome of everything that has come before. They are the measuring stick by which we validate the changes occurring on the inside and a snapshot of outcomes of prior changes. Results help us to measure the distances we have traversed in the growth of ourselves and our contribution to those around us. There are three types of results that can occur: 1) Learning Results, 2) Neutral Results, and 3) Positive Results. Once you have measured your results, you must adjust your actions, decisions, beliefs, knowledge and mentors accordingly.

RICHual™ 10: Change the Quality of Your Life

All of these prior changes represent the evolution of our quality of life. This is an evolution bringing us closer to our ideal and in tune with our own internal compass. Evolving into our true potential is seldom easy, and rarely simple, but always necessary if we are to achieve our personal greatness.

In summary, **RICHuals**™ is a process for creating meaningful permanent change in your quality of life. It identifies the relationship between the internal identity and external behaviors that produce the substance of our lives. Any area of life that is not in alignment with your ideal quality of life is almost certainly directly related to some missed or ignored step in the **RICHuals** Path. Challenge yourself to create new **RICHuals**, and watch your quality of life improve dramatically!

Michael Cody brings over 12 years of successful business coaching, and entrepreneurial business leadership in sales, marketing, operations, and systems development in start-up, fast-growth, and mature companies. He is a teacher, certified business coach, and coaches' coach; with his guidance, peak performers reach the next level.

Michael has built, bought, and sold several companies in the technology, services, and banking industry in the last twelve years. He is a J.D. Powers Certified Customer Centered Sales Professional. Through ACTION International(www.action-international.com) the InterBIZ Business School for Entrepreneurs (www.interbizusa.com, www.interbiz.ca), and **RICHuals**™ (www.richuals.biz) Michael coaches business owners on developing practical business skills and the emotional intelligence required to succeed.

Enable Your Success:
Create a Powerful Vision

By Chuck Kocher

Have you ever found yourself wondering, "Where am I really going with my life, my career or my business?" Do you ever feel that your passion, energy and attitude are just not what they used to be? Do you sense a need for change but you are not really sure what to do? Do you finally want to take control of your destiny and your life?

At one point in our lives, most of us have asked these questions of ourselves. But the biggest question of all is what did you do about it – or what are you going to do about it? Sadly enough, most people dream but never really do anything more than that. Those who do something about it are those who set themselves above the rest. As a business coach, author and public speaker, it never ceases to amaze me how few people really have a vision for their life, their career or their business.

My passion as a business coach is helping others achieve their dreams. I teach my clients to do something about it – to take action. I teach them to create very powerful vision for their future. Then we craft a plan and begin the quest to achieve their dreams.

You see, you – and only you – control the keys to your destiny. Creating a powerful vision is the start of it all and will set your life in forward motion toward success. It will unlock your energy, attitude and passion.

One of the most powerful ways to address change is with vision. While change is certainly inevitable, it is how we deal with change that ultimately defines how successful we will be. Creating a powerful vision allows us to have some say on how our destiny plays out. In life, we will have many choices to make. We can choose to be reactive or be proactive. Do you want set the course for your life, or do you want to simply follow a pre-destined map?

Your mindset

When I begin to coach my new clients, one of the first things that we address is their mindset. To make any dramatic change you have to have the mindset and desire to change.

119

You and you alone control how you think. Our mind is the most powerful asset we have. Look at any successful person and you will most likely find a person who has a mindset that is focused on being the very best that they can be. Failure is not an option, or even a part of their vocabulary. If anything, failure is simply a way of learning how to do something better the next time.

Each of the successful people I have been fortunate to touch as clients and as mentors has had all of the following four key attributes:

- **Great Attitude** – What leader and visionary does not have this? A great attitude will help you and your team climb the highest peaks.

- **Absolute Passion** – Passion is infectious to everyone. If you can not be passionate about it, don't do it!

- **High and Positive Energy** – The level and type of energy that you exude will energize others.

- **Determination/Commitment** – To weather your storms you must have this. The path to any great vision will be peppered with obstacles and challenges.

Creating a powerful vision

Essentially, I ask my clients to work on two levels of vision, incorporating both their personal and business/career visions. After all, they are deeply connected. If your personal vision is to retire in the Cayman Islands and your business vision is only going to get you to Kansas, that is simply just not going to cut it.

Your vision is like a Picasso painting. You need to paint a picture of the future that is vivid and colorful. You can leave no detail unturned. You will need to see yourself in your vision. You will also need to feel what it is like to be in your vision. Many people subscribe to the notion of a vision that is just a one-liner: "To create the best company that provides the best products and services." I find nothing wrong with doing this, but only after you put in the thinking and details inside of your vision.

So, let's use a business as an example for creating a powerful vision. Pick a point in time 5, 10, 15 or 20 years in the future. Here are some sample questions that I ask my clients to answer. Answer them both in terms of the present where you are today and in the future where you want to be…

- How big is your business? Revenue/Profit/Income

- Do you have multiple locations for your business?

- How many clients/customers do you have?

- What do clients say about your services?

- Who are your ideal/perfect clients?

- What makes you different and unique as a business?

- What position do you hold in the market that you serve versus your competition?

- How many employees do you have? What are their roles in your business?

- What is your role in the business?

- How have you changed as the leader of your business?

- How many hours do you work "in" and "on" your business per week?

- What is the value of your business if you wanted to sell it?

- Do you own additional businesses?

Push, stretch and challenge yourself. Aim high! Don't forget to put yourself physically, emotionally and mentally in your vision. After all, it is your vision!

Six essentials for actualizing your powerful vision

1. The plan

Now that you have created a powerful vision, having a comprehensive plan is essential for achieving your vision. Your plan must have specific goals that are measurable and achievable. If you have a ten-year plan to achieve your vision, then you will need to have 3 to 5 significant goals and objectives each year. These goals and objectives must move you closer and closer to your vision. Essentially, they are the steps up on your ladder to your vision. Surprisingly enough, each time that I have coached a client through this exercise they have either reduced the steps needed to achieve their vision or expanded their vision to new levels.

2. Surround yourself with trusted advisors

Make sure that you have experts in areas that you are not an expert to offer you counsel and advice. A great set of advisors for a business owner would be an Accountant, Banker, Financial Investments Expert, Attorney and Business Coach.

3. Find a mentor

Find someone who has been there and done it in your industry or related field.

The value is in their wisdom and knowledge of what it really takes to be successful, and don't forget to learn from the mistakes that they made along the way.

4. Jury of your peers

Create a network or group of peers that you can consult with on a periodic basis. Open and honest feedback from a peer group is a fantastic way to learn.

5. Flawless execution

Commit yourself to flawless execution of your plans. To bring your vision to life, a comprehensive plan is a requirement. You must have an action plan that enables execution. Execution will make or break your vision. The devil truly lies in the details of execution!

6. Embrace continual learning and change

A vision is not static, but dynamic. You will change and it will change. Be ready and embrace change. Be a voracious learner. Never stop being that curious two-year-old who is not afraid to ask questions.

Caution! Seven vision killers

Creating a powerful vision is one thing – actualizing it is another. There are many obstacles that you will face in actualizing your vision. Many of these obstacles will be in the external environment. To overcome this, awareness, flexibility and adaptation in your planning will be essential. However, the biggest obstacle that you may actually face might just be you.

The following are the personal vision killers that I see as a Business Coach, time and time again:

1. Procrastination/Indecision – I will eventually make my decision …

2. Lack of total Commitment/Focus – The grass is always greener…

3. Self-belief/Confidence – I just can't do it!

4. Fear of failure and/or success – This is really just an excuse not to be successful!

5. Knowing it all already – If you stop learning, you stop growing and stop living!

6. Trying to do it all yourself – Why would anyone in their right mind try to do it all themselves?

7. Dream, dream, dream – Always living in the future and never making it happen in the present!

Your next challenge

I would not be a great business coach if I did not leave you with a final challenge.

If you really want to change, you can. But first, you must have the desire to and then commit to do so. So I challenge you to take control of your destiny, create a powerful vision and start on the journey to success in your career, your business and your life!

Chuck Kocher is a successful ACTION International Business Coach, entrepreneur, speaker and author based in Colorado Springs. Chuck mentors, motivates and inspires his clients to achieve success both in business and in life.

Visit his website: www.actioncoaching.com

Email: ChuckKocher@action-international.com.

Notes

Section III

Business Tips
for Succes

© 2004 Kim Muslusky

www.mentorsmagazine.com

We get by
With a Little Help
From Our Friends ...

By Lee E. Huffman

*W*ise people know what they don't know and they are not afraid to seek out those who do know!

- Andy Stanley, North Point Community Church, Alpharetta, Georgia, USA

When I was thirteen, my parents owned the Top Hat Restaurant, run by my uncle. The restaurant was in a beautiful old home. Inside this home was a magnificent balcony where someone had hand carved the wood to create a place that simply invited everyone to come up and look around. One day, my mother commented that we should put a shop up there. That quickly, the Top Hat Candle and Gift Shop was born.

This was my first business. Looking back, I can see it was successful because of the advisors that I had around me.

My mother, Pat Huffman, was a successful real estate entrepreneur who taught me how to manage the books, how to select the best products, and how to provide high quality service. My father, Robert Huffman, Sr., was also a successful business owner with his own construction company. Dad taught me that manufacturing my own candles and gifts would improve my profit margins. My aunt and uncle, Ruth and Chuck Potter, counseled me, "If the Top Hat Restaurant is open, the Top Hat Candle Shop should be open." To follow their advice, I had to hire people to help us out. That forced me to learn the basics of how to select, develop and take care of employees.

Looking back, most of my success in business and in life is due to the advisors that I have been blessed to have in my life. In high school and college there were many advisors:

- **Duane "Curly" Osburn:** The track coach who taught me that proper preparation could turn even a group of wild Broncos into winning team.
- **Ray Bayer:** The wrestling coach who convinced me that true success came from getting up quickly when life knocked you down.
- **Larry Rees:** The chess coach who instructed me on how to think ten steps ahead of my competitors, which laid the foundation for my success in potential problem analysis and potential opportunity analysis.
- **Ollene Johnson:** The teacher who taught a little bit of everything in her 40+ years as an educator, and who helped me realize that the pursuit of art, music, and relaxation added spice to life.

These teachers, and many others, laid the foundation for my current success in business. They taught me to work hard and to play hard, to expect success and to never accept anything less than the absolute best.

But, then something happened . . .

Like many young business people, I hit the work force and decided that giving advice was more important than receiving it. It was not overt. I did not rebel against the establishment (although many around me did). I did not refuse help. I simply stopped seeking it.

Twenty-five years later, I had several successful – and a few unsuccessful – businesses under my belt. But, I never enjoyed my business life the way that I did back at the Top Hat Candle Shop.

I found myself inside a Fortune 50 company working for a manager who had no idea what true leadership was, let alone mentorship, and I knew there had to be something better out there in the real world. So, I jumped out of that company into yet another start-up. I was willing to make that change because the Chairman of the new company had something that I wanted: he knew how to invest in people.

Joe Peters was a mentor, an advisor, and a coach. I don't know if he is even aware of this, but Joe was the type of manager I wanted to be. A few years later, I went back into the Fortune 50 company with Joe's blessing and advice. Joe, who had worked for the larger company previously, said, "Lee, if you go back in, make sure they put you into the executive development program and ind yourself a good mentor." Better business advice could not have come along.

Through several fortunate events, I became teamed up with two key advisors: Dilip Saraf and Jeff Davis. These two gentlemen, who gave wise and stern counsel over the years, set me back on the right track. I owe as much of my success to them as I do to anyone since my days in high school.

High quality advisors lead to high quality life

Today, I have even more mentors and advisors. I believe that is the true basis for my success. As figure 1 reflects, the quality of your advisors determines, through a chain of events, the quality of your life.

Mentors, advisors, teachers, and coaches are all there to expand your knowledge and education. If you have a higher quality education, either formal or informal, what you believe about yourself and the world around you expands and your dreams for the future grow. With bigger dreams you ask better questions. The answers to better questions drive you to make better decisions and take more positive actions. These actions give you better results and these results improve the quality of life for you, your family, and those around you.

www.mentorsmagazine.com

It all starts with great advisors, mentors, and teachers because they are the bearers of wisdom.

The wisest man in the world

The key is gaining wisdom. But, how do we gain wisdom? It is simple: just seek it out and ask for it…

The wisest man in the most read book of our era is known as King Solomon. He was a young man when he inherited his throne. But, when the Lord appeared to him and said He would give him anything in the world, the young king did not ask for riches or honor. He simply asked for Wisdom.

This young king's definition of wisdom was *"a discerning heart to govern people and to distinguish right from wrong."* His request made this young man the best leader of his time, and quite possibly the finest leader of all time. To many, King Solomon is considered the wisest man in history. People came from all the nations to hear King Solomon's wisdom.

What does this have to do with getting by with a little help from our friends?

Quality Life

Quality Results

Quality Actions

Quality Decisions

Quality Questions

Quality Dreams

Quality Beliefs

Quality Education

Quality Advisors, Mentors & Teachers

Copyright Action International, 2004

figure 1

---

1 Kings 3   Solomon Asks for Wisdom

⁵The LORD appeared to Solomon … and God said, "Ask for whatever you want me to give you." ⁶Solomon answered, "… give your servant a discerning heart to govern your people and to distinguish between right and wrong …" ¹¹So God said to him, "… ¹²I will do what you have asked. I will give you a wise and discerning heart, so that there will never have been anyone like you, nor will there ever be. ¹³Moreover, I will give you what you have not asked for - both riches and honor - so that in your lifetime you will have no equal among kings."

Wisdom and advisors go hand in hand. Andy Stanley, pastor of North Point Community Church in Alpharetta, Georgia, put it best when he said,

"Wise people know what they don't know … and they are not afraid to seek out those who do know!"

Success in life, including success in business, is all about understanding your limits and reaching out to others who have answers that are different from your own.

These "others" do not necessarily have to be highly successful business people, educators, or pastors. In fact, you will benefit greatly from having business and personal advisors who know nothing about the "technical" side of your business.

King Solomon, the wisest man in the Bible, wrote most of the chapters of Proverbs. He had more to say about seeking wisdom than any author in the Bible. Here are some key points of his wisdom:

- **Proverbs 1:5**   *"A wise man will hear and increase in learning, and a man of understanding will acquire wise counsel"*

- **Proverbs 1:8**   *"Listen, my son, to your father's instruction and do not forsake your mother's teaching."*

- **Proverbs 11:14**   *"For lack of guidance a nation falls, but many advisers make victory sure."*

- **Proverbs 12:15**   *"The way of a fool seems right to him, but a wise man listens to advice."*

- **Proverbs 13:10**   *"Pride only breeds quarrels, but wisdom is found in those who take advice."*

- **Proverbs 15:22**   *"Plans fail for lack of counsel, but with many advisers they succeed."*

- **Proverbs 19:20**   *"Listen to advice and accept instruction, and in the end you will be wise."*

- **Proverbs 20:18**   *"Make plans by seeking advice; if you wage war, obtain guidance."*

- **Proverbs 24:6**   *"For waging war you need guidance, and for victory many advisers."*

And we could go on and on…

Successful people surround themselves with quality advisors

Look around. Every successful athlete has at least one coach, typically more. Every successful Fortune 1000 CEO has a solid board of directors. Even the president of these United States has a cabinet that he looks to for advice in every complex situation.

My mentors, advisors, coaches, and teachers circle the globe. Some who I seek out daily, like Kim, my bride of 15 wonderful years, and my business partner Jonathan are right here near me every day. Others (Jeff, Dilip, Mom and Dad, Mike, Ken, Don, Rob, Steve, and Kenny) are just a phone call or e-mail message away. And yet others, who I visit with or listen to weekly (Kelly, Andy and others), don't even realize how much they influence the lives of those around them.

My wish for you is that you will have the wisdom to know what you do not know and the courage to reach out and surround yourself with the highest quality mentors, advisors, coaches, and teachers you can find. Ask others you respect for advice and, like King Solomon, you will become wise.

- **Ecclesiastes 4:9** Two are better than one because they have a good return for their labor.

- **Ecclesiastes 4:10** For if either of them falls, the one will lift up his companion. But woe to the one who falls when there is not another to lift him up.

- **Ecclesiastes 4:12** And if one can overpower him who is alone, two can resist him. A cord of three strands is not quickly torn apart.

Lee Huffman was a very successful entrepreneur and Fortune 50 executive who retired at the age of 40. At 42, he came out of retirement to help other business owners and community leaders *"Discover and Attain Their True Potential"*™

Today, Lee is an international speaker and trainer, an author, a business and executive coach, a Founding Partner of the John Maxwell Team, a Partner in Lifestyle Architecture, and a Licensed Spiritual Counselor. Lee's most recent business, **Professional Development USA, LLC** can be found on the web at *www.ProDevUSA.com.*

In the area of training and public speaking, Lee has become known as *"The Business Catalyst"* and he is available to speak with your group on a myriad of topics related to business and leadership. To learn more, visit *www.TheBusinessCatalyst.com.*

This book comes with a free 30 minute phone-based coaching session for Business Owners and Leaders with 5 employees or more. For more information, contact Lee and his team at (770) 932-2525 or at Walking@ProDevUSA.com.

BECOMING YOUR OWN BOSS

The Challenge of Moving from "Corporate-ship" to "Entrepreneurship"

By David Carter, MBA

Over the years, I worked for several multi-national conglomerates and achieved what I thought was success. In retrospect, it was hollow. My employers cared more about expanding and acquiring new operations than serving their customers. To improve profitability, they eliminated experienced employees with larger salaries and shifted the burden to a younger staff.

For example, one employer, a large information provider and publisher, had just merged with a similar company in England and top executives were poised to present the new management structure to our team. Tension was high. When I entered the briefing room, colleagues greeted me with uncomfortable looks and hushed whispers. One person almost fell out of his chair.

The meeting started with preliminaries, including a speech about management's commitment to its people. It then transitioned to the presentation of the new organizational chart. To my surprise, I was not on it. Either they forgot to tell me I would not be part of the new company, or they simply didn't care. Either way, I knew my days were finished with this organization.

In one inglorious moment, leadership previewed what lay ahead – ineffective planning, inadequate communication, and incongruent management. Although my boss later apologized for the oversight, he never explained it. I gladly left the company.

The turning point

This was a turning point in my life. It was a catalyst that changed the way I thought about work, my life and my relationships. It reminded me of the old saying, "Some people don't know they're in prison until they get out." I got out.

Now free, I embarked on a venture to become my own boss. However, I knew

131

that I would have to change my thinking. I was an entrepreneur trapped in a corporate mindset.

The change in my thinking

I was no longer comfortable in the corporate environment. Now, the only person accountable for my future actions was me. In order to shift gears, I asked myself several questions:

What are my true passions? I knew in my heart-of-hearts that I had sublimated my passions while working for others. Now I had an opportunity to find work that would foster success, growth (spiritual, family, personal, career, civic), a sense of accomplishment, creativity, energy, fulfillment and more. I wanted to live my true passions.

How can I live a more balanced life? In my "other life" people often said one thing while doing just the opposite. I wanted something different. I wanted congruence – a state where actions, thoughts, goals and other qualities that define my life are all in agreement. I wanted that balance in both my personal and work life.

What is my true identity? I determined that my self-identity is the single most important factor in changing how I think, and what drives change in my life. My values, beliefs, skills and ultimate actions derive from my identity. A close mentor once told me **"I AM"** are the two most powerful words in the English language. He reminded me of the new values and beliefs I added to my identity when I became "I am a husband." I wanted a new identity for my work life.

What kind of relationships do I want? In today's environment of downsizing and re-engineering it is easy for people to focus on the negative elements of their personal and work relationships. I wanted something else. I wanted to find something and someplace that would allow me to focus positively on my relationships.

How do I define success? Success for me had previously been related to money and position. Recently I uncovered a quote by Earl Nightingale that really struck a chord: "Success is the progressive realization of a worthy goal." The journey is as valuable as the goal. I wanted a new journey.

The result

After some intense introspection, my thinking and identity became entrepreneurial. This change did not come about because of my disillusionment with corporate life, but rather because of my desire to have control and accountability over my destiny. As President Truman used to say, "The buck stops here."

I decided that I could take the best practices, systems and learnings from big business and apply them to small business. I wanted to foster change and make a difference. I realized that working with small business owners would bring me more positive relationships. The opening of my business coaching practice in Philadelphia equated with success and congruency for me.

Applying these lessons to your business and your life

Identify what's important in your personal and business life. Start by asking yourself the questions I listed earlier in this article. If you are honest with yourself and challenge yourself, you can change your thinking — you can change your life!

If you find that you would be much happier as an entrepreneur, here are some tips from my experience:

- Don't do it alone. Acquire mentors, establish coaching relationships and build strategic alliances. We rarely reach our full potential by ourselves.

- Envision and intimately define your goal. Your goal will drive your success. It will shape your journey.

- Know your perfect client. Define this person as succinctly as possible. They must be congruent with you and embody the kind of relationship you seek.

- Leverage yourself. Develop an identity that demands you work "on" your business, not just "in" it. Develop strategies to take yourself out of the day-to-day business so that you can ultimately grow it to new levels.

- Define your rules of the game. Determine how you will conduct your business and what you will expect of others. Make your decisions true to yourself and your identity.

- Look failure in the eye. Everyone fails at some point. Learn and move on.

- Continuously update your knowledge and improve your mind. Remember the old adage – you are either growing or dying. There is no middle ground. You are practicing the principle by reading this book!

Open the door

Changing my thinking has led me to greater potential in my personal and business life. It has led me to entrepreneurship. It has not been easy, but where would I be otherwise? Is there a turning point or catalyst in your life that will open the door to a change in your thinking? I hope so!

Remember, noted author Charlie Jones says, "The only difference between you now and you in five years time will be the people you meet and the books you read…" I would add "and how you think" to that equation.

David Carter is President and Owner of Action International-Philadelphia, a business coaching and training company. David is celebrating his 31st year leading small and large organizations in revenue and profit improvement, marketing and business development, new product development, and business planning. He previously founded American Trade Exchange, an import and export company, and a PC systems development and training company. His education includes an MBA and BS in Business Administration from Louisiana State University, and a Strategic Marketing Management Certificate from Cranfield School of Management, England.

David publishes a monthly e-newsletter filled with techniques and practical ideas you can use to energize your business. To subscribe, visit www.imakenews.com/actioncoach. You can contact David at *davidcarter@action-international.com* or 215.752.9880.

A Threat Greater than Terrorism...

By Charlie Douglas

Every day we receive new reports on the growing threat of terrorism. Often we see TERROR ALERT: ELEVATED flash across the TV screen as we view the daily news. It's hard not to be presently troubled about the reports on the War on Terror. And while those unnerving reports pose some serious concerns, is there a greater threat in the not too distant future to our quality of life and the well-being of the American Dream?

The biggest threat to the "American Dream"

To answer that daunting question, we need to first define the "American Dream." The term "American Dream" was first used by James Truslow in 1931, in his book The Epic of America. Truslow's concept of the American Dream was a land in which life should be better and richer and fuller for everyone, with opportunity for each according to ability or achievement. It wasn't just a dream of motor cars and high wages, but a dream of becoming all that you could be. A dream where you would be recognized by others for who you were – not necessarily for your position in life or what you were born into.

Although its foe cannot be found in Baghdad, the American Dream is still very much under attack today. The biggest threat to the American Dream is DEBT, both private and public, that continues to mount at an alarming rate.

Federal spending has been skyrocketing in recent years. At $20,000 per household, it is at its highest levels since World War II. As a percentage of the Gross Domestic Product, federal debt is at levels not seen since the Great Depression!

Although not widely publicized, government spending has increased nearly 24% over the last three years. More alarming is the fact that non-defense related items represented the biggest bulk of the spending increase. Defense and September 11th have accounted for less than half of all spending increases since 2001.

Make no mistake; unrestrained government spending and a swelling public debt are very real threats to be taken seriously. In 1816, Thomas Jefferson wrote, "I place the economy among the first and most important of republic virtues, and public debt as the greatest of dangers to be feared."

135

Learning from our mistakes

Many people I talk to today, however, seem unconcerned with deficits in this debt-based economy. True, there is something to be said for prudent deficit spending to stimulate the economy in times of recession in order to prime the pump. However, excessive spending and inordinate levels of public and private debt threaten the well itself and will surely multiply the economic pressures felt down the road. While I am not an economist, I do believe that history has an important lesson to teach.

During World War II, the Korean War, and the Cold War, real discretionary non-defense spending was curtailed in order to save resources. A notable exception is found in the mid 1960s when the Johnson administration simultaneously fought the Vietnam War and began the programs of the "Great Society." The painful result of having both "guns and butter" felt over the next decade was stagflation, where there was rising inflation in a stagnant economy.

Are we heeding the warnings of the predicted economic train wreck to come? Federal Reserve Chairman Alan Greenspan recently forewarned, "The imbalance in the federal budgetary situation, unless addressed soon, will pose serious longer-term fiscal difficulties." Likewise, scholars with the American Enterprise Institute have predicted that the shortfall in unfunded Social Security and Medicare benefits could exceed $50 trillion!

As people continue to live longer and health care costs continue to rise, there will be a huge burden placed on future generations. Our institutions are not equipped to handle the task. Medicare, the taxpayer-financed trust fund that pays hospital benefits for 42 million elderly and disabled Americans, will be bankrupt in 2019 without reform, according to a recent report by Trustees.

The current pay-as-you-go entitlement system will become unsustainable in future decades as the payroll taxes on a shrinking workforce will not be able to sustain the promised benefits of an expanding elderly base. Why is this happening? The simple answer is that the numbers upon which these programs were founded have dramatically changed. For example, when Social Security was brought into being, the average life expectancy at birth was 62 and benefits began at 65. Today, life expectancy is 77, while benefits can be drawn starting at age 62.

Beyond our vote, we may not have control over fiscally irresponsible politicians who often fail to see past the next election cycle. Whether they will take action soon to turn Social Security and Medicare into savings-based programs with payroll contributions that fund personal health care and retirement accounts remains to be seen. However, there is something that all of us can do to keep our quality of life and preserve the American Dream.

Reduce debt and pay yourself first!

I am amazed by the number of people who are not in touch with the very simple yet profound principle of paying themselves first! We often go to great lengths to pay all our creditors what they are owed, but many never see that they owe it to themselves and society to responsibly pay for their economic needs down the road.

Our national savings rate today is only about 3%, but we need to be saving between 10% and 15% of our income for retirement. Many people are surprised to learn that they will need at least 70% of their pre-retirement income to meet their retirement needs. People never plan to fail, but they often fail to plan.

Many wrongly believe that they have less of a need to save for a rainy day in the future because they are able to meet their current needs by borrowing today. And with interest rates at 40-year lows, consumers have been loading up the debt wagon.

Americans now carry more than $700 billion in revolving debt (i.e., credit cards). In fact, the average amount of credit card debt in households with more than one card is now more than $8,000 according to CardWeb.com. Is it any wonder that consumer debt and personal bankruptcies are at an all time high?

In my professional experience as an attorney and financial advisor, high levels of personal debt and the failure to pay oneself first are the top deterrents to responsibly providing for the future. Yes, the asset allocation of your investments is important for helping you improve your rate of return. However, focusing primarily on asset allocation instead of savings and debt levels is like tending the bloom instead of nurturing the roots. There is no substitute for boosting your savings rate and reducing personal debt – they are the best ways to feather your nest egg.

Since 9/11, however, there has been a notion that it has been our patriotic duty to stimulate the economy. Consumers, who account for two-thirds of our economy, were urged to spend in order to prevent the U.S. economy from going deeper and deeper into a recession.

A friend of mine, Dr. Jeffrey Rosensweig, a finance professor and economic commentator for CNN Headline news, wrote a book shortly after 9/11 entitled, Patriotic Economics. In the book Dr. Rosensweig wrote, "the only thing we have to fear is fear itself: our faith can overcome recession and restore prosperity. Consume Now!"

Obviously, the fragile confidence of the consumer was important to bolster at that critical time and I whole-heartedly support Dr. Rosensweig's courageous message. However, the 9/11 crisis has long since passed and a future crisis surrounding debt looms large on the horizon. And please note, I'm not against spending – I'm against getting into an artificial lifestyle that we can't afford through the use of debt. The piper can only be postponed for so long, but in the end he must get paid.

Will Rogers once said, "If you find yourself in a hole, the first thing to do is stop digging." We need to quit digging, both publicly and privately, and start responsibly saving for our future and for future generations. If not, the repercussions to our quality of life and to the American Dream may well be greater than the threat of terrorism today.

As a former business, tax and estate planning attorney, and now practicing CERTIFIED FIANNCIAL PLANNER ™, **Charlie** has been empowering others to realize the American Dream! As the author of the newly released book, Awaken the American Dream, Charlie is a frequent lecturer and keynote speaker on wealth-related issues and mentors others on developing their spiritual and financial capital.

Visit Charlie at www.awakenthedream.com

Leadership

By Brian Tracy

Leadership is the most important single factor in determining business success or failure in our competitive, turbulent, fast-moving economy. The ability to step up to the plate and provide the necessary leadership is the key determinant of achievement in all human activities. And there has never been a greater need for leaders at all levels then there is today.

Perhaps the best news is that leaders are made, not born. A person becomes a leader when a leader is needed, and the individual rises to the occasion.

You become a leader in your business and in the world around you by practicing the qualities and behaviors of leaders who have gone before you. Like any set of skills, leadership is developed by practice and repetition.

The rewards for becoming a leader are tremendous. As a leader, you earn the respect, esteem, and support of the people around you. You enjoy a greater sense of control and personal power in every part of your life.

The laws of Leadership have been identified and discussed over and over throughout the centuries. They are taught in military schools, colleges, and universities. They are taught in business schools and practiced every day in the businesses and organizations of our society.

When you begin to think and act the way leaders do and you apply the Laws of Leadership to your life and work, you will attract to yourself opportunities to use more of your talents and abilities at ever-higher levels.

The Law of Integrity

Great business leadership is characterized by honesty, truthfulness, and straight dealing with every person, under all circumstances.

This law requires that you impeccably honest with yourself and others. As Emerson said, "Guard your integrity as a sacred thing. Nothing is at last sacred but the integrity of your own mind."

139

Perhaps the most important thing you do as a leader is to be a good role model. Lead by example. Walk the talk. Live the life. Always carry yourself as though everyone is watching, even when no one is watching.

A key mark of integrity in human relations is consistency, both internal and external. The best leaders are consistent from one day to the next, from one situation to the next. People know what to expect. There are no surprises.

Being consistent also means that you treat everyone the same. You do not have one persona for an important client and another for a subordinant. As Thomas Carlyle wrote, "You can tell a big person by the way he treats little people."

There are two basic types of leadership in business today, transactional and transformational. Transactional leadership is the ability to direct people, manage resources, and get the job done. But transformational leadership, the most important form of leadership today, is the ability to motivate, inspire, and bring people to higher levels of performance.

Transformational leadership is the ability to touch people emotionally, to empower them to be more and to contribute more than they ever have before. This ability enables transformational leaders to elicit extraordinary performance from ordinary people.

Leaders think about the future. They think long term. They think about how they want to be viewed by others, now and later in life. Because of this long time perspective, they never sacrifice their integrity or their reputations for short-term gain or profit.

The Law of Courage

The ability to make decisions and act boldly in the face of setbacks and adversity is the key to greatness in leadership.

Winston Churchill once said, "Courage is rightly considered the foremost of the virtues, for upon it, all others depend."

Leaders have the courage to make decisions and to take action in the face of doubt and uncertainty, with no guarantees of success. Your ability to launch, step out in faith, even when there is a chance of loss or failure, is the mark of leadership. Leadership is not a lack of fear or absence of fear. Leadership is control of fear – mastery of fear.

The Law of Realism

Leaders deal with the world as it is, not as they wish it would be.

Your ability and your willingness to be completely *realistic* in your life and work are among the most important qualities of leadership. The measure of how realistic you really are is demonstrated by your willingness to deal straightforwardly with the truth of your life and business, whatever it may be.

Peter Drucker refers to this quality of realism in a leader as "intellectual honesty." Jack Welch, president of General Electric, calls it the "Reality Principle." He approaches every problem or difficulty with the question, What's the reality?

Concentrate on getting the facts. Facts don't lie. The more facts you gather, the better will be the picture of reality that you can develop. The quality of your decisions will be largely determined by the quality of the information on which those decisions are based.

Never trust to luck or hope that something unexpected will turn up to solve a problem or save a situation. You are the leader. You are in charge. Deal with your world as it is, not as you wish it would be.

The Law of Power

Power is the ability to influence the allocation of people, money and resources. It exists in all human relationships and situations. It is essential for the effective functioning of human life and society. It is neither good or bad. It just is.

Power can be used in business in two ways: (1) to advance the interests of the organization or (2) to advance the interests of the individual. When power is used skillfully to advance the interests of the organization, it is a positive force. It can improve the situation of all the people who are affected by it.

Four kinds of power

There are four major types of power you can develop. The first is expert power. This is where you start. You concentrate on doing your job in an excellent fashion. When you are recognized as being very good at what you do, you acquire greater power and influence than people who are only average or mediocre. With the expert power, you attract the respect and attention of the important people in your organization. You receive more opportunities to do what you do well. Doors open for you.

The second type of power you can develop is personal power. This form of power comes from being liked and respected by the people around you. This type of power if often called "social intelligence" or "emotional intelligence." It is the most helpful and ultimately the highest paid ability in our society.

The third type of power, position power, is the power that goes with the job title. Position power includes the ability to hire and fire, to reward and punish. Position power can be separate from ability or personality. There are many incompetent people with position power who got it for reasons other than their ability to get the job done quickly and well or their ability to get along well with others.

Perhaps the best type of power, the fourth, is ascribed power. This is power you have when the people around you willingly grant you authority and influence over them because of the person you are. You attract this power to yourself by being very good at what you do and, at the same time, by being liked and respected by the people around you.

Brian Tracy is one of America's leading authorities on the development of human potential and personal effectiveness. He's a dynamic and entertaining speaker with a wonderful ability to inform and inspire audiences toward peak performance and high levels of achievement.

Prior to founding Brian Tracy International, Brian was the chief operating officer of a development company with $265 million in assets and $75 million in annual sales. He has had successful careers in sales and marketing, investments, real estate development and syndication, importation, distribution and management consulting. He has conducted high-level consulting assignments with several billion-dollar-plus corporations in strategic planning and organizational development.

Excerpts from "100 Absolutely Unbreakable Laws of Business Success" by Brian Tracy. Copyright© 2000, 2002, Brian Tracy. All rights reserved. Used here by permission.

The Marketing Maven

By Bill Glazer

A strong marketing strategy is the key to your business success. I've collected here, for your education and enjoyment, some of my key insights into marketing. Putting them into practice will change your business – for the better! Enjoy!

In the jungle, tigers starve last

We are hearing a lot – too much, actually – about a "slowing" or "soft" economy. Every one is sitting on their hands waiting to hear what Greenspan or Bush is going to do about it. I'm even starting to hear it as an excuse from some of the members of my Marketing System.

I say, "Bull!" And here's why…

In tough times, exactly the same marketing methods apply – just more so. Incredibly, when the economy slows, the first place where a lot of gun-shy business owners cut costs is in advertising and marketing. That's naive for several reasons. First of all, it's the only expenditure that directly produces profit (and if you're still spending money on marketing that's not profitable, you should've axed it long before now.) Second, it's what the herd does, so for that reason alone, it's wrong. And third, because your competitors are doing it, it leaves them especially vulnerable to an aggressive marketer – like you. Or like you should be.

So actually, the correct reaction to a slow-down in the economy is to become even more aggressive and innovative. Here are three such things you can do:

1. Increase the frequency and quality of communication with customers to reward their loyalty, and incentivize their patronage. During tough times, your competitors quickly resort to price-cutting, so your customers will have cheaper prices shoved in their faces even more than usual. If you aren't countering this with "quality relationships," you'll lose.

2. Make appropriate adjustments in products, services, payment options, etc. to be attractive to your customers. It may mean arranging more, better-suited financing options to make paying easier. It may mean adding a wider price range of products.

143

3. Crank up your marketing aimed at new customers, to take full advantage of your competitors' fears and timidity. A little "salt in the wound" goes a long way. Now, I'm not suggesting you should become arrogant, just clever. Their timid "counter-response" to the changing economic conditions means more opportunity for you.

Uncover the hidden wealth in your customer database

As we enter the new millennium, competition is fierce. Fewer and fewer entrepreneurs are doing more and more business. Why is that? It's partly because the leading business people in this country are always investigating new and innovative systems to increase the productivity of their business. One system is the use of VOICE BROADCAST.

Voice Broadcast enables you to record a powerful voice message from your own phone and send it to a predetermined database of customer's, client's or patient's phone numbers...automatically. You can practice your message, perfecting it until you have just the right inflection and enthusiasm. Once satisfied, this technology searches out answering machines and leaves your message. If a live person answers, you even have the option of disconnecting without the recipient ever knowing who called.

How much additional business would you generate? Clients report an average of 30% when adding it as a follow-up to their current advertising, while enhancing loyalty and good will. Best of all, the cost is only about a dime a call – much less than the cost of direct mail.

Voice Broadcast is a valuable system that helps you run your business. You run the Voice Broadcast system. You run your business...your business doesn't run you. You're working smarter – not harder. You can reach tens-of-thousands or more of your clients in a single "Fell swoop!" that takes just a couple of minutes!

How to turn customers who love you into...money in the bank

You've got 'em. Everybody's got 'em... at least some. (And, if you really stink, you've at least got your mother.) I'm talking about that precious core group of customers who really adore you and think your business is the best thing since sliced bread. They happily sing your praises and make you sound so good that you even want to buy from yourself.

But, did you know your clients' honest adoration can put additional money in your bank account? It can. Harness your customers' affection – have them put it in writing or record their voices, and you've got yourself a "testimonial."

So, what is the big deal about testimonials? They are so important simply because of this truth: What others say about you is infinitely more believable than

anything you could say about yourself. Think about it. Would you trust your life to a surgeon who says he's the best, or a surgeon who everyone else says is top notch? Testimonials add credibility. They make your company seem more believable.

And that is why the power of your clients' words is worth its weight in gold. Where should you use them? Everywhere! Put them in every direct mail piece you send out. In every newspaper, radio, or TV spot.... everywhere. In my own retail stores, I don't even stop there. When customers call and are placed on-hold, they listen to a recording of other customers singing our praises. How many should you use? As many as you have! You can't possibly overuse them. But you can seriously under-use them. In fact, it's a safe bet you're probably already doing just that.

You will see immediate results when you let your customers tell others about the benefits of shopping your company. So, get busy! Capture your customers' testimonials. You will find their words are as good as money in the bank.

How every entrepreneur can boost their advertising's pulling power

You can boost the response of any ad or promo piece, whether it is for newspaper, direct mail, TV, radio, billboards (whatever) by creating a strong, compelling headline. The sole purpose of the headline is to grab and hold the reader's attention, demanding that they read or hear the rest of the ad. Your headline must make an immediate impression on the reader about what your offer is going to do for them. Face it... we are a society of skeptics. We all read and listen to ads, ready to tune out or turn the page in a nano-second unless we instantaneously are told what's in it for us. Accomplishing this task is no small feat; in fact, at times it's one hell of a challenge.

When I write an ad, I usually write several headlines. Then I select the one that is great. The most powerful headline you can write contains your biggest reader benefit. One of the best ways to write a benefit-oriented headline is to ask: What is the biggest benefit of responding to this offer? Within that answer lies the headline for your ad.

When writing a headline consider the following:
1. Promise a benefit or provoke curiosity.
2. Know one of your prospect's main obstacles or problems--address it and solve it for them. Pick their scab, so to speak, then offer them a band-aid.
3. Put the name of the promotion, offer, or product in the headline if possible.
4. Long headlines pull just as well (and often better) than short headlines.
5. Don't be cute. Try not to fool the reader.
6. Don't confuse the reader with multiple ideas. Keep it simple.
7. "Flag" your targeted prospect. This will weed out the readers or listeners you DON'T want.

www.mentorsmagazine.com

8. Add a deadline to get the reader to respond NOW!

For example, let's say you own a Big & Tall store that is conducting a half price sale. You might write in your headline, "FINALLY... BIG & TALL MEN CAN DISCOVER THE SECRET OF SLASHING THEIR WARDROBE COSTS IN HALF... But only until May 27th."

Or, if you need another example of a great headline, just look at the one at the top of this section. It got you to read it, didn't it?

The most profitable piece of mail you can send any customer

When was the last time you received a "thank you" note from anyone you did business with? Most businesses just don't bother. This is good news for you – and bad news for your competition.

All too often, we tend to focus on "getting the new sale," and then forget the customer by the time he or she gets to the door. But for 37 cents, you can create a good feeling for you and your company. This is one of the cheapest ways you can build loyalty, trust, and most importantly…referrals!

Let's take a deep look into why the "thank you" note is so vital, so powerful. The reason should be rather obvious. It makes the recipient (your customer) feel good about doing business with you. This in turn elevates you from the pack of businesses (the majority) who NEVER express their appreciation.

A note is a permanent record of your special thanks. It took time to write it – time YOU invested to show your customers that you really do appreciate their business. You even cared enough to find an envelope and a stamp. Then you went the extra mile to put it all together and mail it. Now your effort will sit on the recipient's desk as a lasting memento of your gratitude. Here's a brief example of a well-written thank you note:

> *Dear (customer's name)*
>
> *I want to express my sincere gratitude for investing with (name of your business). My commitment does not stop with your purchase. Your total satisfaction is my highest priority. So, please call me when I can be of further assistance. I would also like to offer my service to anyone you could recommend who may be interested in purchasing (your product or service) in a professional manner.*
>
> *Sincerely,*
>
> *(your name)*

Write that "thank you" note today to every customer who shops your store and watch your business grow!

Increase your sales...OVERNIGHT!

Think about what happened the last time that you went to a professional baseball game. The first batter walked up to the plate and the big electronic screen posted his name and all his relevant statistics. It gave you his batting average, how many home runs he hit, how many games he has played this year, and a host of other statistical information.

You probably always thought that this was a way for all the people in the stands to evaluate how good a player the batter is. But even more important, the statistics also serve as a huge motivation to the batter. Don't you think that he wants to have really good personal performance numbers up there on the huge screen for the thousands of fans to see, including his manager, his fellow players, and the team owner?

Well, the same principles apply in business. You should track everything that's important and post it for you and everyone else in the company to see.

For years, I have worked with top management consultants to develop a performance management system that diagnoses what specific statistics make sense to track. These stats, displayed like a billboard on the interstate, lead to increased productivity and performance by our sales associates.

Every day, information such as individual sales, average sale per transaction, and average units per transaction are posted. Actually, we post 13 different statistics. And all of them, I tell you, lead to increased performance!

Of course, when we first introduced this program, it met a lot of resistance. Salespeople told us that it wasn't right for other people to see their performance. Ironically, these were the same salespeople who had lower performance figures.

We found that in a short period of time, two very interesting things happened: First, we experienced some turnover among the under-performing sales associates, which was okay. But more importantly, those sales associates who remained with our company had sales performance figures that rose significantly, causing the company's overall sales to skyrocket.

Thus, we discovered that – just like the batter at the plate – good sales associates are naturally competitive. They're "major league." They'll always want to be at the top of each category measured.

Have a big, bold, solid guarantee

You should guarantee everything you do... That's right...EVERYTHING. Now, your first reaction might be, "I can't afford to do that, I'll have customers calling me all the time wanting this and asking me to fix that...Or worse yet, they'll want their money back and they'll rip ME off!"

This is a natural reaction, but here's my guarantee to my customers: 100% "NO-RISK" GUARANTEE. Simple, isn't it? But very solid, very easy to stand behind. Let me tell you why.

A recent survey of consumers across the country were asked the question, "Why do you buy where you buy?" And folks, the number one answer was NOT "price" (actually "price" was number five). The number one reason people buy where they do is CONFIDENCE.

By the way, after "Confidence" the other reasons in order were "Quality," "Selection," "Service," and then "Price."

Put yourself in the customer's role – after all, you do buy things, don't you? People want to do business and be taken care of – the same way you do. And, practical experience continues to prove that (1) a guarantee boosts sales, and (2) the better the guarantee, the higher the sales.

So what does my BIG, BOLD, SOLID GUARANTEE mean? Basically, if the customer isn't happy with my product or service, I'll make it right – or the customer can have his/her money back.

Is it bold? YES. Is it risky? NOT AT ALL. Think of it this way...

I may encounter a situation where the customer isn't happy perhaps only two or three times a month. And if I have to give their money back, it just shows the customer that my company is trustworthy and it gives them the confidence to come back.

I don't think anyone should be in business if they can't guarantee what they sell. But still, many do not. And those who do, give a wimpy guarantee anyway. All this does is present your competition the chance to "one-up" you. Believe it, during these tough times, a rock-solid guarantee is an excellent way to set yourself apart from your competitors. It reverses the general lack of trust customers have built in their minds to begin with. Why would you not want the upper hand in this situation?

And here's the best news...The numbers will always work in your favor to offer a "100% 'NO-RISK' GUARANTEE." It's less likely that people will take you up on it...and much more likely that lots of people will be convinced to shop with you if you have one. And…(NOW PAY ATTENTION) if you guarantee it…FLAUNT IT! Go ahead and flaunt it shamelessly. Let the world know. You won't regret it.

Here's an analogy: Overall last year, most major users of direct mail saw increases in response. Why? Because many companies cut back on direct mail in favor of e-mail, and others cut back because of the postal increase. As a result, there was less competition, less clutter in the mailbox. So the "tigers" ate even better than usual! The exact same thing occurs in a soft economy: the herd thins, but the tigers eat even better.

It's time to belly-up to the table!

Bill Glazer is the #1 most celebrated marketing advisor to the retail industry in the world. Information about his Retail Business Building Products are available at bgsmarketing.com. In addition, he is the publisher of Dan Kennedy's "No BS Marketing Letter," considered the best marketing newsletter on the planet. Information is available at www.dankennedy.com.

The Elements
of the Deal

By Donald Trump

My style of deal-making is quite simple and straightforward. I aim very high, and then I just keep pushing and pushing and pushing to get what I'm after. Sometimes I settle for less than I sought, but in most cases I still end up with what I want.

More than anything else, I think deal-making is an ability you're born with. It's in the genes. I don't say that egotistically. It's not about being brilliant. It does take a certain intelligence, but mostly it's about instincts. You can take the smartest kid at Wharton, the one who gets straight A's and has a 170 IQ, and if he doesn't have the instincts, he'll never be a successful entrepreneur.

Moreover, most people who do have the instincts will never recognize that they do, because they don't have the courage or the good fortune to discover their potential. Somewhere out there are a few men with more innate talent at golf than Jack Nicklaus, or women with greater ability at tennis than Chris Evert or Martina Navratilova, but they will never lift a club or swing a racket and therefore will never find out how great they could have been. Instead, they'll be content to sit and watch stars perform on television.

When I look back at the deals I've made – and the ones I've lost or let pass – I see certain common elements. But unlike the real estate evangelists you see all over television these days, I can't promise you that by following the precepts I'm about to offer you'll become a millionaire overnight. Unfortunately, life rarely works that way, and most people who try to get rich quick end up going broke instead. As for those among you who do have the genes, who do have the instincts, and who could be highly successful, well, I still hope you won't follow my advice. Because that would just make it a much tougher world for me.

Think big

I like thinking big. I always have. To me it's very simple: if you're going to be thinking anyway, you might as well think big. Most people think small, because most people are afraid of success, afraid of making decisions, afraid of winning. And that gives people like me a great advantage.

My father built low-income and middle-income buildings in Brooklyn and Queens, but even then, I gravitated to the best location. When I was working in Queens, I always wanted Forest Hills. And as I grew older, and perhaps wiser, I realized that Forest Hills was great, but Forest Hills isn't Fifth Avenue. And so I began to look toward Manhattan, because at a very early age, I had a true sense of what I wanted to do.

I wasn't satisfied just to earn a good living. I was looking to make a statement. I was out to build something monumental – something worth a big effort. Plenty of other people could buy and sell little brownstones, or build cookie-cutter red-brick buildings. What attracted me was the challenge of building a spectacular development on almost one hundred acres by the river on the West Side of Manhattan, or creating a huge new hotel next to Grand Central Station at Park Avenue and 42nd Street.

The same sort of challenge is what attracted me to Atlantic City. It's nice to build a successful hotel. It's a lot better to build a hotel attached to a huge casino that can earn fifty times what you'd ever earn renting hotel rooms. You're talking a whole different order of magnitude.

One of the keys to thinking big is total focus. I think of it almost as a controlled neurosis, which is a quality I've noticed in many highly successful entrepreneurs. They're obsessive, they're driven, they're single-minded and sometimes they're almost maniacal, but it's all channeled into their work. Where other people are paralyzed by neurosis, the people I'm talking about are actually helped by it.

I don't say this trait leads to a happier life, or a better life, but it's great when it comes to getting what you want. This is particularly true in New York real estate, where you are dealing with some of the sharpest, toughest, and most vicious people in the world. I happen to love to go up against these guys, and I love to beat them.

Protect the downside and the upside will take care of itself

People think I'm a gambler. I've never gambled in my life. To me, a gambler is someone who plays slot machines. I prefer to own slot machines. It's a very good business being the house.

It's been said that I believe in the power of positive thinking. In fact, I believe in the power of negative thinking. I happen to be very conservative in business. I always go into the deal anticipating the worst. If you plan for the worst –if you can live with the worst-the good will always take care of itself. The only time in my life I didn't follow that rule was with the USFL. I bought a losing team in a losing league on a long shot. It almost worked, through our antitrust suit, but when it didn't, I had no fallback. The point is that you can't be too greedy. If you go for a home run on every

151

pitch, you're also going to strike out a lot. I try never to leave myself too exposed, even if it means sometimes settling for a triple, a double, or even, on rare occasions, a single.

One of the best examples I can give is my experience in Atlantic City. Several years ago, I managed to piece together an incredible site on the Boardwalk. The individual deals I made for parcels were contingent on my being able to put together the whole site. Until I achieved that, I didn't have to put up very much money at all.

Once I assembled the site, I didn't rush to start construction. That meant I had to pay the carrying charges for a longer period, but before I spent hundreds of millions of dollars and several years on construction, I wanted to make sure I got my gaming license. I lost time, but I also kept my exposure much lower.

When I got my licensing on the Boardwalk site, Holiday Inns came along and offered to be my partner. Some people said, "You don't need them. Why give up fifty percent of your profits?" But Holiday Inns also offered to pay back the money I already had in the deal, to finance all the construction, and to guarantee me against losses for five years. My choice was whether to keep all the risk myself, and own 100 percent of the casino, or settle for a 50 percent stake without putting up a dime. It was an easy decision.

Barron Hilton, by contrast, took a bolder approach when he built his casino in Atlantic City. In order to get opened as quickly as possible, he filed for a license and began construction on a $400 million facility at the same time. But then, two months before the hotel was scheduled to open, Hilton was denied a license. He ended up selling to me at the last minute, under a lot of pressure, and without a lot of other options. I renamed the facility Trump's Castle and it is now one of the most successful hotel casinos anywhere in the world.

Maximize your options

I also protect myself by being flexible. I never get too attached to one deal or one approach. For starters. I keep a lot of balls in the air, because most deals fall out, no matter how promising they seem at first. In addition, once I've made a deal, I always come up with at least a half dozen approaches to making it work, because anything can happen, even to the best laid plans.

For example, if I hadn't gotten the approvals I wanted for Trump Tower, I could always have built an office tower and done just fine. If I'd been turned down for licensing in Atlantic City, I could have sold the site I'd assembled to another casino operator, at a good profit. Perhaps the best example I can give is the first deal I made in Manhattan. I got an option to purchase the Penn Central railyards at West 34th Street. My original proposal was to build middle-income housing on the site, with government financing. Unfortunately, the city began to have financial problems, and money for public housing suddenly dried up. I didn't spend a lot of time feeling sorry for myself. Instead, I switched to my second option and began promoting the site as ideal for a convention center. It took two years of pushing and promoting, but ultimately the city did designate my site for the convention center-and that's where it was built.

Of course, if they hadn't chosen my site, I would have come up with a third approach.

Know your market

Some people have a sense of the market and some people don't. Steven Spielberg has it. Lee Iacocca of Chrysler has it, and so does Judith Krantz in her way. Woody Allen has it, for the audience he cares about reaching, and so does Sylvester Stallone, at the other end of the spectrum. Some people criticize Stallone, but you've got to give him credit. I mean, here's a man who is just forty-one years old, and he's already created two of the all-time-great characters, Rocky and Rambo. To me he's a diamond-in-the-rough type, a genius purely by instinct. He knows what the public wants and he delivers it.

I like to think I have that instinct. That's why I don't hire a lot of number-crunchers, and I don't trust fancy marketing surveys. I do my own surveys and draw my own conclusions. I'm a great believer in asking everyone for an opinion before I make a decision. It's a natural reflex. If I'm thinking of buying a piece of property, I'll ask the people who live nearby about the area what they think of the schools and the crime and the shops. When I'm in another city and I take a cab, I'll always make it a point to ask the cabdriver questions. I ask and I ask and I ask, until I begin to get a gut feeling about something. And that's when I make a decision.

I have learned much more from conducting my own random surveys than I could ever have learned from the greatest of consulting firms. They send a crew of people down from Boston, rent a room in New York, and charge you $100,000 for a lengthy study. In the end, it has no conclusion and takes so long to complete that if the deal you were considering was a good one, it will be long gone.

The other people I don't take too seriously are the critics – except when they stand in the way of my projects. In my opinion, they mostly write to impress each other, and they're just as swayed by fashions as anyone else. One week it's spare glass towers they are praising to the skies. The next week, they've rediscovered old, and they're celebrating detail and ornamentation. What very few of them have is any feeling for what the public wants. Which is why, if these critics ever tried to become developers, they'd be terrible failures. Trump Tower is a building the critics were skeptical about before it was built, but which the public obviously liked. I'm not talking about the sort

153

of person who inherited money 175 years ago and lives on 84th Street and Park Avenue. I'm taking about the wealthy Italian with the beautiful wife and the red Ferrari. Those people – the audience I was after – came to Trump Tower in droves.

The funny thing about Trump Tower is that we ended up getting great architectural reviews. The critics didn't want to review it well because it stood for a lot of things they didn't like at the time. But in the end, it was such a gorgeous building that they had no choice but to say so. I always follow my own instincts, but I'm not going to kid you: it's also nice to get good reviews.

Use your leverage

The worst thing you can possibly do in a deal is seem desperate to make it. That makes the other guy smell blood, and then you're dead. The best thing you can do is deal from strength, and leverage is the biggest strength you can have. Leverage is having something the other guy wants. Or better yet, needs. Or best of all, simply can't do without.

Unfortunately, that isn't always the case, which is why leverage often requires imagination, and salesmanship. In other words, you have to convince the other guy it's in his interest to make the deal.

Back in 1974, in an effort to get the city to approve my deal to buy the Commodore Hotel on East 42nd Street, I convinced its owners to go public with the fact that they were planning to close down the hotel. After they made the announcement, I wasn't shy about , pointing out to everyone in the city what a disaster a boarded-up hotel would be for the Grand Central area, and for the entire city.

When the board of Holiday Inns was considering whether to enter into a partnership with me in Atlantic City, they were attracted to my site because they believed my construction was farther along than that of any other potential partner. In reality, I wasn't that far along, but I did everything I could, short of going to work at the site myself, to assure them that my casino was practically finished. My leverage came from confirming an impression they were already predisposed to believe.

When I bought the West Side railyards, I didn't name the project Television City by accident, and I didn't choose the name because I think it's pretty. I did it to make a point. Keeping the television networks in New York – and NBC in particular – is something the city very much wants to do. Losing a network to New Jersey would be a psychological and economic disaster.

Leverage: don't make deals without it.

Enhance your location

Perhaps the most misunderstood concept in all of realestate is that the key to success is location, location, location. Usually, that's said by people who don't know what they're talking about. First of all, you don't necessarily need the best location. What you need is the best deal. Just as you can create leverage, you can enhance a location, through promotion and through psychology.

When you have 57th Street and Fifth Avenue as your location, as I did with Trump Tower, you need less promotion. But even there, I took it a step further, by promoting Trump Tower as something almost larger than life. By contrast, Museum Tower, two blocks away and built above the Museum of Modem Art, wasn't marketed well, never achieved an "aura," and didn't command nearly the prices we did at Trump Tower.

Location also has a lot to do with fashion. You can take a mediocre location and turn it into something considerably better just by attracting the right people. After Trump Tower I built Trump Plaza, on a site at Third Avenue and 61st Street that I was able to purchase very inexpensively. The truth is that Third Avenue simply didn't compare with Fifth Avenue as a location. But Trump Tower had given a value to the Trump name, and I built a very striking building on Third Avenue. Suddenly we were able to command premium prices from very wealthy and successful people who might have chosen Trump Tower if the best apartments hadn't been sold out. Today Third Avenue is a very prestigious place to live, and Trump Plaza is a great success.

My point is that the real money isn't made in real estate by spending the top dollar to buy the best location. You can get killed doing that, just as you can get killed buying a bad location, even for a low price.

What you should never do is pay too much, even if that means walking away from a very good site. Which is all a more sophisticated way of looking at location.

Get the word out

You can have the most wonderful product in the world, but if people don't know about it, it's not going to be worth much. There are singers in the world with voices as good as Frank Sinatra's, but they're singing in their garages because no one has ever heard of them. You need to generate interest, and you need to create excitement. One way is to hire public relations people and pay them a lot of money to sell whatever you've got. But to me, that's like hiring outside consultants to study a market. It's never as good as doing it yourself.

One thing I've learned about the press is that they're always hungry for a good story, and the more sensational the better. It's the nature of the job, and I understand that. The point is that if you are a little different, or a little outrageous, or if you do things that are bold or controversial, the press is going to write about you. I've always done things a little differently, I don't mind controversy, and my deals tend to be somewhat ambitious. Also, I achieved a lot when I was very young, and I chose to live in a certain style. The result is that the press has always wanted to write about me.

I'm not saying that they necessarily like me. Sometimes they write positively, and sometimes they write negatively. But from a pure business point of view, the benefits of being written about have far outweighed the drawbacks. It's really quite simple. If I take a full-page ad in the New York Times to publicize a project, it might cost $40,000, and in any case, people tend to be skeptical about advertising. But if the New York Times writes even a moderately positive one-column story about one of my deals, it doesn't cost me anything, and it's worth a lot more than $40,000.

The funny thing is that even a critical story, which may be hurtful personally, can be very valuable to your business. Television City is a perfect example. When I bought the land in 1985, many people, even those on the West Side, didn't realize that those one hundred acres existed. Then I announced I was going to build the world's tallest building on the site. Instantly, it became a media event: the New York Times put it on the front page, Dan Rather announced it on the evening news, and George Will wrote a column about it in Newsweek. Every architecture critic had an opinion, and so did a lot of editorial writers. Not all of them liked the idea of the world's tallest building. But the point is that we got a lot of attention, and that alone creates value.

The other thing I do when I talk with reporters is to be straight. I try not to deceive them or to be defensive, because those are precisely the ways most people get themselves into trouble with the press. Instead, when a reporter asks me a tough question, I try to frame a positive answer, even if that means shifting the ground. For example, if someone asks me what negative effects the world's tallest building might have on the West Side, I turn the tables and talk about how New Yorkers deserve the world's tallest building, and what a boost it will give the city to have that honor again. When a reporter asks why I build only for the rich, I note that the rich aren't the only ones who benefit from my buildings. I explain that I put thousands of people to work who might otherwise be collecting unemployment, and that I add to the city's tax base every time I build a new project. I also point out that buildings like Trump Tower have helped spark New York's renaissance.

The final key to the way I promote is bravado. I play to people's fantasies. People may not always think big themselves, but they can still get very excited by those who do. That's why a little hyperbole never hurts. People want to believe that something is the biggest and the greatest and the most spectacular. I call it truthful hyperbole. It's an innocent form of exaggeration – and a very effective form of promotion.

Fight back

Much as it pays to emphasize the positive, there are times when the only choice is confrontation. In most cases I'm very easy to get along with. I'm very good to people who are good to me. But when people treat me badly or unfairly or try to take advantage of me, my general attitude, all my life, has been to fight back very hard. The risk is that you'll make a bad situation worse, and I certainly don't recommend this approach to everyone. But my experience is that if you're fighting for something you believe in – even if it means alienating some people along the way-things usually work out for the best in the end.

When the city unfairly denied me, on Trump Tower, the standard tax break every developer had been getting, I fought them in six different courts. It cost me a lot of money, I was considered highly likely to lose, and people told me it was a no-win situation politically. I would have considered it worth the effort regardless of the outcome. In this case, I won, which made it even better.

When Holiday Inns, once my partners at the Trump Plaza Hotel and Casino in Atlantic City, ran a casino that consistently performed among the bottom 50 percent of casinos in town, I fought them very hard and they finally sold out their share to me. Then I began to think about trying to take over the Holiday Inns company altogether.

Even if I never went on the offensive, there are a lot of people gunning for me now. One of the problems when you become successful is that jealousy and envy inevitably follow. There are people I categorize as life's losers who get their sense of accomplishment and achievement from trying to stop others. As far as I'm concerned, if they had any real ability they wouldn't be fighting me, they'd be doing something constructive themselves.

Deliver the goods

You can't con people, at least not for long. You can create excitement, you can do wonderful promotion and get all kinds of press, and you can throw in a little hyperbole. But if you don't deliver the goods, people will eventually catch on.

I think of Jimmy Carter. After he lost the election to Ronald Reagan, Carter came to see me in my office. He told me he was seeking contributions to the Jimmy Carter Library. I asked how much he had in mind. And he said, "Donald, I would be very appreciative if you contributed five million dollars."

I was dumbfounded. I didn't even answer him.

But that experience also taught me something. Until then, I'd never understood how Jimmy Carter became president. The answer is that as poorly qualified as he was for the job, Jimmy Carter had the nerve, the guts, the balls, to ask for something extraordinary. That ability above all helped him get elected president. But then, of course, the American people caught on pretty quickly that Carter couldn't do the job, and he lost in a landslide when he ran for re-election.

www.mentorsmagazine.com

When Trump Tower became successful, a lot of developers got the idea of imitating our atrium, and they ordered their architects to come up with a design. The drawings would come back, and they would start costing out the job.

What they discovered is that the bronze escalators were going to cost a million dollars extra, and the waterfall was going to cost two million dollars, and the marble was going to cost many millions more. They saw that it all added up to many millions of dollars, and all of a sudden these people with these great ambitions would decide, well, let's forget about the atrium.

The dollar always talks in the end. I'm lucky, because I work in a very, very special niche, at the top of the market, and I can afford to spend top dollar to build the best. I promoted the hell out of Trump Tower, but I also had a great product to promote.

Contain the costs

I believe in spending what you have to. But I also believe in not spending more than you should. When I was building low-income housing, the most important thing was to get it built quickly, inexpensively, and adequately, so you could rent it out and make a few bucks. That's when I learned to be cost-conscious. I never threw money around. I learned from my father that every penny counts, because before too long your I pennies turn into dollars.

To this day, if I feel a contractor is overcharging me, I'll pick up the phone, even if it's only for $5,000 or $10,000, and I'll complain. People say to me, "What are you bothering for, over a few bucks?" My answer is that the day I can't pick up the telephone and make a twenty-five-cent call to save $10,000 is the day I'm going to close up shop.

The point is that you can dream great dreams, but they'll never amount to much if you can't turn them into reality at a reasonable cost. At the time I built Trump Plaza in Atlantic City, banks were reluctant to finance new construction at all, because almost every casino up to then had experienced tens of millions of dollars in cost overruns. We brought Trump Plaza in on budget, and on time. As a result, we were able to open for Memorial Day weekend, the start of the high season. By contrast, Bob Guccione of Penthouse has been trying for the past seven years to build a casino on the Boardwalk site right next to ours. All he has to show for his efforts is a rusting half-built frame and tens of millions of dollars in lost revenues and squandered carrying costs.

Even small jobs can get out of control if you're not attentive. For nearly seven years I watched from the window of my office as the city tried to rebuild Wollman Rink in Central Park. At the end of that time, millions of dollars had been wasted and the job was farther from being completed than when the work began. They were all set to rip out the concrete and start over when I finally couldn't stand it anymore, and I offered to do it myself. The job took four months to complete at a fraction of the city's cost.

Have fun

I don't kid myself. Life is very fragile, and success doesn't change that. If anything, success makes it more fragile. Anything can change, without warning, and that's why I try not to take any of what's happened too seriously. Money was never a big motivation for me, except as a way to keep score. The real excitement is playing the game. I don't spend a lot of time worrying about what I should have done differently, or what's going to happen next. If you ask me exactly what the deals I'm about to describe all add up to in the end, I'm not sure I have a very good answer. Except that I've had a very good time making them.

Donald Trump is a billionaire real estate developer that has amassed a fortune through owning key New York properties, and Atlantic City casinos. He has gained fame for his flamboyant deals and lavish lifestyle. He is the author of four books and most recently an immensely popular TV show.

Article reprint from *Trump, The Art Of The Deal* ©1987. Printed here by permission.

Every *CHAMPION* Has a COACH...**Do YOU?**

By Alan Edelmann

Remember back to those hormone-infested teenage years when you were... learning to drive!?! You probably weren't aware of it then, but there are distinct steps to learning. The **Unconscious Incompetence** stage happened quite a few years earlier, when you didn't even know (or care) that you couldn't drive. As puberty left its mark and you began to notice the 'freedom' that a vehicle offered, you started to want to learn how to drive. You then became conscious of the fact that you didn't know how to drive. That's called **Conscious Incompetence**.

With some coaching and training, the mechanics and subtleties of operating a vehicle became more and more familiar. With your coach's guidance and some more practice, you became **Consciously Competent**. These days, you may notice 6 blocks or perhaps 60 miles down the track that you weren't even paying attention to the pedals or the gas gauge or speedometer or watching intently for traffic. Now you have reached **Unconscious Competence**! These are the four stages of learning.

So, what would happen if you moved to another level? For instance, what if you went out to a race track with a high performance race car? I, for one, would be back at the level of **Conscious Incompetence** again and would need some practice and coaching to gain **Conscious Competence**! This cycle of learning repeats itself throughout life – for those who choose to grow and develop their potential as Human Doings... and sometimes as Human Beings as well!

How do you move from lack of knowledge to competence, success and excellence?

You would agree that a Coach or Trainer is a critical ingredient. Just as with learning to swim or drive a car – Business Skill and Knowledge have the same four stages of learning.

I've come to the conclusion that every Champion has a Coach... Do **YOU?**

Have a *check-up from the neck up...*

A pre-requisite is Attitude!

Another experience you may recall, if you've ever been a teenager, is the MINDSET of *I KNOW*. Possibly, YOU were immune from this affliction, or maybe there are a few remnants of this left over that affect your current life from time to time…

This *I KNOW* mindset is a state of mind where I am NOT open to changing my opinion – or learning any more… at least about a certain area or topic. In my experiences of life and business so far, I've noticed that when I changed my MINDSET from *I KNOW* to *I DON'T KNOW*, further learning came into my life. Sometimes I had the opinion that I knew a lot about a subject and even considered myself an "expert." Until I changed my mind, I couldn't learn anymore.

Many business owners have years of experience in their business and industry. There may be a certain level of success and proficiency – a certain amount of routine and continuity and perhaps then some boredom. Does success and proficiency equal mastery? Or sustainability? In an ever-changing world and business environment, business leaders must continue to learn and grow in order to maintain their competitive edge.

How can you re-ignite the passion in your business?

Simply put – Change Your MIND! After the *check up from the neck up*, a decision is required. For the business to change, I must change. For ME to change, I must decide to change. Until I become OPEN to learning again, I will be stuck in the *I KNOW*. Without an outside force to stimulate, motivate or create a change of mindset, I'll remain STUCK.

Often a crisis will assist that decision. This is the hard road. An easier road is to get a COACH!

Enter the coach

Throughout History – and sometimes HERStory – the concept of Coaching has primarily been focused on the sports and athletic arenas. From the days of the Gladiators and early Olympians to more recent Olympians and sports teams and individual athletes, the concept of having a "COACH" has become totally 'normal.' Today's professional players – be they Tiger Woods, the Williams sisters, Michael Schumacher, the Lakers or the Yankees – ALL have Coaches working with them week after week.

Ten to fifteen years ago you might have noticed the proliferation of "Personal Trainers" at local gyms and sports and health clubs. That entire industry has exploded to where there are literally thousands of "personal trainers" working within the fitness industry.

Then there are the "performance coaches." This has evolved into another giant industry of developing the "Human Potential" of various individuals in whatever arena they strive to achieve, be it sports, fitness, beauty, image, public speaking or at

161

last ... **business!** This movement has been developing since the '70's and is gaining critical mass – as we speak!

In more recent times you may have noticed that Coaching has taken on a broader perspective and come to be used in the corporate business world as well. Lately, this has been probably more in name than reality, because COACHING has become a "Buzz Word". It seems many people I speak with who used to be "managers" are now saying they've actually been COACHES. In other words, they're assisting their fellow colleagues to achieve better results. These results have generally been focused on the benefit of the company – and occasionally include the benefit of the employee.

This has evolved into the business coaching world. There is no instruction booklet when you go into business. Often the theory you get in university courses is not the practical nuts and bolts knowledge and information that you need to run a business. So, the evolution of the industry of coaching has been from the sports model through the personal guidance counselling model to the business coaching or performance coaching model. If you look at the likes of Anthony Robbins and the NLP industry, these are great success stories of how personal coaching and development can be implemented into anyone's life.

Currently you may be noticing the introduction of Life Coaches, Executive Coaches and Leadership Coaches. This shows you the development of the overall industry of COACHING – and the particular Niche of BUSINESS COACHING – that a few companies have developed. This is just the beginning of the merger between traditional business Consulting and the Human Potential movement.

Who would a Business Coach work with?

You would work with the leader of the organization. The person who makes the decisions, the person who can make and implement changes at short notice rather than companies that have Boards of Directors and a Committee approach to making decisions.

Business coaching is all about identifying the personal and business goals of the owner, educating them about their areas of need, creating leverage, building the Team and developing synergy. That can take anything from six months to six years depending on the size of the company and the willingness of the people that we're dealing with. Getting the right people in the right place and enrolling the team in the vision will get you a 30 to 40% increase in revenue without doing anything other than just working with the people. Throw in systemization, greater efficiencies and sales and marketing and you can end up with 1000% increases in bottom line profits!!! COACHING IS AN INVESTMENT...GREAT COACHING WILL DEFINITELY PROVIDE YOU WITH AN ROI!

What sort of person makes a great Coach?

A great Business Coach will work with Business Owners to re-ignite their passion for their business – and quite often for their family, their dreams…and consequently their passion for Life!

A great coach is someone who:
- enjoys people and likes to understand what makes us tick.
- has experienced a level of personal transformation and change and wants to assist others in growing and learning.
- has passion and spirit and can infuse others with those qualities.
- is interested and passionate about using the coaching vehicle for their own personal change and development.

A Coach's world is one of never ending improvement. This is the concept of Kaizen – constant and never ending improvement.

The FUTURE big picture…people will ask each other, "Who's YOUR Business Coach?"

My prediction for the 10 to 20 years ahead is that most of us in business will be asking… "Who's YOUR Business Coach?" The coaching arena as I see it is going to be a part of everyday life. It will continue to grow. It's a requirement for people who gain in their consciousness and want to expand and grow and develop themselves. I believe that people are gaining in awareness that their diet, nutrition, health, wellbeing, learning, success and leadership are integral to life. This is a global phenomenon. Often people need some outside assistance to achieve the change they want to make.

Consequently, in the next few years there will be a huge demand for great Business Coaches. Are you the type of person that has a dream of running your own business? Of creating your own destiny and lifestyle? Of assisting others to achieve their full potential while you fulfill yours as well? Of making a difference to the lives and economies of people in your community?

Business Coaching is a new, leading-edge career path that will lead you to the knowledge of Entrepreneurship and Wealth Creation at the level of Unconscious Competence.

Are YOU ready to step back into the next cycle of learning and expose yourself to Conscious Incompetence?

If so – Get a Coach! Every Champion has one.

Alan Edelmann is an Action International Business Coach and Master Licensee both in the USA and in New Zealand. He facilitates people in developing their full potential through the vehicle of Business Coaching. His passion and mission is to learn and grow and then teach what he needs to learn…To Awaken YOUR Consciousness Contact: *alanedelmann@action-international.com*.

How to Achieve Your Business Goals
Faster Than You Ever Thought Possible

By Jeevan Nadchatiram Sahadevan

A key ingredient to achieving any business goal you want is enlisting the help of others. This type of leverage is extremely powerful and enables you to attain your goals quickly and easily. Many entrepreneurs take achieving goals as an individual private activity. What I am about to share with you will change the way you think about setting and reaching your goals forever! I call this my **"Other-Focus Goal Setting Method."** It has transformed not just my business, but those of all my clients as well. However, to do this well, there are several steps you must follow.

The famous Zig Ziglar once said, "You can get everything you want in life if you can help enough other people get what they want." This forms the basis for the 'Other-Focus Goals.' Whatever you want to achieve in business should be tied directly to your customers achieving their objectives. In other words, if they don't get what they want, you don't get what you want.

Let me give you an example. Let's say you run a pest control company and you want to make $1 million in sales within 12 months. First, identify how many people you must help in order to make that one million, and identify what 'help' you are going to give. Let's assume you price your termite treatments at $1,000 per client. For you to make a million dollars, you would need 1,000 clients. No client is going to care about 'helping' you get 1 million dollars. But imagine for a moment that you explained a powerful vision to your client and tied it to your sales approach. For instance, you mention that your goal is to make 1,000 homes in Malaysia (or California or Sydney), completely termite free. You explain to your client that he or she is a part of your 'Termite FREE 1000' program. Suddenly, they're a little more excited about working with you because your services are about THEM and NOT you – at least not directly. As you and your team also focus on this goal of doing whatever it takes to make your customers' homes termite free, you start to bring in a lot more business. For instance, when you ask your clients for referrals they will be more than happy to give them to you and they will make sure they're quality referrals. This sort of thinking will start a whole chain reaction of excitement in your business.

Let us take another example. One of my clients decorates homes with beautiful pictures in exotic hand made frames. His goal is to have 1,000 beautifully decorated homes and happy homeowners by a certain date. As a result of this he has put in satisfaction and money back guarantees that allow customers to preview pictures in their homes for up to 30 days before buying. This ensures that not only are these homes beautifully decorated, but that the home owners are extremely happy with their purchases. This thinking has exploded his business with tons of customers, referrals and repeat business.

Moving the focus of the goal from you to the 'other person' is the key in getting everything you want in business. There are 7 steps to creating powerful other-focused goals. These steps will help you achieve any business goal!

The Other-Focus Method

Step 1: Clarity: Decide what you want specifically out of your business, and by when.

Most people have the greatest challenge here. Unless you have absolute clarity on what you want, you're missing out on powerful emotions that come with that clarity, such as passion, excitement, determination and courage. A realistic 'by when' deadline ensures your goal is not just a wish, but an achievable vision you will work towards.

Step 2: Macro Other-Focus: Create a vision of how many customers in total you must impact in your territory or niche to achieve your above goal.

This is where you find out exactly how many customers you must help and how you must help them in order to achieve your goals. In other words, you will ONLY reach your goals if these people or organizations reach theirs. When people or businesses buy your products or services, they have certain objectives that need to be met. Build your goals around these objectives and they will materialize! For instance, you have a men's tailoring business and you target young executives who want to look good, but not at a massive expense. Your macro other-focus goal could be to have 750 elegantly dressed and well-groomed executives in your town, state or country.

Step 3: Micro Other-Focus: Outline how you will impact the individual customer, whether a person or organization.

From the example above, this is where you spell out what well-groomed and elegant is to you and your clients, and how you are going to achieve that on an individual basis. For instance, my client, the picture decorating specialist, gave out feedback forms upon doing a job asking for his ratings on various areas, from staff friendliness to quality and type of pictures to customer satisfaction levels. Each 5-Star rating puts him closer to his goal of 1000 beautifully decorated homes.

Step 4: Marketing Action Plans: Design specific strategies, tactics and implementation dates for the steps you are going to take to achieve your Macro and Micro Other-Focused Goals.

This is where you plan out your various campaigns and investment amounts and 'who is going to do what by when.' Break down your other-focused goals to yearly, quarterly, monthly and weekly segments and decide how you plan to tackle them.

www.mentorsmagazine.com

Step 5: Take action: Make public your Other-Focused Goal and take action on it.

From here on, everything you do in your business is about this goal. It is all about helping your clients reach their objectives so you reach yours. Focus single-mindedly on it and publish this everywhere, from your USP (unique selling proposition) to your flyers, advertisements, press releases, referral strategies, name cards and so on.

Let people know that this is what your business is all about. Get people excited about how easy it is to achieve their goals by doing business with you. Every staff you hire must subscribe to this other-focused goal of yours as a condition of employment. Invest in whatever is required to accomplish this goal, from marketing knowledge and systems to customer service and team building systems. Bring in technology to help you better achieve your other-focus goal, such as powerful contact management software, etc. You will be surprised how much fun and easy all this is!

Step 6: Review and Inform: Constantly review your progress and inform your customers of it.

Have periodic audits on your progress – what needs to improve, what else needs doing, what new methods are available to try, how close you are to achieving your customers' goals and total numbers of such customers. Involve your customers constantly in your progress, because their progress means your progress. You will be amazed how much their feedback can help you, since this is all about them. Most importantly, this constantly keeps you on their minds and makes your business a very 'talked about business,' which simply means more referrals and repeat purchases – and more business.

Step 7: Celebrate: Celebrate your wins, from each monthly or quarterly customer impact target reached to fully achieving your other-focus goals.

Decide how you are going to celebrate upon achieving your other-focused goal by the due date. Make a massive deal about it. Also make a great deal about reaching sub-goals within your main goal. For instance, let's say you have a secondhand car sales business, with the other-focused goal of 3000 happy and satisfied car owners by December 30, 2005. Each time you hit sub-goal increments of 500 cars sold to satisfied customers, celebrate with a huge party, or by getting together car accessory businesses to give out free gifts to your customers, or by giving out huge pay bonuses to your staff, going on an exotic vacation with your family, etc. This will make you enjoy your business.

These 7 steps will ensure you have an other-focused goal that gives meaning and purpose to your business and all who encounter it. It has made me and my clients LOVE and PROFIT from what we do. Each lead or customer of yours has only one question on his or her mind when he or she encounters your business: "What's in it for me?" Your other-focused goal not only answers that question, but also sets you apart from everyone else in your industry!

Now that you know the seven steps to creating powerful other-focused goals, stop reading and immediately get started on Step 1. This is your first step towards achieving your business goals faster than you ever thought possible!

Jeevan Nadchatiram Sahadevan, winner of ACTION's coveted "Most Improved Coach in Asia 2004" award, is one of Asia's youngest and top ACTION coaches. He only works with business owners willing to do what it takes to make a million ringgit and above in their business within 12 months! Contact him at: (+603)- 21684493 or (+606)-7616846 or nadchatiramsahadevan@action-international.com

Weight, Pulse and Business KPIs

By Randy Paulson

It was 12:15 AM on a Sunday. I had just laid my head down for a good night's sleep, when the ringing phone suddenly broke the silence. The feeling in my stomach and the chill down my spine instantly indicated something was wrong. Was this the call that no one ever wants to receive? I picked up the receiver. It was the local hospital. In a somber but caring voice, the nurse's words still echo today: "Please, get to the hospital immediately." I grabbed my concerned mother and rushed to the emergency room. My heart was heavy as the doctor spoke. "I'm sorry, we did everything possible." Tears began to flow…my father was gone.

Obviously, I will remember that day forever. I often reflect on that experience, and each time I learn something new. One such lesson did not surface until years later, after I had become a Business Coach. As a Business Coach, I teach business owners how to leverage their business – how to manage their businesses to create the lifestyle they truly desire. Some of the lessons that I teach come from everyday life.

So what is this lesson that I've learned? Let me start at the beginning.

The beginning

Years ago my father was diagnosed with a rare lung disease. I often escorted him to the clinic for routine examinations. Every visit began with the same routine: the nurse checked his height, weight, pulse rate, blood pressure and so forth. After this initial assessment, the doctor conducted a more thorough examination…listened to his lungs, checked his breathing capacity, analyzed his blood, and then finally prescribed the next treatment plan.

The doctor was operating in a reactive mode. Why? Because my father had delayed. He had waited too long. He thought he could "overcome" or "shake off" his symptoms. However, with his health deteriorating, he was finally compelled to make the visit where his illness was diagnosed. Unfortunately, the damage had already been done. The doctor's hands were tied.

The lesson

The lesson is quite evident. Although it's a familiar story, most of us still don't take prevention seriously. We need to be proactive! We need to be aware of problems, catching them *before* they become serious.

One big problem I often encounter is business owners who simply try to "overcome" or "shake off" the symptoms of illness in their businesses without diagnosing the root cause. These are symptoms such as too few hours in the day, enormous stress, high turnover, cash-flow headaches, falling revenues…the list goes on and on. Sound familiar?

Let's not kid ourselves. Operating a business can be draining, quite draining. Fantasies of success and freedom can quickly evaporate into nightmares of drudgery. Businesses that once elicited dreams of excitement and passion suddenly transform into nightmares – beasts of chaos. Instead of owners driving their business, their business drives them. Control has disappeared. Owners are in a reactive mode. They're working 60+ hours per week just trying to keep their business barely alive. What happened? What went wrong?

Maintaining a healthy business is just like maintaining health through routine check-ups. Remember my father's visits to the clinic? Without fail, the doctor checked his basic vital signs before determining a course of action. Let's examine the health of your business.

Key Performance Indicators (KPIs)

Do you know how healthy your business is right now – this instant? This can be a tough question to answer. Who is your "business physician?" Is it your tax accountant, your banker, your employees? What are the "vital statistics" that indicate the well-being of your business? These vital statistics are called KPIs (Key Performance Indicators).

Envision your car's dashboard. On that dashboard are gauges. These gauges indicate the status of your car's key systems, such as the electrical system, fuel level, mechanical condition, oil pressure, and cooling system. The gauges tell you how well the car is operating at any moment and also forewarn you of any impending failure. By heeding the information they provide, you can prevent breakdowns. And just as you can with your car you can be proactive with your business. You just need to watch the KPIs on your business dashboard.

What are some examples of business KPIs? Some key functional areas in a business that should be measured include marketing, sales, operations, accounting, finance, and human resources. Depending on the type of business, some areas are more critical than others. I trust this makes sense. So, how do you develop and use KPIs in your business?

How do you develop KPIs?

You can develop business KPIs by following these five simple steps.

Step 1: Define the KPIs.

Look at each major function and ask this one question: "What key information do I need to know about this functional area to tell me how well it's doing?" Take marketing as an example. What do you need to know about the marketing function of your business to determine its effectiveness? It might be the number of new leads being generated, the return on investment (ROI) for each advertising campaign or the average acquisition cost for each new customer. How about sales? KPIs might include the overall conversion rate, the number of quotes issued, or maybe the average dollars collected per sale. The first step is to discern what is important about each major function that can be measured.

Step 2: Establish a system to track and measure each KPI.

Next, ask yourself, "How do I track and measure each KPI?" Some will be easy, others more difficult. Tracking could be manual, like actually counting the number of customers daily. It may be asking people when they call, "How did you hear about our business?" Technology can certainly help. Point-of-purchase software, spreadsheets, and accounting programs can simplify tracking. Although a KPI might be difficult to track, that doesn't make it less important. If it's a critical function in your business, track it. If you don't, you're losing valuable information.

Step 3: Define the most appropriate format to report each KPI.

Once data is gathered, the information must be assembled, consolidated, and reported in a clear and concise fashion. Some reporting tools include graphs, tables, charts, and listings. Different KPIs lend themselves to different reporting tools. For example, the number of quotes issued might be best presented in a simple table, while cumulative sales are best depicted in a graph and a listing can clearly define the number of new customers. Keep it simple to avoid "analysis paralysis."

Step 4: Define the frequency with which each KPI must be reported.

While data should be collected continuously, it is not always necessary to report everything immediately. Daily reporting may be necessary in some cases, while in other cases weekly or monthly reporting may better suit your needs. For example, in a retail business it may be best to report total sales daily, the number of new leads monthly, and employee turnover rate quarterly.

Step 5: Assign responsibility for each KPI.

Just as someone is accountable for each and every function in the business, someone needs to be accountable for each KPI. This individual is responsible for tracking, measuring and reporting.

Top KPI mistakes

Listed below are some of the top mistakes made when implementing KPIs.
• Lack of clear definition.

- Lack of discipline to execute.
- Lack of a systemized process to track and measure.
- Making the KPI either too vague or too detailed.
- Failing to assign responsibility for each KPI.
- Failing to communicate to the team the value of KPIs.

While good intentions usually exist, I often see KPIs transform into "sporadic" activity. Data is not accurate because it's not consistently collected or reported. When this occurs, the business reverts to being reactive instead of proactive. Don't be a victim. Your business too important. Make the commitment and stay ahead of the curve.

Benefits of KPIs

The value of KPIs can never be overstated. Some of the key benefits include:
- Providing continual monitoring of business health.
- Enabling the business to operate proactively instead of reactively.
- Enhancing quality decision making.
- Helping to manage resources.
- Improving communication.
- Measuring functional as well as individual performance.

When properly instituted, KPIs are very powerful. In fact, they are a necessity. Could you imagine my father's doctor prescribing a treatment plan before understanding his basic condition? It would be ludicrous. But, I see it every day – business owners prescribing treatment based on outward symptoms without diagnosing the root cause. Stop the nonsense. Be proactive. Establish KPIs in your business. Start monitoring the health of your business and enjoy both a fruitful business and a more rewarding personal life.

Randy Paulson is an extremely talented Business Coach. He is a successful entrepreneur who has launched several companies. He is an international speaker whose presentations draw raving fans. His personal mission is to bring out the greatness in people and their businesses. If you'd like to be one of the select few that Randy coaches, contact…

Action International
10467 Brentmoor Drive
Cincinnati, Ohio USA
(513) 677-9683
randypaulson@action-international.com
www.actioncoaching.com

The Six Figure Job Search

By Rob Waite

Before we start discussing how to search for a six figure salary job, let's set a goal. The goal I suggest is to double your income every five years. That may sound like a stretch. Well, it is…but it is a do-able stretch goal.

I set this goal for myself twenty years ago when I graduated from a small public college. I grew up an average kid from Philadelphia. I had average grades in high school and college. And I never went to graduate school. At the time I graduated from college, I had never been west of Harrisburg, Pennsylvania. Twenty years later, I have lived and worked on three different continents and I'm Vice President of a large, publicly traded company.

The difference

What made the difference for me were two things.

First and foremost was my college sweetheart. She always felt that I could do and be what ever I wanted. Her faith was a driving force that ignited my ambition. The best decision I ever made was to marry the woman who first lit that spark in me. We have been happily married, with three great daughters, ever since.

Second was the director of the placement office at my college. He spoke to the senior class about the job market in 1983…which was bad. He spent three-quarters of his presentation telling us what we couldn't do and what we shouldn't expect. While I recognize that he was trying to manage our expectations so that we wouldn't become frustrated or disappointed in our job search, his negativity, frankly, pissed me off.

One of the things he told us was that we should forget about applying to Armstrong World Industries. Armstrong was headquartered in the same town as my college. The director told us that since the job market was tight Armstrong was going "up market" to the bigger name schools, so we should forget about wasting our time chasing them.

Right then and there I made up my mind that no one was going to tell me what I can't do when it comes to achieving success. Since Armstrong was not interviewing on campus, I had to figure out how to land an interview with their college recruiter.

I targeted a job with them in their sales organization. I thought it would impress them if I made a cold call on the college recruiter. I planned my approach: I would go over at lunch time when the main receptionist wouldn't be on duty. I figured the person covering during lunch wouldn't take their gate-keeping duty as seriously. I thought if I could just get into the Human Resources Department, I could wait for the college recruiter to get back from lunch.

My planning worked better than expected. The college recruiter was having lunch at his desk and he was happy to sit with a student who had cold called him.

I had my two minute pitch and my questions to gather more information as to their needs all polished up and ready to go. I was very relaxed since I figured I had nothing to lose, which is true in any job interview. If the interview you are on doesn't work out, learn from it and move on.

After spending an hour with the college recruiter, I was offered the opportunity to join Armstrong's training program. The first thing I did when I got back on campus was to see the director of the placement office. I told him how I got into my beat up 1977 Datsun B-210, wearing the brand new navy blue polyester suit I bought at Sears the night before, drove over to Armstrong and landed a job offer to join their college training program. You could have knocked him over with a feather. Then I told him that I would double my salary every five years…

Three lessons for life

I learned three things from this experience:
- First, don't let anyone tell you what you can't do.
- Second, anyone who learns how to successfully conduct a management level job search can significantly advance their career.
- Third, anyone who is willing to learn, stretch themselves and who isn't a quitter can achieve their goals.

I applied these three lessons twenty years ago and I haven't looked back…doubling my income every five years along the way.

Since I always felt like the original "Average Joe" who found out how to break through the ceiling of mediocrity, I wanted to share what I learned. What led me to wanting to share the lessons for finding a six-figure salary position were two things.

First, I landed as a senior executive at three different large publicly traded companies before I was forty. And second, I saw on the news that the number one New Year's Resolution is to get a new job or to advance your career.

The Six Figure Job Search

So I began work on *The Six Figure Job Search* CD, launched in July 2003 on www.sixfigurejobsearch.com. This CD leads the executive job searcher through the entire process, from planning the campaign to negotiating the offer. I will share the overview of the techniques here.

For a six figure salary search, you have to understand that it is a numbers game. You are now approaching the narrower points in the pyramid and the demand for six figure jobs always outstrips the supply. Your resume has to hit at exactly the moment that a company or a recruiter needs a person with your particular skill and experience. So you can see that you will get very few hits…and that is why we need to get you up to bat as often as possible.

A mistake I've seen executives make is that they believe the process will be easier than it really is. They believe that once they get their name out there and send their resume to 50 or 100 companies, the world will beat a path to their door. Understand right up front that this process is going to be tough and time consuming. That is why knowledge of how to manage the process and how to diligently prepare are going to be the major keys to success.

The further up the ladder you climb, the more items other than just your functional skills will come into play as part of the hiring process. The hiring company will screen your functional skills, but that is just the minimum ante.

The first thing the hiring executive will want to assess is what kind of person you are. Are you the kind of person they want to work with? If the hiring executive doesn't have a good feel for you personally, then it will be difficult to win them over. This may seem unfair, but it is human nature.

Next, the hiring executive will be looking at your functional skills. Suffice it to say that you will have to be able to point to specific successes and experience that will demonstrate that you do have the functional skills for the position.

At this point, the hiring executive will likely be seeing if you will fit with the company's culture and environment. You need to learn as much as you can about the company's culture. No sense in going to work somewhere you won't feel is a good fit.

Another thing they will be evaluating is whether or not you will be a risky hire. A bad hiring decision costs significant time and money for both the candidate and the company. If this job will be a big step for you, that is an added element of risk. Also, if this job is in a new industry to you, that too is a risk. The prepared searcher can deal with these types of objections.

The bottom line question in the hiring executive's mind is this, "Will you bring value to the company that far exceeds the compensation they will pay you?" That is the magic formula upon which you will need to focus the whole process.

Many executives have contacted me seeking employment and have started by telling me what they thought they deserved and were worth. You know what? I couldn't care less. If they can't sell me on the value they can deliver first, then why should I be interested in what they want?

Let me tell you from experience on both sides of the desk, if the hiring executive is convinced of the value that you can deliver, you will likely get an offer that is higher than what you felt you "deserved." But you have to unequivocally demonstrate tangible value that you can deliver.

Most people do have great value that they can offer. However, they are poor at communicating what that value is. Therefore, often it is not the person with the most innate talent that gets hired; it is the person who can best articulate, in a winning way, what their talent is that gets them the job offer.

Take responsibility

Some common mistakes many searchers make are lack of preparation and a lack of understanding of the ins and outs of the search process. There are also two traps that you should be aware of:

- The misconception that the outplacement consultant is responsible for getting you a job.
- The misconception that the job broker or resume distribution firm you hired will find you a job.

These things could happen, but DON'T COUNT ON IT!!!

It is much more likely that you will have wasted time and money by not taking full responsibility for your search.

If you have been put out of your job and your company provided outplacement service, push them hard – they're getting paid whether you find a job or not. Even better, try negotiating an arrangement with your former employer in which they would give you an amount in cash equal to what they would pay the outplacement service. You are much more likely to focus the money in ways that address your needs.

I am not a big fan of outplacement services. I compare executives going through outplacement to the walking dead. Outplacement is reminiscent of poorly conceived government entitlement programs that drain any motivation from people who are forced to rely on them.

This really isn't surprising, given that most of the executives you will mix with in outplacement have been pushed out of their jobs. They tend to be bitter, and also feel that they are owed a new job by the outplacement firm. The smartest thing you can do is to get over it as quickly as you can. Instead of becoming bitter, look forward and focus on what is important to you and your family. Bad things happen to good people and good companies, but how you react to the situation is 100% within your control. Being a savvy and knowledgeable job seeker can help you preserve your health and sanity while opening up better opportunities for you.

Regarding Job Brokers – happiness isn't the only thing that money can't buy; it can't buy you a job, either. I also recommend avoiding resume-distribution firms with wild claims of success. You can learn to do the same things yourself with a little time and effort, while saving yourself a great deal of money.

Here's the number one six figure level job search tip: don't go it alone. Advancing your career and fulfilling your aspirations are too important to take chances with…or for that matter to leave to chance. Underselling yourself or not properly selling yourself will cost you in not reaching your potential. It will also cost you tens of thousands of dollars in annual compensation. Over the course of 10, 15 or 20 years that adds up to hundreds of thousands of dollars.

Seek out a reputable career coach or mentor that has demonstrated experience in the area of six figure salary executives and job searches. You, too, can be on your way to reaching your goals – even doubling your income every five years!

Rob Waite is a senior executive with leadership experience in domestic and international businesses. His successes include start-ups, turnarounds, and multinational strategic partnerships. Rob's resume includes service with Fortune 500 companies and worldwide leaders.

His hit program "The Six Figure Job Search" can be found at:
www.sixfigurejobsearch.com.
www.robwaite.com

176

Copyology™

How To Connect With Your Client

By Nick Wrathall

Have you ever struggled to write a sales letter?

We've all been there. It's getting late, that sales copy has to be written, and you're staring at a blank page wondering what to do next...

If you've ever found yourself in this position (and I know I have!) then don't worry. There are proven strategies you can use for writing sales messages to attract all the customers you'll ever need.

Why copywriting is the best business in the world

What other business is so easy to run? You don't need offices, staff or expensive equipment, and your 'overheads' run to all of 50 cents – for a pen and paper. You can also write copy from anywhere in the world and work the hours you want.

With that in mind, I'm going to share with you the exact techniques I use to write copy for my clients.

Don't worry if you've never written copy before. It's not rocket science. You have to start somewhere. But if you follow the advice below you'll see an improvement in your copy skills. That's a promise.

OK. Let's get cracking!

Before you start writing any copy, you have to lay the foundations, by studying your target market and doing the necessary research.

This doesn't have to be a 500-page report. Just ask and answer simple questions like "who is my target market? What do they believe in? What is their age/demographic? Is there a proven desire for what I want to sell them?" That kind of thing.

But there's something else you must do to capture your prospect's attention.

And that's where my Copyology™ system comes in...

So what is Copyology™? Let me explain.

We now live in the 'connected' age. High-Tec IT systems have seen to that. But while we're connected in one sense, more people than ever are DISconnected from their feelings and desires. And since 9/11, people are questioning what they do. They're seeking spiritual and emotional answers to questions they didn't even think about before.

So your job as a marketer is to find and meet the needs and wants of these people. Connect with them on a personal 'me to you' level, as if you were writing to a cherished family member. Make them feel special, like they're not just a number.

That's why I've set up my Copyology™ system: to write compelling sales copy incorporating the principles of classic advertising from a modern perspective – all with the human touch. So to help you get started writing great copy, I've drawn up a list of factors to consider every time you write a sales message.

Let's start with a big one...

1. Headlines

Master UK marketer David Ogilvy spent 80% of his time on headlines, and yes, they are very important. Their aim is to capture attention in your target market and persuade them to read the rest of your message.

Contrary to popular belief, you want your headline to narrow down the number of prospects who read your message. What's that? "But everyone wants to buy my product!" Not so!

As a marketer you want to 'get rich in your niche.' The more focused your headline is on attracting your core niche buyers, the greater your long-term profits.

Think about the headlines you see at supermarket checkouts on the cover of Cosmopolitan or The National Enquirer. These magazines employ the best copywriters around. They know they only have a split second to capture attention and persuade prospects to buy. Think carefully about your headline and you'll reap big rewards.

2. Body Copy

Words are the most powerful forces in the world. They can make you happy or sad, laugh or cry, and even help you fall in love! With that in mind, here are just a few general guidelines for writing copy…

• Keep your sentences and paragraphs short. No more than 23 words and 6 lines respectively.

• Write in a personal 'me to you' style and don't be too formal.

- Don't use ten-dollar words when five-cent ones will do. In other words, don't use long words unless you have to. Keep them simple to avoid confusion. After all, no one has ever complained that something is too easy to understand!

- Once you've finished writing your copy, read it out loud. That way, you'll instantly find any 'speed bumps' in your piece. If you stumble over words, the chances are your prospects will too. So take note and make it easier to understand.

3. How to overcome writer's block at any time

The best way to get over "writer's block" is simply to write. A lot. Sounds like a contradiction, doesn't it? Not really. You see, actually getting started and writing your copy is half the battle. Once you've written your first draft, you can always come back to it later.

4. Bullets

Bullets are the little 'nuggets' of information or 'mini headlines' you often see in sales letters. They're a great way to include the benefits of your product in bite-size pieces. It's not unusual to see some sales letters made up completely of bullets. And tests have proved that sales have increased because prospects responded to just one bullet.

5. Offer/Price

The offer or price you make to prospects is vital. Together with finding the right market, it's the most important part of your entire campaign. Another point to remember is that price is elastic. If you educate your prospect correctly as to the benefits of your product, and think hard about putting together an irresistible offer, price will not be an issue.

6. Guarantee

Every piece of copy you write should have a guarantee. Let's face it, if you don't stand 100% behind your product with a money-back guarantee, you shouldn't be selling it. Period.

7. Bonuses

Bonuses must provide value to your customer, and enhance the product you're selling. The golden rule is simple. If the bonus product won't sell on its own, then don't use it as a bonus.

8. Testimonials

Glowing reports from delighted customers are worth their weight in gold. They're a great way to credentialize your product, especially as claims are more powerful (and believable) when somebody else is making them – and not you. For example…

179

"Anyone who doesn't take advantage of Nick's Copyology™ wisdom is running their business with their eyes closed."
–Jerry Wilson, CSP (Author of worldwide bestseller "Word of Mouth Marketing")

9. PS

Putting a PS in your sales copy increases response dramatically. Together with the headline and the order form, the PS is the most-read part of your sales letter. It's also a great place to remind your prospects of the benefits of your product.

10. Order Form

This is the most neglected, but vital part of the entire sales process. When writing copy, you should always start with the end in mind. Namely, 1) who am I trying to sell to? and 2) what do I want to sell to them?

That's why you should start by writing out the order form BEFORE you write your headlines and sales letter. This way, you'll still have plenty of 'juice in the tank' and have down on paper exactly what your offer is.

11. Model, don't copy

Being inspired by other people's work is perfectly natural, and something to be admired. But outright copying of someone else's intellectual property is illegal and immoral. My advice is simple – don't do it.

Instead, look at the great sales letters of the past and see how you can adapt them to your marketing campaign. For example, I recently wrote some copy for fellow Walking With The Wise contributor Brian Smithies of the Longwater Group in England. I wanted to help him sell a steel-coated trunk bracket called LoadLock.™

I remembered a successful headline used to sell face cream which was "The Amazing Facelift In A Jar." So I adapted it for Brian's product to read "Announcing LoadLock.™ The Amazing Anchor In A Car." Not copying, but a great way to promote Brian's product by reworking a tried and tested headline.

12. Testing

In real estate, the mantra is "location, location, location" – in copy it's "test, test, test."

And remember what business you're really in. No, not the marketing business. The ARITHMETIC business. Yes – you have to know your 'numbers' cold, like lifetime value of your customers, cost of production, ROI, and a whole host of others.

Make sure you always have them on hand. Otherwise, how will you be able to know how successful your campaigns have been, or what to invest in future roll-outs?

Once you've sent out your sales piece you'll start to get results. Whether they're good, bad or somewhere in between, it's vital to TEST elements of your copy in every piece you produce – but only one at a time. If you don't, you'll never be able to improve on your percentage of conversions.

And last but not least…

13. Have fun!
The great thing about writing copy is the ripple of prosperity you send out into the world. You've not only helped yourself but a whole host of other people in the world - printers, suppliers, clients, your database – who can also enjoy the benefits of the marketing of your product or service.

What you've just read are my basic guidelines on how to write copy that increases your sales. But I've only scratched the surface. I could go on for another 50 pages at least!

So if you'd like to find out more about how to write sales copy and my Copyology™ system, please e-mail me at *copyology@tiscali.co.uk* . I'd love to help you.

Nick Wrathall is an information publisher, copywriter and the world's leading Copyology™ expert. His books include *How To Write Killer Adverts* and *Sun, Sea, and Sexy Football* (the 'Think and Grow Rich' of Soccer).

To contact Nick directly, go to *copyology@tiscali.co.uk.*

Renewing Main Street

By John Kernan

It appears to me that consumers held the US economy together by force of sheer will and bravery when Wall Street crumbled; first over the dot com mess, and when the corporate greed merchants stole, and lied, and got caught, memories screamed back to the Milken Junk Bond swindle. What that shows is that "Main Street" – the old way of shopping at neighborhood merchants – still has tremendous value to consumers. We at Action International foresee the redistribution of wealth through re-education. We are in the coaching business to make sure small to medium business owners receive the best advice available from the downsized, talented corporate experts – the best education offered by any business. Big Companies are doing their part to help us by shedding their most expensive, most marketable and experienced people to cut their costs in order to improve shareholder return.

I made a very decent living working in the smallest divisions of large corporations, and by doing so I was able to put my mark on our brands. As part of Kraft/General Foods, I was lucky enough to bring a 200-year-old product out of retirement and make Altoids a $170 million brand. I was also a player in the acquisition of Balance Bar and its integration into my Callard & Bowser Company. We called that CB2. When we were turned over to Nabisco as Kraft Confections, I ended my career there as VP of Broker Sales, using a small, highly creative team to multiply the $64 million business to $350+ million.

There is a point to this, which is the focus of my article. My knowledge can be used help the small-to medium-sized businesses out there today. The power of the growth I spoke about came from some very creative ideas and even more committed people. The key point I want to drive home today is the absolute need for a "Unique Selling Proposition," or even better, a "Strategic Competitive Advantage." Price competition is the road to bankruptcy. Small to medium operators, or even owners of a huge hyper mart, can not demand the volume discounts, free labor and the luxury that owners of super centers enjoy. This is what attacks most hometown, family owned businesses when the "Category Killers" move in.

Strategy One – Add variety that would never fit the "bigger is better" formula

I wonder if the writer who coined the phrase "Category Killers" did so when talking about CATEGORY PROFITS. Wal-Mart, Toys R Us, Costco, Petco, Home Depot, and on down the list are entrepreneurial dreams come true – if you own them or work in them. For small to medium businesses, Category Killers are your worst nightmare – but there is hope. Because of their immense size and the high inventory turns needed push cash in through their stores, product assortment suffers horribly. Their goal is maximum volume.

In order to take advantage of their limited assortment, the merchant who built a store over generations should make way for a strong, varied assortment which fills the needs of the local population – but more importantly, your core customer base. I can not tell you how many times our family and friends frequent stores or shops that sell products we remember from childhood, because they fit special tastes, or meet organic standards. Holding core customers is a key to some of the promotional ideas I want to get into later.

Strategy Two – Discontinue price matching or deep discounting

By using the Category Killers' tactics, you will cripple your profit dollars at the end of the day. What, then, do you do to draw customers? Get creative. Think about what you have always done best and turn that into your "Unique Selling Proposition." "Sustainable Competitive Advantage" has been claimed by the big companies that can drive huge volume through automated systems or build the best distribution system. New, larger stores built from the ground up give the other guys the edge over a real estate-constrained, small distribution operation.

The Agricultural, Industrial and Technological revolutions have pretty much been played out. The key to any future hyper growth is through a knowledge-based company where everyone knows what is going on in the business and any individual can get on a network site to answer a customer's question. Action International has that dynamic system, linking coaches around the world to help establish the strategies I am discussing. Being in a small business, you must still develop your ownable difference from your competitors. Pull together your team and start working on ideas to find a way to draw people to your business. You need to define how your service is different or better than anyone else providing the same service. For example, if you own an inner-city take out restaurant, have bike messengers deliver fresh food faster than pick up. Remember the Dominoes Pizza delivery promise to get there in 20 minutes or the pizza was free?

Strategy Three – never compete with larger competitors in the high, fixed cost game of TV and paper advertising.

Use free, low priced products as give aways to bring people in. Make sure you develop bundled promotions that can not be price shopped, but offer a true consumer value.

I want to go back to my Callard and Bowser days for a couple of examples. Among the best commercials run by C & B starred John Cleese. He rambled on about the great toffees and butterscotch candies but never used the brand name – he pretended he forgot it but told the consumer, you know what I mean. It created "badge value" for the users of the brand – they were "Monty Python" cool. During my tenure there, the factory in England could not make a competitively priced butterscotch product so we were forced to discontinue the main product in the range. The Callard & Bowser Toffee line died quickly.

A good example of small competing with large is our experience selling Terry's Chocolate Orange, the first Chocolate Brand to exceed $50 million in annual sales before Mars, Nestle and Hershey could react. We ran commercials that showed people whacking the orange to separate the 20 pieces. The Whack and Unwrap commercials, product sampling and the orange essence of the chocolate gave us several unique selling propositions. At some retailers, Terry's two flavors were the best sellers in the category against heavy competition. This was done on a small regional scale before we burst into international distribution. I overheard two Mars reps at an Industry Convention asking where those orange things came from.

Using a variable cost reduction, like a buy two, get one free, can drive your business efficiently but would on a large scale, cost the Category Killers by forcing them to shed more margin and spend more money they can afford; you only spend when you complete the sale. When your special deal brings customers in, hook them on your Unique Selling Proposition!

Strategy Four – Develop and nurture your team

There are other weaknesses you can see in large operators. They have stopped training their people to meet shareholders' earnings expectations. They are also cutting training of their bright young stars in favor of cost savings. As a small-to medium-sized organization you can develop and foster teamwork in several ways. Putting written descriptions of each position together helps a new employee start up faster. Personality understanding through testing and off -site leadership meetings to develop your company's culture each form stronger personal bonds and help people understand their roles in their organizations.

Pay attention to details

There is a growing dependence among large manufacturers to service the newest trade class: Dollar Stores. Originally they were set up to sell close outs, marketing

www.mentorsmagazine.com

overruns or failed product launches. Volume teams need to reproduce or grow that volume every year so they are granting hot deals on perfectly good product. Watch the prices on your top suppliers. If the key items retail at Dollar Stores for prices lower than you can buy them from your Sales Rep, threaten to buy competitive, fairly priced products. You will get a reaction – or take your business to the outlet with the best price offered.

You can also recycle golden oldies in terms of ideas to compete against the huge retailers. Nostalgia is big in the World markets, especially in consumable or collectable products. Look at the resurrection of Harley Davidson. They stood by their quality and design long enough to capture a core customer base, what Action International calls "raving fans." They were able to do what Ford and GM could not do – fend off the European and Japanese machines no matter how cool, fast or comfortable they made their bikes. E-tailers are another threat to all brick and mortar retailers, but they will now have to reward their investors with real profits not paper promises.

So our biggest strategy to renewing Main Street is to make your business special in some significant ways. I gave a few examples above that large companies used, but they are food for thought for your ideation sessions. As I said, I think our core age-old downtown businesses are set to take back their fair share of the consumer spending A great way to inflict mortal wounds on the enemy is to have the happiest, most knowledgeable, and talented people service your shoppers. Even if you need to sell at a higher price, the personal touch will build a relationship that is not about money.

Feature special products; specialize in fresh produce, unique toys, free pet exams at your local pet shop, or free ski sharpening to keep people in your shop to see the new products. They will continue to buy from you, my friend. We all want to save money but not at the expense of the American dream. The average American shopper still likes to shop, or our economy would have died with the Wall Street mess. So take back your business and customers. Use the ideas I have shared with you to develop your own niche, then sell for all it is worth!

John Kernan is a Master Licensee for Action International who spent twenty years in large corporations, like Kraft and Pfizer. His main strengths are his abilities to train and direct strong cohesive teams. He spends more time than most Sales Execs in the leadership chair because of his strong sense of vision, creativity, and profit & loss management skills. He now brings corporate battle scars from the big company trenches to the advantage of small-to medium-size businesses. In fact, John has started to build a couple of small businesses himself in New England. You can contact him at *johnkernan@Action-International.com*.

Essential Business...
Learning to Forget!

By Stephen Marino

Small businesses are successful to the extent that the business owner is willing to get old thoughts out of their mind. Success includes letting go and forgetting what no longer applies to the future. It is what you know today that prevents you from achieving further success. Picture your "I know" cup filled to the brim, without room for tomorrow's knowledge. Unless you let go or forget the "I know" contents, there won't be room for the knowledge that governs your new circumstances. Yet forgetting is darn near impossible, because you have a vested interest intellectually, emotionally, spiritually and physically into "I know." After all, it got you this far. Forgetting means change and has implications affecting how others view who you are and how you view yourself. In essence, your identity and ego are at stake.

Difficult as it was, I learned to forget these limiting "I know" beliefs about business-building in order to attract more success:

1. Forget about being the best business "doer," the perfectionist, believing "no one" can do it as well as myself

2. Forget about re-enrolling in the "school of hard knocks" where by the time I discover success, it is going to be too late, and

3. Forget about knowing "how to" when it is getting it done that matters.

Forget about being the best business "Doer"

Often, business ownership leaves you vulnerable to an "I know" attitude. Your strong need to express entrepreneurial creativity and independent autonomy means you are passionate about what you are doing. And this is where you get entrapped – doing vs. being the business owner. If you are like most business owners, you have the key relationships to vendors and customers while simultaneously performing most of the key operations. This is an expensive job, not a business. You are the chief business "doer" and not a business owner.

Before I became the owner of a business coaching firm in Texas, I was an

186

entrepreneur with several start-up companies. Meanwhile, I was reviewing over 838 companies with the intent of acquiring a company about which I was passionate. During that extensive research, I met nearly one hundred business owners at that pinnacle point in business ownership. My conclusion was that very few sellers were going to see any significant financial reward for their efforts. Why? Because these business owners were the chief business "doers." The value of a business is the sustainable discretionary cash flow under new ownership. In over 90% of the companies I reviewed, without the original owner, the cash flows were appreciably less. These business owners forgot that to get full economic value, the business-of-business is to be profitable regardless of who owns it. There was no trained team nor system to have the company operate effectively and efficietly without the business owner always being there.

These chief business "doers" worked hard, defied long odds of success, and assumed a large amount of debt to earn less and sacrifice more – only to receive a meager return on their life's energy. Certainly, you went into business to achieve loftier goals, not to drain your energy for the title of "employer and employee." This is an expensive lesson. Nationwide statistics from the Department of Commerce continually show approximately one million business failures a year. Specifically, 40% of new businesses fail in the first year and 80% over five years.

There are hundreds of thousands of businesses with 3 to 75 employees in the USA that perform below their capabilities. Often the chief business "doer" lacks the people and systems to play the game of business better. Your ability to play up to your potential is not only about your "doer" ability. It is about your ability to attract, select and retain a team dedicated to and aligned with your vision who can serve clients with your distinct products and services in order to win. I recognized this in my own businesses. My strengths at doing were my strongest shortcomings at being a more effective leader – business owner. Without changing my mindset from chief business "doer," I limited myself and any significant business success.

Sports teams and athletes have long recognized the benefit of a coach, whether they are winning or not. Why would the coaching benefits to business owners be any different? Business coaches identify what you need to forget and place you on a predictable success path. They help you attract more business, learn how to lead your business and become a better business owner by coaching you on time-tested and proven methodologies.

Isn't this definition more like what you had in mind when you started your business: A commercial, profitable enterprise that operates without you always being there. This definition provides you the business ownership freedom you were seeking. Even if you are committed to working the hours, at least earn more for your labor. Working hard yourself does not get you further ahead long-term, as you saw in the above example when it came time to sell the company. You need to forget about

187

doing it all and begin harnessing your team and systems.

Business coaches see the business objectively from an outsider's perspective and recognize when the owner is being the chief "doer."

- Key Thing to Forget – Being the chief business "doer."

- Key Thing to Learn – Be the best business owner – leader.

Forget about re-enrolling in the "School of Hard Knocks"

Prior to business coaching, I enrolled and re-enrolled into the "school of hard knocks." That cost me tens of thousands of dollars in tuition for several years to earn this difficult degree. From my academic, corporate and family backgrounds, I believed that originality, complexity and difficulty was better, more true, more important, and made the most difference in success. Furthermore, my mindset was of economic scarcity. The world was a zero sum game. In order for you to win I had to lose and vice versa. I did not trust the concepts of simplicity and abundance. I was looking for the hard way – no, the hardest way – to success. After several years of seeking, I found the better knowledge. I had exhausted my ways and discovered that easy was better than hard. What is it in your beliefs that makes discovery of success difficult?

The knowledge was out there. Why wasn't I receptive enough to tap into it? I did not believe in the altruism of people willing to publish their success and share it in such explicit detail. Yet, when I finally decided to seek, I discovered that there were numerous laws of success as true as the laws of nature and philosophy. The law of correspondence – cause and effect – was most significant. I learned that if I did the same things others have done, I should get similar results. I was delighted to have discovered these laws and eagerly wanted to begin applying them in my businesses. These laws generate the same result each time, regardless of who applies them, plus they do not wear out. I do not fight these laws any longer. I work with them. I'm still learning what and how to apply them – when, how much and/or how fast. I willingly forgot my old beliefs, ate "crow" and chose to enroll as a student of success vs. re-enrolling in the "school of hard knocks." Do you believe you can learn these laws of success from what others have done, and can you do as well by applying them?

Business coaching brings you this business literacy while accelerating your learning effectiveness.

- Key Thing to Forget: Re-enrollment in the "school of hard knocks"

- Key Thing to Learn: Be a student of success

Forget about just knowing "How To" when it is getting it done that matters

I've spoken to hundreds of business owners who state that even when they want the reward and they finally know what to do to get it, they are not willing to implement and pay the price. Instead, they wait for things to be easier. They tend to forget the hidden price they pay by remaining where they are. They are willing to maintain the perception of security and comfort at the loss of personal freedom. By failing to invest in their team, they spend more hours working, earn less and generally receive less of life's rewards. What is this worth to you: getting your time back, working with a higher quality team and making more money? Priceless. Then discipline yourself to do the small things today to achieve the big things tomorrow.

Business coaches specialize in holding you accountable to your dreams.

- Key Thing to Forget: Knowing without acting

- Key Thing to Learn: Discipline yourself to be accountable to your dream and get it done – invest in your team and systems.

Stephen D. Marino is an entrepreneur, business coach, author, speaker, and business owner. He is attracting, selecting and leading a team of Texas business coaches with the vision of Lone Star Abundance Through Business Re-Education.

We coach you to Think Big – Think Win/Win – Be First!

Visit Stephen at www.ActionCoaching.com/StephenMarino or email him at *StephenMarino@Action-International.com.*

PEOPLE PAY FOR IDEAS AND SOLUTIONS

... THE BETTER THE IDEA, THE BIGGER THE PAYCHECK!!

By Stu McLaren

As an entrepreneur, your future depends on creating great ideas all day, every day. The world needs big ideas and small ideas, ideas that make money, solve problems, bring people closer together or keep relationships fun and electrifying!

People pay for ideas and solutions.

Whether you are looking for more customers, ideas for your marketing, or exciting press coverage, generating fresh, unique ideas is vital for every entrepreneur. The quality of these ideas will determine your success.

The better the idea, the bigger the paycheck.

As you can probably tell by my picture I am a little "age deprived" compared to most of the AMAZING contributors in this book. But being young forced me to take a different approach to business as an entrepreneur.

I didn't have the money. I didn't have the experience. And I certainly didn't have the contacts. I had to learn how to use my creativity - a skill that can overcome all three of the obstacles I just mentioned.

That's why I am FIRED UP!!

This is a skill that any entrepreneur can learn, and a skill that every entrepreneur should learn. If you want your results quicker, easier and cheaper, you need to learn how to generate creative solutions for your business.

The good news – times are tough

Yes, that is good news!!

People are always going to have problems.

Competition can steal your market share with a revolutionary idea. Customers can lose interest in your products or services. An interoffice divorce can split your staff into friends and foes. A natural disaster can change the way you do business

forever. The point is, we just don't know what can or will happen.

This is good news for the creative entrepreneur because there will always be problems that people want solved.

So how do you think creatively?

Thanks for asking.

The creative thinker follows a definite set of rules in order to increase their odds of success.

The word "rules" brings an implied set of restrictions. In the case of the creative thinker these rules actually set you free. By following these creative guidelines, your mind is free to think beyond your ordinary day-to-day viewpoints and it jumps into a world of imagination and creation.

Research from the renowned creativity hotspot, The Eureka Ranch, confirmed an earlier study published in the Harvard Business review. Your ideas, if dramatically different from the status quo, actually have a higher probability of success in the marketplace by over 350%.

Your success goes up the more your ideas are dramatically different.

So to develop ideas that stand out, you need to think differently. Here are some simple rules to guide you through that process.

1) THERE ARE NO RULES!!
The best ideas flow when your thoughts are not limited by boundaries or restrictions. Therefore it is imperative that you emphasize anything is possible. Great ideas shake the world. They defy the ordinary and redefine what is possible. If it doesn't, it's been done before. Stretch your thoughts to new levels. No limitations and anything goes. That includes getting rid of money limitations and time boundaries. There are NO rules!!

2) RESPECT THE CATERPILLARS
Ideas, when they first occur, aren't full-blown polished products. In the beginning, they're ugly caterpillars – but in the end they could be beautiful butterflies. Phrases like "that'll never work," "it's not reasonable," or "only in a million years" are extremely toxic to your creative environment. No idea is a bad idea. Give your ideas a chance. Defer judgment on all ideas until the end.

3) GO WHERE NO ONE HAS GONE BEFORE
Let your mind go numb to reality. In order to create fresh, new, eye-opening ideas

you need to push the envelope of "what if?" What has never been done before in your industry? Think B O – BIG and Original!! You may not know all the details to make it happen, and that's ok. Ideas first, details second.

4) GO BIG OR GO HOME
Great major league baseball players like Mark McGwire, Barry Bonds and Reggie Jackson are famous for one thing – homeruns. However, you'll also notice that these players, and many of the other top home run hitters, are also very high on another list – strikeouts!! Mark McGwire is 20th all-time, Barry Bonds 10th and Reggie Jackson is 1st. The lesson here is swing for the fences and swing often!!

The same principle applies to creativity. You need to strive for LOTS of raw ideas. Greg A. Stevens and James Burley confirmed this concept in their May-June 1997 Research Technology Management review of the results of ten major venture capital firms. They found it takes roughly 3,000 raw ideas or 125 formal projects to generate 1 success.

Swing for the fences and go big – we are looking for quantity, not quality. Quality will naturally come with quantity.

5) LET LOOSE
Having fun throughout the creative process naturally sparks an infusion of ideas. Let go of any worries, inhibitions or timidity. Without fun, there's no enthusiasm. Without enthusiasm, there's no energy. Without energy, there are only shades of "what could be." Let go of your fears and have a good time – it doesn't have to be hard work if you don't want it to be!!

Stimuli

With the rules in hand, it's now time to create. There are plenty of exercises you can use to help push your thinking (you can find a bunch of them for free at www.ideastu.com).

Throughout my presentations and workshops you will notice plenty of wacky pictures, words, toys, magazines, music and food. My mission is to engage your senses!!

Generating ideas is nothing more than making connections or associations between ideas that have never been made before. The secret ingredient is gathering and surrounding yourself with rich sources of STIMULI.

Picture a long line of dominos all lined up one after the other. It winds itself around the corner, on objects, and up your stairs.

In order to set off this HUGE chain reaction, a little nudge is needed on the first domino. Then as the first one falls, every domino after that falls in a beautiful display of one reaction after the other.

The creative process is very similar. A piece of stimuli acts as the first domino. It sets off a chain reaction of idea associations and creations. Stimuli is the nudge that helps your brain start creating.

Stimuli can take many forms including sights, sounds and scents, all the way to competitor products, customer feedback and firsthand experiences. The world in which we live in is a playground for the creative thinker, because essentially everything around you can act as some type of stimuli. Knowing that, you can see why some people are able to always generate ideas no matter what the circumstances.

Creativity in action - one quick exercise

Put on some music. If it's been a rough day put on something that will get your energy going. In fact, put on your favorite song and let loose with your best karaoke effort!!

Then define your challenge in one sentence. What do you want to generate ideas for? Put the challenge at the top of a fresh sheet of paper.

Now grab a picture from your favorite magazine. Start looking at the picture and write down your immediate thoughts, observations, reactions, or impressions about what you see.

What does the picture remind you of?

How does it make you feel?

What are the characteristics of the people or objects in your picture? Are they big, small, hairy, plump, juicy, smooth, energetic, or colorful?

How might you use what's in the picture to solve your challenge?

What is completely opposite to what you see in the picture? How can that help you solve your challenge?

Who does the picture remind you of and how can that help you with this challenge?

Now listen to the music that you have playing in the background. What does it remind you of? How can you use music to solve your challenge? What kind of music would you use?

www.mentorsmagazine.com

The purpose of using a picture is the picture lends itself to one idea reaction after another. Let your mind wander and write EVERYTHING down!!

The major mistake people make is they don't write their ideas down. By writing your ideas down you can sometimes set off another idea reaction.

The effectiveness of this process is multiplied when you add some brainstorming buddies. As you come up with an idea, say it out loud. By doing that you might trigger an idea in someone else.

Always, always, always keep the momentum going.

If the ideas start slowing down you need to grab another picture. When you have enough raw ideas, stop writing and start combining. Sort through your ideas and see if you can combine any together. Often times you can make a single idea much juicier by introducing it to a few other smaller ideas.

Learning to be more creative is easy once you tap into the resources that you already have around you. The downside is you need to be deliberate when you want unique ideas. Generating ideas is a process. Trying to brainstorm without engaging your senses with stimuli will decrease your odds of success. So will violating any of the creativity rules. Follow the rules, go through the process, and watch the magic happen!!

Stu McLaren works with entrepreneurs who want fresh, creative ideas that make life easier and put money in the bank. He has presented his creativity material to audiences all across North America and he continues to coach people through teleseminars, books and other learning resources.

Visit www.ideasforentrepreneurs.com to grab a report exclusively for readers of *Walking With the Wise* entitled "11 Creative Ideas Every Entrepreneur Must Know."

To contact Stu, visit:
www.ideastu.com
www.ideasforentrepreneurs.com

Writing Your Book @ The Speed of Thought

By Dan Poynter

Writing a book provides you with more credibility than anything else you can do; more credibility than an audiotape, videotape, a seminar, a screenplay or a song. People place a higher value on a book than on a tape – even though the same amount of work may have gone into the production.

There are many justifications for investing your time and money in writing a nonfiction book. Some good reasons are: fame, fortune, to help other people and/or because you have a personal mission.

> "For a person who has never led an army into battle, been elected to higher office, acted in movies or committed a heinous crime, a good book is the way to bridge the credibility gap."
>
> —Rick Butts, author and speaker

Few things can boost a company's image like a book. Look at what Lee Iacocca's books did for Chrysler, John Sculley's book did for Apple Computers and what Harvey Mackay's books have done for his envelope company. Marriott, Hilton, Volkswagen and many politicians have books. They all know a book will advance a cause, give them more credibility, bring in more business and/or provide a new profit center.

Invest your time in your future. The foundation for the rest of your life is your book. Your books give you credibility and are the underpinning for your other business.

Writing your book

Books are changing – for the better. There is a New Model for book writing, producing, selling and promoting. Now you can break into print faster, easier and cheaper. One part of this revolutionary change is in book writing.

195

Gone are the days of manuscript boxes holding boring sheets of paper with double-spaced lines in Courier typeface. Gone too are dull manuscripts without photos and drawings. Today's manuscripts look like books. In fact, they are books, with four-color soft covers, single-spaced lines, words that may be bolded or italicized and headers with page numbers. New printing techniques let you produce books faster and cheaper – and this changes the way the books are written.

Today, authors "build" their books; writing is just part of the assembly. Building your book is like building a speech with PowerPoint. The computer simply provides you with more visual aids to help you get your point to your reader. Now, in addition to the printed word, you can add digital photos and scanned drawings to your manuscript as you write, pull information from the Web, add resource URLs to your text, and search encyclopedias for background information, art sites for illustrations and quotation sites for quotations. You draw from all these visual-aid sources as you draft the manuscript.

First, set up your book in a binder with frontmatter pages, dividers for each chapter and a backmatter section. You fill in as much as you have for the title page, copyright page, acknowledgements, about the author, etc. Then build the manuscript by filling in the pages. For a complete description and page layout instructions, see Writing Nonfiction at http://ParaPub.com.

Editing your book

You will save time if you submit your completed manuscript to your copy editor on a Zip disk or rewritable CD. Have the editor make changes on the disk and return it to you. Then re-read the manuscript to make sure the editor improved the copy without making material changes. If the corrections are made to a printout (the old way), you will have to enter the changes and then proof them. This is time consuming and provides more opportunities for error.

Preparing for print

Following this New Model, your manuscript looks like a typeset book from the start. Then, with a click of the mouse, you will convert the word-processing file to an Adobe Acrobat PDF and you are ready to send the disk to a POD (print on demand) or PQN (print quantity needed) printer for a single or a small quantity of perfect-bound or hardcover books.

For information on PDF, see http://www.adobe.com/products/ acrobat/main.html.

For information on PQN printing, see http://www.PQNbooks.com.

Editions

You can wring maximum value out of your work by re-purposing your core content into other products. Those versions may be for Web-based downloadable books, ebook readers, compact discs, articles, special reports, compatible (non-info) products, seminars, consulting and digital audio.

The electronic edition of your book will have even more features than the print version: color illustrations, sound, video and hyperlinks. Your e-edition will take up less space, be even less expensive to produce and will provide a richer experience to your reader.

Approaching agents and publishers

With POD and PQN printing, authors may send their book to agents and publishers. A finished book is more portable and a nicer presentation than a bunch of loose sheets.

Promoting your book

With POD and PQN printing, publishers may send copies to major reviewers, distributors, catalogs, specialty stores, associations, book clubs, premium prospects, foreign publishers suggesting translations and various opinion molders. In the future, books will not be printed on spec in the hope they will be sold. Books will not be produced in great quantity until after they are sold.

New computer programs, new printing processes and the Web are transforming the writing, producing, disseminating and promoting of information. Books will never be the same. The winners are authors, publishers and readers.

For more details on *The New Book Model* and how to get your book out, see http://ParaPub.com.

Dan Poynter has written 114 books since 1969, including *Writing Nonfiction and The Self-Publishing Manual* published by Para Publishing. See http://ParaPub.com.

How to Deliver an Effective Sales Presentation

By Eric Lofholm

I began my sales career the same way millions of other salespeople all over the world did, not knowing how to deliver an effective sales presentation. When I first started, my manager handed me a stack of 100 leads and said, "Now go make me some sales."

During my first year, I was the bottom producer because I didn't know what I was doing. On the verge of being fired because I couldn't sell, a miracle happened. The top producer in the office, a man named Tony Martinez, taught me how to deliver an effective sales presentation. Dr. Donald Moine, author of Unlimited Selling Power, had trained Tony. With Tony's help I became the top producer in the office. I then hired Dr. Moine to train me.

In this article I am sharing with you the five components of an effective sales presentation. By mastering these five components, you too can become a sales superstar! Once I began delivering sales presentations with this formula, my results became extremely consistent. I began to share this formula with others. The metaphor that I now teach to help others understand how to deliver an effective sales presentation is a sales mountain.

1. Trust and Rapport

At the base of the mountain is trust and rapport. Trust and rapport is the cornerstone of the sales process because people do business with people that they like and trust. Rapport reduces resistance.

2. Identify Customer Needs

The next step is identifying customer needs. The easiest way to persuade or influence someone is to find out what they want and give it to them. The way you find out what they want is to ask questions. Go into each sales presentation knowing what questions you are going to ask the customer.

3. Share the Benefits

The next step is to share the benefits. One of the most powerful techniques to use during this section of the presentation is telling stories. One of the traits of sales superstars is that they are great storytellers. Stories suspend time. Stories make you more interesting. Stories act as invisible influence.

4. Close

The next step is to close. The close takes place at the top 25% of the sales mountain. Imagine starting off with your customer at the base of the sales mountain and going up together. You are leading the entire way. You are now—of the way up the mountain, and it is time to close. The close is where you ask for commitment. Many salespeople try to close below the—line. They then begin to apply pressure to the customer. This is very poor technique by the salesperson. The salesperson does this because they don't know any better. They don't know about the sales mountain. Understanding the sales mountain would change their life forever.

5. Objection Handling

After asking for the order, sometimes objections come up. Objections are reason the customer gives for not buying. There are many techniques for handling objections. Here is one: isolate the objection. If the customer says they don't have the money, then you say, "Other than the money is there anything else preventing you from moving forward today?" The purpose of this technique is to eliminate other objections that they might bring up.

These five steps will help you successfully climb the sales mountain and can turn you into a top performing salesperson!

Eric Lofholm is the president of Eric Lofholm International, Inc., a sales training firm located in San Diego. Eric trains sales professionals all over the world. To receive a free copy of Eric's book, *21 Ways to Close More Sales Now*, go to www.ericlofholm.com.

Run Your Business...

Don't Let It Run You!

By Bruce Luecke

Y ou've started a business. You may be following a dream or acting out of necessity. I've been at that point myself and have known others who have traveled down that path. Recently someone shared with me the personal experience of one such individual.

Phil had served as a high school principal for almost 20 years when he inherited some money from his family estate. The challenges of working in a bureaucratic administrative job had left him desiring more autonomy, and now he had the money to do something about it. On summer break from school, he went looking for a company to buy. After a brief search, he found a small utility trailer manufacturer whose owner wished to retire to Florida. He bought the company and even convinced the former owner to stay as a consultant for a short time. Phil finally found what he had always wanted…his own company. He remodeled the offices, hired an office manager and salesman and stepped up the marketing program. Despite his enthusiastic approach, the company started losing money. Unfortunately, in less than 9 months, the company was seriously 'in the red' and his inheritance was gone. Less than one year after buying his dream, he lost the business. Even though Phil was able to land on his feet as principal of another high school, the failure he experienced with the business continued to haunt him. If only he had prepared himself better…

There are many reasons why a person like Phil wants to start and run his own company. He may want the independence that comes from setting his own schedule or the desire to have more control. The individual might just have a great idea and intuitively know that he is the only one with the passion to make that vision come alive. No matter the reason, vision or type of business, new companies are started and, unfortunately, closed every day.

The definition of a successful business

From our experience working with over 4,000 businesses around the world, we have identified three factors that define a successful business: they are profitable, they are growing and they work without the owner.

Profitable and growing seem obvious, but why create a business that works without its owner? Quite simply, at my company, *Action International,* we believe that owning a business must give you more life, not less. It exists for the purpose of the owner and should support his or her personal goals and dreams. Without the ultimate objective of having a growing, profitable company that works without you, then you own a job, not a business.

As business owners, we know that building a business that works without you does not happen overnight. Companies grow a step at a time…one building block upon another. Investor Warren Buffett says: *"You don't need to have extraordinary effort to achieve extraordinary results. You just need to do the ordinary, everyday things exceptionally well."*

Mastery

The first step in building your company is to turn chaos into control. In other words, become a master at the fundamentals of your business…managing time, money and consistent delivery of your product or service.

Great business leaders understand that in order to consistently improve, one must set goals or benchmarks – called Key Performance Indicators (KPIs) – and then measure results in order to diagnose the health of the company. Calculate your profit margins and use your financial measuring systems – income statement, balance sheet, cash flow statement and key ratios – to measure your effectiveness. You can compare your company to others in your industry. As a leader, make sure your team also understands the significance of your benchmarks. Their actions should be driven by the goals you set. Your KPIs become the 'vocabulary' your team uses when measuring results.

Make sure you are delivering your product or service in the manner you want. What's the best way to find out? Walk around and observe. Ask a lot of questions and listen for key issues. Talk to your customers. Finally, test and measure.

Time is a finite resource. You can't create more. Your goal and the goal of your team is not to stay busy, it is to get results. As a leader, it is your responsibility to set an example. Spend your time on the tasks that make a difference, not on the ones that are the easiest. Spend time on the tasks that yield the best return on the investment of your time. Hold your team accountable for doing the same.

Create a Market Niche

The objective of this stage is to generate sustainable cash flow by creating value in the minds of your customers. The first place to start is to have a Unique Sales Proposition, or USP. Your company's USP must be clear and to the point: What do we do or offer that is better than any of our competitors and will create a perceived difference in the minds of our current and prospective customers? Or, as stated from the customer perspective: "I would be crazy not to do business with them."

If you are constantly measuring the effectiveness of your USP, it will keep you from becoming complacent. Bill Gates says it best: "Success is a lousy teacher. It seduces smart people into thinking they can't lose." In business, it is all about the customer…build a culture that encourages constant improvement.

The next step is to exploit your USP. What marketing strategies and tactics will most effectively communicate the message and profitably reach your target market? Don't be dependent upon one or two. You should have eight to ten different strategies in place at any one time. And, since you learned from the mastery stage that testing and measuring is the foundation of a successful business, remember to measure the return on your investment in marketing.

Creating Leverage

You are mastering the fundamentals and are generating profitable cash flow by creating value for your target market. If you are like many companies, you are also starting to split at the seams handling the workload. It is now time to build scale into your business. Effectively building scale means you need to employ leverage. In business, there are four ways to leverage:

- Using systems and operations. Systematize the routine and humanize the exceptions. Examples include scripts, workflow processes and automated systems.

- Through people – your greatest asset. At this stage, train them to run the systems you have built. Delegate clearly, provide the tools needed for your people to succeed and hold them accountable for obtaining the results expected.

- With money. Ideally, your company's cash flow will fund growth. Of course, when appropriate, it may also pay to use credit or other funding options.

- Building your marketing system. It is now time to systematize your marketing. Rather than depend upon one or two strategies, build a system of eight to 10 that are constantly creating leads for your business. Constantly test and measure to ensure you are getting a return on your marketing investment.

At this stage, you are learning how to plan for growth by creating the infrastructure needed to profitably handle your business volume.

Developing Your Team

The fourth step in the process of getting massive results in your business is developing your team. People times process equals profits. As the owner, it is your job to make sure your team understands how their performance affects the bottom line. At this level, having a vision, mission and a set of values and ground rules start to pay dividends. Collectively, they form the culture of your company. Reinforce the unique culture of the company through your recruitment practices, your new employee induction process, regular communication and education and consistent company and team goals.

Note that this step comes after creating systems. Far too many companies depend upon key individuals instead of systems. In the leverage stage, you created systems and taught your team to use them effectively. During this Team stage, it is now time to ensure that you have the **right** people running your company's systems. The business goal of this stage is to have a happy and motivated group of employees who all understand the goals of the business and take action congruent with them.

Synergy

Just as a symphony conductor creates beautiful music from the contributions of individual artists, so too must the owner create synergy in the business. The owner provides the systems that the motivated team needs to delight the customer with its unique offering. At this stage, the customers create value for the business by purchasing services and by referring others to buy. And, the company's success is measured by the key performance indicators and financial reporting that has been implemented.

Only through the combination of mastering the fundamentals, creating and maintaining a unique niche, using leverage to build scale and building the right team to run the systems does the owner get to the stage where the business can run without him or her. The synergy created can now lead to the final step...

Getting the results YOU want

Having a successful, growing business that runs without the owner provides options. Whether your goal is more time and money to pursue other interests, buy additional businesses, support charitable causes or simply spend more time with your family, you can now take advantage of the results you've earned through your hard work.

Building a great business takes time, planning and execution. Fortunately, there are a number of ways to get help and support. Start with a vision and never stop learning...improve yourself by reading, networking, and testing and measuring. Finally, seek out the help of a business coach or mentor to guide you, motivate you and hold you accountable for taking the actions needed to get the results you want. Achieving your dreams is hard work, yet it does not have to be complicated. Use the '6 Steps' as your guide to building the business and life you want.

Bruce Luecke is a certified Action International business coach located in Columbus, Ohio. He helps business owners obtain results by sharing his successful experience as a business owner and leader and by using Action's unique mentoring approach. Reach him at *bruceluecke@action-international.com.*

It's All In The Numbers

By Terri Argue

Operating a business is like being a juggler in the circus of life. There are three main balls to juggle in business: Operations, Sales & Marketing, and Finances. A well managed, efficient, profitable business operates in the intersection of all three spheres – in the center overlapping portion of the diagram below. At times, this juggling of priorities can be overwhelming – but it doesn't need to be. All you have to do is FOCUS on these main areas, learn what to watch for in your business, keep tabs on the important numbers, and take ACTION when adjustments are needed.

Finances

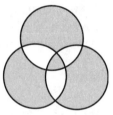

Operations

Sales & Marketing

Let's take a closer look at each area, and at the functions within those areas that require your attention…

Operations

1. **The people in your organization.** First and foremost, everyone in your business should have specific responsibilities so that it is very clear what is expected. Everyone should be kept accountable. Measure the numbers that are most important for the success of your business. These are sometimes called Key Performance Indicators, and may include the number of goods produced, the number of sales made, number of items serviced, etc. Monitor the number of staff you have in the various positions. Changes in volume versus the people in your organization can trigger actions that may need to be taken regarding hiring policies, training issues, even possibly the need to downsize the staff or labor hours.

2. **Getting the product in your door.** This can mean bringing in a product or service to the marketplace or it can be the manufacturing itself. In either case, it is important to know the actual time and dollar value involved. Measure the cost of goods sold. A change in cost of goods sold can trigger actions that may need to be taken regarding inventory control, quality control of production, and maintenance schedules, just to name a few.

3. **Getting your product out to your customer**. The various forms of distribution can have a huge impact on costs. You need to establish what the expense is for your product or service, and monitor it for discrepancies or changes. A change in distribution costs may require action to be taken in areas such as logistics and warehouse support, quality of management systems for distribution, etc.

Sales & Marketing

1. **Diversification is the key.** There should be ten different strategies for generating new leads to your business. All businesses will find that some lead-generating strategies will work better for their business than others. However, you want to maintain at least 10 different strategies so that if there are extenuating circumstances during a given period of time, or if one of the strategies becomes ineffective, you still have the others to rely on. Out of the ten strategies, you will find about five to be the most effective. It is most important to monitor the source of all your leads. This will tell you not only where you are getting the most visibility, but also where you either have to adjust what you are doing or where you are doing it. For example, if you get very few or no leads from your yellow pages advertisement, it may mean that your ad is not effective. You need to adjust it, or it may be that for your type of business, yellow pages are not effective and you should use your marketing money elsewhere.

2. **Monitor specifics of each sale.** We already discussed that all marketing strategies should be tracked. Likewise, all sales should be tracked as to how the prospect initially found out about your business, the dollar amount brought in, and the time it was brought in for seasonal variances. Another important stat that is vital to monitor regarding the sale are spin off sales that result from the initial sale. This will help track the lifetime value of each customer, as well as whether they are a good referral source for your business.

3. **Individual sales personnel and their successes**. This can both help and alert the business owner. By tracking the number and the dollar value of sales by each salesperson, you, the business owner, can determine who the successful salespeople are. You can use their knowledge and ability to establish "Best Practices" in your business, and they can help train the sales people that need it the most. Keeping track of these stats can also help identify those that are just not cut out for sales at all.

www.mentorsmagazine.com

Finances

1. Incoming revenue. This is the MOST important number to watch in any business. To quote Brad Sugars, founder of Action International, "You Have To Make The Sale, You Have To Make The Sale!" This is the lifeline of any business, and as a result should be tracked daily. What you want to watch for are trends from day to day, week to week, month to month, year to year – and in particular the same time periods over several years (i.e. first quarters, second quarters, etc.). There may be isolated circumstances why sales vary from one period to another period. As a result, when doing comparisons, a minimum of three consecutive periods and preferably five should be looked at for analysis purposes. However, as a business owner, keeping track on a daily basis will keep you on top of any changing situations and give you the opportunity to make changes quickly.

2. Cash flow. You must be aware of the money coming in versus the money going out in the way of expenses, as well as the timing of these movements of funds. There is a saying, "You have to spend money to make money." Although it is important to track total expenses, it is equally important to track when these expenses are due for payment versus the timing of incoming revenues. Being proactive and planning for shortfalls or allocating surpluses more effectively is a sign of good business management.

3. Profitability. Operating profits are basically the money left over from the sales after the costs of bringing in or producing your product or service. Total profitability is after all expenses have been accounted for. To put it another way, profitability is the percentage out of every dollar sold that goes into your bottom line – your pocket. Remember, a business has to be profitable or it just doesn't make sense to keep it going!

To summarize, the key numbers to watch for are:

1. Individualized Key Performance Indicators

2. Cost of making your product or service ready for the marketplace

3. Cost of getting your product or service to the customer

4. Lead generating strategies

5. Sales details

6. Salespersons stats

7. Total revenue

8. Cash flow

9. Profitability

When you start FOCUSING on and tracking the "Numbers" in your business, you will have greater control over your business. Soon, you will know what the acceptable levels are, what is not acceptable, and when to take ACTION. The sooner you start the better…YOU Can Do It!

Terri Argue is President of Action International Edmonton, Inc., director of Alsask Learning Resources, Inc., at a multi-million dollar, international educational franchise company, and director / treasurer of Alsask Learning Resources – Nevada, Inc. She has almost 23 years experience in the financial industry and over 16 years in business.

Terri has a strong belief in watching the "Numbers." Visit her website at www.actioncoaching.com/terriargue or www.action-international.com/terriargue. She can be reached at *TerriArgue@action-international.com*, (780) 461-9494 or toll free at 1-877-441-9494. You can request your FREE BUSINESS DIAGNOSTIC by mentioning Walking With the Wise in an e-mail to *ClientDevelopment@action-international.com*.

A Communicator Looks at Corporate America

By F.X. Maguire

Both the original Adam and Adam Smith could concur that this indeed is a period of transition and shake-out for the American Industry. Those organizations which are ready and have planned might make it. Those which are ready and have not planned won't make it.

If corporations respond in a timely fashion, there is unquestionably a unique window of opportunity in the coming decade. Many of the pieces are already in place: a highly competent sales force, willing workers, experienced management, a proud history, and loyal customers.

We have all been impressed by what has been accomplished to date. But I am also impressed by the magnitude of what remains to be done. If I had to begin with only one impression, it is that it is doable. Whether or not it will be done depends entirely on an openness and willingness on the part of senior management to change.

The crisis of morale

As I see it, Corporate America has a major communications problem. It is a crisis of employee morale. The work force is confused. They do not feel that they are getting the full story of what is happening within their company. They see constantly changing management teams. They perceive senior management as remote and often indifferent. They receive a wide variety of conflicting messages. And, in the absence of solid information, they are open to all kinds of misinformation, rumor, undigested data, and speculation about their company and its future.

These perceptions become their reality.

It adds up to a significant and pervasive problem.

This "reality" – these perceptions – more than any other factor, smothers enthusiasm and winning attitude, which are vital parts of any successful enterprise, and erodes confidence in the company.

These problems are systemic in any organization doing business on a national or global scale. They all have to do with communications in one form or another.

Cumulatively, they can sap the productive energy of a company. If dealt with and resolved, they can release a surge of positive energy and imagination, which can transform an ordinary workplace into a hub of participatory excellence and quality.

The rising tide lifts all boats. Effective communication is a multiplying force within a company. Everyone benefits.

At the core is the need for a company-wide culture, which incorporates:

- Shared vision
- Shared knowledge
- Shared responsibility

If this positive corporate attitude is sometimes hard to identify and define, there is little problem in sensing its absence in an individual or group. A losing team mentality is devastating. It turns active and creative human energy into cynicism and hostility. It puts an end to pride of achievement and to initiative. It isolates people from one another and fosters the "us against them" mentality at all levels of the organization.

"The most important ingredient in winning wars is morale."
–Dwight D. Eisenhower

We cannot not communicate

Communications will be the test of the modern world. We are the communicating species. As individuals and in groups we employ an elaborate system of symbols and signals to create an environment of ideas, emotions, and attitudes.

We are always sending out messages. We might not always do it well, but we always do it. We communicate by our presence, by our choices, by our words, by the complex nuances of our silent language. Basic to all of its forms is the fact that human communication has to do with an interactive process in which a message is sent, received, and responded to. To understand our organizations and ourselves it is critical that we understand this most complex of human activities. We are the communicating species.

A corporation is a communicating entity with many audiences – customers, suppliers, shareholders, employees, the competition, governments, and the public.

The perceptions these groups have of the company are critical to its ability to operate and to thrive in a complex and competitive environment. Communication deals directly with these perceptions. That is why productivity and profitability are so directly dependent on communication. That is why no company can be much better

than the quality of its communication. That is why communication will be the critical test of the modern corporation.

The Information Age is characterized by the democratization of information and a decentralization of decision-making. They go together. Technology has speeded up the flow of information. Customer expectations have brought about the need for on-the-spot decisions. Today's employees need information, which is candid, timely, and thorough.

Eighty-five percent of productivity problems are due to management policy and procedures, said W. Edwards Deming, the late celebrated management guru.

Experience confirms that many corporations look upon communication as a kind of cosmetic overlay on the serious business of the company or as a bag of techniques designed to keep the public and the employees at peace. It is my conviction that the communication dimension is an integral part of the business of the corporation and that it can be the quickest and most cost-effective way of advancing the goals of any corporation.

There are no people-proof systems. Getting the most out of your people is the clearest and most direct path to increased earnings and profitability.

Managers are the key

The manager is the mediator, teacher, motivator, and model. The manager knows the realities of the local workforce and its increasing diversity. There will be little productivity, improvisation, initiative, or enthusiasm unless there is a manager who exemplifies these values,

Communication is the process.

The manager is the agent.

Effective communication is the central nervous system of the corporation. At every level, the manager should be looked to as the source of information and inspiration. If the managers are credible, the company is credible. The manager is the key factor in the triad of management, employees, and customers.

Most companies presume that they are already communicating through a manager-based structure. Realistically, this assumption often has more to do with the organizational chart than with the functional activity of the company. Today's manager should be perceived by employees as the personnel department, the communication department, the safety department, the benefits department, and the training department. The manager becomes the key player in the network of speeded-up information, the initial contact for advanced and privileged information, and the primary source for both information and motivation for employees.

The manager is the messenger and the message.

These principles were developed in the founding of Federal Express and they have served that company productively for all these years. It's not that the system has been tried by many organizations and found wanting; most often it has not been tried.

Great workplaces are defined not so much by wages and working conditions as by feelings, attitudes, and relationships.

Look at the manager through the eyes of the employees. Workers don't show up in the morning with the idea of doing a mediocre job. They want to make a difference, to contribute to the enterprise, to feel good about themselves.

In a time of disintegrating institutions, they want to belong to a group that does meaningful work and does it well.

The world asks them: "What's your name and what do you do?" The answers to both questions are important to your employees.

Once again, the point-of-contact manager becomes the soul of the corporation. The manager is the one who personalizes the strategy, who injects the passions and feelings into the task. And although sports metaphors have often been overused, it can be helpful to look upon today's manager not as a boss but as a coach, a leader, a teacher, a motivator, a trainer, and a model. He/she stands up for the employees. He/she sets the tone. He/she monitors the execution of the plan in an informed and improvisatory fashion. And, in all situations, the manager should remove obstacles from the path of the employees.

There is an advertising agency in San Francisco which has a simple Latin motto taped to each of its manager's telephones:

NE SIM OBEX

"May I not be an obstacle"

Employees working in this special kind of environment will inevitably approach their work in a more positive and productive way.

The challenges before us

The challenges at the beginning of this new century are three: the management challenge, the employee challenge, and the customer challenge.

• Management Challenge

There must be developed a sense of urgency in managers to nurture a will to win, to get the juices flowing by putting employees on a war footing for a battle in which they are assured they will prevail because of superior planning and strong leadership.

• Employee Challenge

Employees must be convinced that they are the company, that they are not manual laborers, but professionals operating with a sense of the whole company and with knowledge and decision-making power of their own; that they are needed, wanted, and respected.

• Customer Challenge

The customer must be made to know that your employees are part of their experience, that your employees are on their payroll. The Team must be customer-driven, customer-sensitive, and customer-centered.

The communication strategy employed by your company will be the key to embracing these challenges and successfully conquering them. Be sure that your company is one that is ready and has planned for the future, so that you will be one of those still standing in the end!

Francis X. Maguire, chairman of Hearth Communications Group, Los Angeles, California, was a founding officer of the Federal Express Corporation and former senior vice president for the company. Currently, he is a popular keynote speaker, author and mentor to top corporate management teams on leadership, management and effective communications.

Losing Ground in the Innovation Race

By Bill Gates

Computers will change our lives more in the next 10 years than they have in the last 20.

Not only are people relying on them for more of the things they do every day, but the pace of computing innovation has never been faster. Processing power continues to advance, while network bandwidth, wireless, storage and graphics capabilities are growing at even faster rates.

This is revolutionizing how we live. Many of the things we use every day – from entertainment systems and telephones to kitchen appliances and even wristwatches – are morphing into computers capable of communicating with PCs or any other computerized device in our homes. The result is that computers are becoming so ubiquitous, they are literally disappearing into the fabric of our lives – and becoming so intuitive to use that we hardly notice them. The next generation of scientists, engineers and researchers will really make this happen.

All this makes it a great time to be in the computer industry. The abundance of hardware and connectivity is making it possible to tackle some of the biggest challenges in computer science.

Can we make tomorrow's computers unfailingly reliable and secure? Is it possible to create computers that can see, listen, speak and learn like human beings can?

Can we find new ways to seamlessly connect the technology in our lives – so that, for instance, the minute you add new songs to your digital music collection, you'll be able to listen to them on everything from your portable media player to your car's stereo system?

Can we create innovative new technologies to help people navigate the growing world of digital information to find the data they really need?

These kinds of breakthroughs are the engine of our country's economy, and they depend on a number of key factors. Federal support for research and development, particularly through our universities, is crucial. It drives long-term technology

213

advances that help create new companies and jobs – or entire industries--which, in turn, generates tax revenue that can be invested in further innovation.

The Internet boom was the result of this cycle of innovation: as a product of government, business and academic work, it accounted for more than one-third of economic growth in the United States during the late 1990s.

But we're losing ground in another part of the innovation process: finding the smart, motivated people that can make these breakthroughs happen. Fewer young people are choosing to study computer science, despite all the challenging problems we have yet to solve and the incredible potential of the technology industry. We need talented computer scientists more than ever. We need new ways to understand the large-scale computer systems of tomorrow and new ways to program them.

The abundance of hardware and connectivity is making it possible to tackle some of the biggest challenges in computer science. Software and hardware advances have cleared the way for more natural interfaces, yet we still have lots of work to do in bringing the speech and vision capabilities of the computer closer to that of humans. Computers are becoming better learners, distinguishing legitimate e-mail from spam and translating simple documents or modeling specific areas of human knowledge.

Many of these challenges are software problems, and I think that the solutions are within reach. Moreover, the commitment of government and the private sector to invest in the future remains strong. This year, for example, Microsoft will invest $6.8 billion in research and development, working alongside governments and universities to create the fundamental software breakthroughs that will help push computing forward.

But it's the next generation of scientists, engineers and researchers that will really make this happen. That's why I'm spending this week visiting some of our country's best universities, talking to students and faculty about how we can work together and encouraging a larger and more diverse pool of computer science students.

Some of these students might join technology companies like Microsoft after they graduate, while others may stay and teach, work in other industries or launch their own ventures. My priority is to help them realize their own incredible potential – and that of America's computer industry. The future won't happen without them.

William (Bill) H. Gates is chairman and chief software architect of Microsoft Corporation, the worldwide leader in software, services and Internet technologies for personal and business computing. Microsoft had revenues of $32.19 billion for the fiscal year ending June 2004, and employs more than 55,000 people in 85 countries and regions.

Corporate Executive to Successful Entrepreneur

By Tom Maier

Little did I know that the paper route I started when I was 9 years old would be the business that I still refer to when I am working with clients. When I started my paper route, I walked, pulling a wagon to pick up my papers and then delivering them to 85 houses. From my early earnings, I purchased a bike which I used to pull the wagon. I finished much faster each day, and realized I had more time to have fun. I later convinced my dad to drive me in his car on Sundays, which eliminated me making 2 trips – the papers on Sunday were very big and would not all fit in the wagon.

When I entered high school and played on several sports teams, I did not have time to do both, but delivering papers was my only income. I wanted both. I hired several friends to deliver the papers for $2 per day. I collected the payments from customers in between practice and games. I made $35 per week and paid out $14 per week to have the papers delivered, clearing $21 per week – with plenty of time for fun. That was total leverage of time and money, in its purest sense. It was my first encounter with being an entrepreneur.

My corporate experience

After I graduated college, I went right into the corporate world like so many others. My corporate experience has always been very rewarding. I learned from the ground up how all aspects of a business operated. Once my basics in business were developed, I continued to rise through management to become a very successful executive. The thing I learned very early on was how to "step on people's toes without scuffing their shoes." I was paid very well to fix problems and quickly make a business profitable and run more efficiently. Along the way I was very fortunate to have some great mentors who not only taught me, but who gave me a lot of freedom to make decisions and implement my strategies into the organization.

In most of the corporations I was with, training was the first item cut when companies were fine tuning expenses. I have always felt training – good training – needs to be looked at as an investment, not an expense. Corporations constantly promote people to a level beyond their competence. Without proper training, the performance standards of many companies have suffered.

Itching to be an entrepreneur

I have always wanted to have my own business, and with the help of

215

several corporate buyouts, I decided to take control of my life. I felt with all my business experience, I was ready to invest my own money in my dream.

The first question I had to answer was, "Am I committed to being an entrepreneur?" The only way to be successful in any venture is to give it your full commitment – not just doing it until that big job offer comes along. Without the commitment, you will become the "Victim," like so many business owners. Victim corresponds with three words: Blame, Excuses and Denial. Problems are never their fault and something or someone else is always to blame. Progress can not be made in this state of mind.

Progress can only be made if you approach life and business as a Victor. The three words that correspond to a Victor are Ownership, Accountability and Responsibility. A Victor takes ownership for his situation, is accountable for results and responsible for his actions. Setbacks are challenges, and they stimulate ideas that improve the situation.

When my answer was a resounding, "Yes, I am completely committed," I moved on to looking at why I wanted to be an entrepreneur. Buying a business does not make you an entrepreneur. Many people lose their job or get tired of working for someone else, so they start their own business and do everything themselves and end up working more hours than ever before. All they have done, in this case, is to have bought a job - usually making less per hour than anyone else in the business.

I sat down and worked out my personal mission statement, which is what you want people to say about you during your funeral. If you are contemplating starting a business, you should have a personal mission statement and one for your business. Then look at both mission statements and see if they support each other. You can not go forward unless these two are compatible.

The change

My corporate career success had always come from jumping right into problems and determining quick solutions. I knew that my way had always worked – but that wasn't the case when I was building my own business. Not only did I have to deal with not having enough paper clips, office supplies and computer support readily at hand, but I now had to re-educate myself about listening.

I had to start over and learn not to be so anxious to impose my solutions (although I have many in my tool box) on potential clients and internal staff and support. Listening to my clients was critical in finding out their real needs. I needed to dig deep and find out why they started in business, what their goals were and what was holding them back from reaching their goals. Not until those questions were answered could I start providing successful solutions.

As my business grows, I apply the same listening skills to my staff, whom I call associates. I have seen many business owners make the mistake of thinking they are the business. They feel the Owner needs to take care of the Business, the Business will handle the Customers, the Customers will take care of the Team and the Team will take care of the Owner. This common scenario is why an owner often finds himself always working IN the business – every day, all night and on weekends, with no vacations.

To be a successful entrepreneur, the business cycle needs to be: the Owner takes care of the Team, the Team takes care of the Customer, the Customers take care of the Business and the Business takes care of the Owner. When this is in order, you truly are a business owner. Brad Sugars' definition of a business is a "commercial, profitable enterprise that works without you!"

The growth

Becoming an entrepreneur needs to be fed by a desire to constantly grow and get better. If you were allowed to make one investment in your business to help it grow, it would have to be in yourself. The better you are, the better your business will perform. Jim Rohn says "Don't wish your job were easier, wish that you were better."

Imagine you have a child in 5th grade and every year, they do the same things. They would have to repeat 5th grade year after year until they could actually drive to 5th grade. That sounds ridiculous and would never happen to my child. Well, many business owners do the same things year after year and the business never changes. You need to spend at least 4 to 5 hours a week in training, whether in sales, marketing, or with your particular products and services. You can do this by reading, listening to tapes or CDs and attending seminars in sales, marketing, personal development or industry-specific training.

Personal development is critical in understanding your strengths so they can be maximized and your weaknesses so they can be improved. Learn by talking to the most successful people in your business. Tap into their knowledge and listen to the ways they became successful. Chances are their tactics will also work for you. Find a mentor or business coach to take you to the next level. I always point out that Tiger Woods has a coach, so why not you?

You must become a sponge, constantly learning from everyone you meet and everything you do. Don't be afraid to try new things. The only failure is the failure to try things. Constantly make yourself better!

The goals

Every successful entrepreneur needs to set goals and monitor them. Your goals need to be specific, measurable, attainable, results-oriented and have a timeframe.

www.mentorsmagazine.com

Without these components they are just wishes. There is a saying, "If you don't know where you are going, you will end up someplace else."

Your goals need to be written and completed yearly, monthly and weekly. By doing written goals you are activating your subconscious to be looking out for them. This is called using your Reticular Activating System, or RAS. It is like when you are shopping for a new car, and after you leave the dealer you suddenly see hundreds of that same car on the road, when you barely noticed them before.

The strategy

Once your goals are set, you need to have an Action plan. I don't mean just a business plan, which usually ends up in your bottom drawer. Specifically, a 90-day action plan starts by determining what your 12-month goals are for revenue, clients and profits. Then you need to have at least ten different lead generation strategies and any other strategies that are needed to reach your goals. The strategies need to be specific and measurable, and they all need to have a due date. Then you break down these strategies over the next 90 days. Do this exercise every 90 days in order to make any necessary adjustments. Finally, test and measure all your results, such as where all your leads are being generated, what your conversion rate is and your average dollar sale. Do all these things and you will keep on the right path to reach your goals.

The fun

Don't forget the fun! You get into business for yourself to give yourself a better life, more financial freedom, more time and whatever else is important to you. You can't let it be anything different. You must have fun!

Tom Maier is an entrepreneur and a licensed business coach. He is also president of Action Business Coaching, NE, Inc. If you would like to learn how to reach the dreams you have for your business, or would like to enter a profession where you can help change people's lives, contact Tom at *tommaier@action-international.com.*

The Secret To Achieving Your Financial Goals

By John Assaraf

Have you ever asked yourself what your highest income-producing activity is?

If you're like most people, you probably go about your day-to-day business never really thinking about the moment-to-moment activities that consume your day. I'd like to walk you through an exercise that has helped me and my clients stay focused on earning their highest possible revenue per hour.

We each start with 365 days in a year. If we take away weekends (104 days), 5 major USA holidays, 2 weeks of vacation, and personal religious holidays (average 3), that leaves each one of us with approximately 238 days in which to earn the income we desire. Of course, we can add or delete days based on our own schedule and desires.

If you multiply these 238 days by an average of 10 working hours per day, you are dealing with 2,380 hours of real work time for the year. So, let's do some math.

If your yearly income goals are:

- $25k = you must be earning an average of $10.50 for every hour of work.
- $50K = $21 per hour
- $100k = $42 per hour
- $250k = $105 per hour
- $1 million = $420 per hour
- $5 million = $2100 per hour
- $10 million = $4200 per hour

In order to earn the income per year that you really want, you absolutely must be doing activities every hour that cause your income to line up with this chart. If you catch yourself doing anything that isn't your absolute highest-producing income activity all the time, you are, in effect, making it much harder to achieve your desired financial goals.

www.mentorsmagazine.com

Ask yourself the following questions:

- What activity or activities generate your highest producing income?
- What are you spending your time doing?
- Are you focused on the real money-makers or the real time-wasters?
- Are you making it easy for yourself to be a high income earner, or are you doing the things that can be done by someone whose income goal or ability is less than yours?

I can tell you that when you start to look at each hour this way, you'll stop doing the small stuff and start doing the real stuff that yields results.

Just look at your most recent 3-5 days and count the number of hours you spent really making the big bucks vs. all the stuff that creeps up on all of us. What you discover will amaze you.

Here's To You Having It All!

John Assaraf, aka **The Street Kid** New York Times & Wall Street Journal Best-Selling Author, Trainer & Entrepreneur. *Discover My Secrets To Building Multi-Million Dollar Businesses – Guaranteed!*

Go to www.TheStreetKid.com/seminars and get your free 5 lesson course on *The Science Of Making Tons of Dough and Being Happy Doing It.*

For more information please visit: www.TheStreetKid.com.

Market Dominance

By Joe Polish

There is a secret that the Real Estate Industry has known about for years. The secret has been used for decades to gain market dominance. Let's take a look "outside the box" and see what we can learn from an industry other than our own.

First of all, before I go revealing this amazing secret, I have to admit that the majority of real estate agents are pretty clueless when it comes to marketing. Most of them are products of "marketing incest." (Everyone does what everyone else in their industry is doing and everyone winds up real stupid.) Another case of the blind and dumb leading the blind and dumb. Granted, there are a few bright marketers in the real estate industry, but the majority of them don't know how to drum up business any better than the average carpet cleaner does. So, what is this amazing secret that you can learn from a group that is 90% marketing illiterate?

Real estate agents have a marketing technique, and if they knew exactly how to properly exploit it using direct response marketing systems, they could kiss working 80 hour weeks goodbye forever. You are about to get the inside scoop on how to take this brilliant concept and apply it with effective marketing strategies to dominate whatever market you choose to dominate. The amazing technique is called "farming."

Perhaps you've heard this term before. Perhaps you've even been "farmed" before. New agents are told to pick their "farms," and then they usually waste a lot of time and money sending ineffective business cards, flyers and postcards to their farms in hopes of dominating that particular group of people. To make matters worse, most of them do tons of manual marketing – which is door to door, cold-call grunt work. If they used Marketing "systems" instead, they would end their pain and stop wasting their time. Like I said, this is a brilliant concept, and with the right tools, you can turn it into a brilliant marketing SYSTEM.

Old MacDonald had a farm

Just in case you haven't figured it out by now, a "farm" is a niche market you relentlessly target market to in an effort to gain market dominance. Farms can be a particular neighborhood, a social club, a doctor's list of clients, a business's clientele, or a group of businesses or business people.

221

So, your first step is to choose your farm (or farms). Let's say there is a particular neighborhood in your area where the people live in large homes (with lots of carpet), they drive nice cars, and by the looks of their yards and homes on the outside you can bet they keep them looking just as good on the inside. This would be a great target market for you to farm. So, you begin an effective direct marketing campaign. It may start with a series of sales letters, and next it may be postcards or flyers (all Direct Response, of course). Once you've cleaned for a few of the neighbors, you get their testimonials, you get them to refer their neighbors, and you print the neighbor's testimonials in your letters, flyers, and postcards.

You work the neighborhood like a farmer works his fields, planting seeds, watering growth and reaping the harvest. I guarantee that in a matter of a couple of months you will be the carpet cleaner of choice in that neighborhood. That is called market dominance.

The beauty of owning the farm

Once you have chosen and properly farmed your niche markets of choice you will find that you "own" your farms. In other words, you dominate the market and no one else can touch it (as long as you take excellent care of your clients, of course.) And, as long as you are worthy, when you own your markets, you don't compete by price. As a bonus, you will find your farm naturally grows, because your farmed clients are generally farms of their own. In other words, they have colleagues, they have lots of friends and families. The farm just keeps getting bigger and bigger.

So, steal the secret real estate agents have been sitting on for years. After all, the greatest marketing concepts are often found when you look outside your own industry. (Where do you think McDonald's got the drive through ideas for their restaurants - think banks!) So, find the farms in your area and start farming. By harvest time you will be reaping the rewards of market dominance.

Joe Polish is the President of Piranha Marketing,. Visit his site at www.joepolish.com.

Section IV

Keep Your Health...
To Keep Your
Abundance

© 2004 Kim Muslusky

Mind Over Body

By Christopher Reeve

Before my injury I believed that our overall health is affected by our state of mind, but I was highly skeptical of those claiming to be healers. The damage to my spinal cord and all the ensuing complications led to a reconsideration of those beliefs. I've had pneumonia, blood clots, broken bones, and reactions to drugs, which have all required medical care ranging from pills to IV antibiotics to hospitalization. I've also been approached by many well-meaning individuals who have professed the ability to heal me noninvasively, using only their "special powers."

"Healing" Experiences

An emergency, such as a blood clot or a collapsed lung, has always led me immediately to the ER. Long-term issues of gaining strength and recovery of function have made me wonder if there are indeed genuine healers who can, as they claim, effect change simply by touch. Most have been easy to dismiss because their claims of past success seemed dubious at best and their proposals for treating me sounded very far-fetched. But twice I let my guard down and allowed myself to be examined and treated. The first healer arrived from Ireland – a short, friendly character in his late fifties wearing a bright green jacket. My first thought was that a leprechaun had come to save me. He claimed that acupressure along my spinal cord would release endorphins that would relieve the pain and create "a new environment." I told him that there was no pain, but that didn't seem to faze him in the least. Suddenly my right arm twitched and moved a few inches. He immediately took credit, but everyone in the room knew that it was only a routine spasm – an involuntary movement caused by nerves seeking a connection to the brain. Score: Medicine 1, Healer 0.

Supernatural health provider number two actually made a house call. (Try getting a regular doctor to do that.) He had been recommended by an acquaintance who told me that he had successfully cured people of ulcers and cancer, as well as one spinal cord injury. Will answered the doorbell, and down the hall came a banker or a stock-broker in his mid-thirties, dressed in conventional business attire. My first thought was, "I'm glad he has a day job." He accepted a glass of water and settled into a chair in my office. I soon learned that he had been in the business world until he was "called" to change his life's work (though apparently not his wardrobe) five years earlier. He began his assessment of me by looking at my hands and noticing that the little finger on the left was broken. I told him that it was an old fracture from a family soccer game and I'd never bothered to have it set. He announced that we should do "first things first" and that he would heal the finger right away. I sat silently for over an hour with my eyes closed because I didn't want to disrupt his concentration. He massaged the finger, kneaded it, moved it in all directions, but kept trying to start a conversation. How did I like living out in the country? Any new film projects? I see (looking at a picture of our boat on the wall) that you're a sailor. Me too! I kept my answers short, instinctively not wanting to give him too much information. At last he announced that he was done. I looked down and saw that indeed the little finger was lying flat on the armrest of my chair instead of in its usual contracted position. I have to admit I was pretty impressed – especially because, like the leprechaun, he didn't charge anything for the session. We made plans for another visit the next week. But even before he had reached the front door on his way out, my finger began to curl up again. It has remained that way ever since. (It seems that both times I got what I paid for.) Score: Medicine 2, Healers 0.

The mind-body relationship

In the quest for a cure from disease or relief from psychological and emotional distress, you could put pure medicine at one end of the spectrum and supernatural interventions at the other. I've always been fascinated by the possibility that the treatment of disease and the cause of disease lie somewhere in the middle. I share the widely held belief that there is a relationship between the mind and the body that can both create a physical condition and enable us to recover from it.

As a teenager I suffered from occasional asthma and a variety of allergies. For some reason the worst attacks came on when I went to visit my father. Was that because of mold spores or mildew or the tall grass around his nineteenth-century farmhouse? A few of my friends near my home in New Jersey lived in similar houses, but I never I had a reaction when I visited them. The only logical explanation had to be that I was extremely anxious to please my father. It was difficult to relax, be myself, or literally "breathe easy" when he was around. Since these issues were never discussed, it might have been tension building up inside that often left me gasping for breath and sneaking off to use my inhaler.

Perhaps the level of stress in the mind determines the severity of its manifestation in the body. There is overwhelming evidence that stress can be linked to hypertension, ulcers, and a compromised immune system. Many researchers agree that some forms of cancer are caused or made worse by repressed anger. When President Nixon was embroiled in the Watergate scandal in 1973, he faced the nation and told us, even as beads of sweat formed above his lip, "I am not a crook." At the same time he developed phlebitis – a condition that causes pain and swelling due to partially blocked circulation – in one leg. Was this a coincidence, or was it caused by the mental stress of maintaining a cover-up? Whenever we don't feel well we tend to blame it on external causes: the weather, contact with others, the environment, or even something we ate. These may well be contributing factors, but we should acknowledge that the source of many ailments is within ourselves.

If we accept that the mind/body connection can produce harmful effects, then we can assume that the same connection has a healing power as well. Before my injury, a positive attitude probably helped me bounce back from various injuries and illnesses. But nothing that had gone before could have prepared me for an experience I had two years after I was paralyzed.

In the spring of 1997 a small red spot appeared on my left ankle, probably caused by irritation from my shoe. Within a month the red spot had become a serious wound. It was only an inch and a half wide, but the skin had broken down, layer after layer, until the anklebone itself was exposed. Then the site became infected and turned septic as it spread up my leg. I was examined by specialists and told that there was the potential for a systemic infection, which might prove fatal. If they detected any indications of that scenario, the only recourse would be to amputate my leg above the knee. I remember my immediate reaction, which I did not hesitate to share with the experts: I told them that was absolutely unacceptable, because I would need my leg in order to walk. I remember mentally drawing a line in the sand, establishing a barrier that could not and would not be crossed.

I was put on a ten-day course of a powerful antibiotic administered intravenously. As I sat on the porch of our summer home in Massachusetts, gazing for hours on end at the hills surrounding our property, I kept picturing my ankle as it used to be. Slowly but surely new layers of skin began to form. Six months later the wound had closed. Within a year the ankle appeared perfectly normal. I don't claim to understand precisely why my wound healed and my leg was saved. Certainly Fortaz, the prescribed antibiotic, is an aggressive therapy. But even the strongest antibiotics don't always work. I had learned that from other treatments when I was in rehab. Looking back at it now, I believe that I wouldn't have recovered without the drug. But I also believe that I wouldn't have recovered without an ironclad agreement between my mind and my body that I had to keep my leg.

There were many times during the healing process when I still felt very anxious about the outcome. It was much like the decision not to commit suicide after my accident – the decision created consequences of hard work, sacrifice, and the beginning of a journey into the unknown. It was relatively easy to tell the doctors that I would refuse amputation. My response was instinctive and probably irrational, driven by my aggressive and competitive personality. It was far more difficult to sit on the porch with my leg propped up on pillows constantly trying to push doubt and negativity out of my mind. One minute I would think, "I can do this – I can heal this wound." The next minute I would think, "What are you talking about? You don't have any special powers." Then I would try yet again to picture my ankle as it used to be and tell myself that it deserved to be whole. I reminded myself that I had always recovered from all kinds of setbacks. There was even good reason to believe that sooner or later my spinal cord could be repaired and the nightmare of paralysis would be over. Why shouldn't this ankle come with me as I moved forward?

Internal chatter after a brave decision is probably the rule rather than the exception. When NOTHING IS IMPOSSIBLE field commander gives his troops the order "Follow me!" he might be extremely anxious or down-right terrified. But he has to project confidence and authority, or the troops will only reluctantly do their duty without rallying behind him. In some cases the old adage "Fake it until you make it" is actually helpful. You make a choice or set a goal and let people know about it. Then just getting started leads to the discovery of internal resources that help us go farther than we ever thought we could.

Expanding comfort zones

My friend David Blaine is perhaps the best example of an individual who has used those internal resources to go farther than ordinary people can imagine. A slender, soft-spoken young man, he performs unbelievable magic with an air of nonchalance that almost borders on lethargy. But what sets him apart are his feats of endurance. He has been buried alive, frozen in a block of ice, and most recently, in May 2002, he stood on top of an eighty-foot pole for thirty-four hours before jumping into a pile of cardboard boxes. He has been described as a thrill seeker, a nut case, a guy who will do anything for publicity and money. As someone trying to overcome the limitations of a disability, which requires exercise and discipline, I take exception to those who so readily dismiss his achievements.

The truth about David is that he was pushing the limits of his endurance long before the media had ever heard of him; that he lived for years just above the poverty line; and that he prepares for every "stunt" with rigid self-discipline. He trained for the pole for over a year, starting at twenty feet and learning from the best Hollywood stunt-men how to fall safely into airbags. Once he was comfortable standing on a twenty-two-inch platform and jumping from that height, he moved up to forty feet and gradually worked his way up to eighty. He never used a harness or a safety net. Why did he do it? Because he was always afraid of heights and wanted to free himself from that fear.

The vast majority of people live within a comfort zone that is relatively small. The comfort zone is defined by fear and our perception of our limitations. We are occasionally willing to take small steps outside it, but few of us dare to expand it. Those who dare sometimes fail and retreat, but many experience the satisfaction of moving into a larger comfort zone and the joyful anticipation of more success. A person living with a disability may find the courage to leave the comfort zone of his own house for the first time. An able-bodied individual might decide to face claustrophobia by taking up scuba diving. Even as our country tries to cope with terrorism, most of us know intuitively that living in fear is not living at all.

www.mentorsmagazine.com

David's physical preparation included daily up hill climbs on a mountain bike so that he would have enough strength left in his legs to control his jump off the pole at the end of thirty-four hours. He also learned to fast for long periods of time. In fact, he didn't eat anything during the entire performance.

The most extraordinary use of his own resources was the power of his mind. He used his mind to overcome his fear of heights and to summon the willpower to go without food. His mind kept his body from failing. When he did jump, he imagined that he was falling into air mattresses, which he had done almost exclusively in practice. The result was a perfect landing.

The victory over the ankle in 1997 was a landmark for me. Since then I've been much less concerned about what else could go wrong with my body. I've also found the self-discipline to exercise when I don't feel like it, which is extremely important because overall health and any hope of recovery can't be achieved without it. I've learned to stick to a conscientious diet; keeping my weight under control makes muscular and cardiovascular conditioning much easier. Since 1997 my skin has stayed intact; as a result I have the freedom to sit in my chair for as many as fourteen to fifteen hours. In the old days I was often limited to five or six. I have been able to avoid many urinary tract infections and keep the bases of my lungs functioning almost normally.

All of that is extremely hard work, and many times I don't succeed. Just recently I suffered from severe bloating of my stomach and difficulty breathing. X-rays showed that huge pockets of air had formed in my large intestine, which was putting pressure on my diaphragm. The remedy didn't come from the mind/body connection; I made changes in my diet and underwent a procedure to clear the blockage.

Perhaps I am still in the early stages of learning to control manifestations in my body with the power of my mind. At this point it seems that I am able to respond to emergencies such as the threatened amputation of a limb. I get the sense that in time I will discover the ability to do more. But now I'm confident that when something comes up, when germs invade and systems fail as they inevitably do, my mind and body, with the assistance of medicine, will keep me healthy and prepared for the future.

Christopher Reeve actor and activist, suffered a fall from a horse in May of 1995. The uppermost vertebrae in his spine, was fractured leaving him paralyzed from the neck down. Reeve has used the intensive interest in his condition to bring awareness to the field of spinal cord injury and to raise money for research into a cure.

Learning Not to Age:

The Link Between Belief and Biology

By Deepak Chopra, M.D.

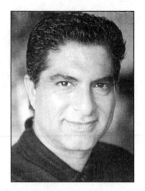

Although awareness gets programmed in thousands of ways, the most convincing are what we call beliefs. A belief is something you hold on to because you think it is true. But unlike a thought, which actively forms words or images in your brain, a belief is generally silent. A person suffering from claustrophobia doesn't need to think, "This room is too small," or, "There are too many people in this crowd." Put into a small, crowded room, his body reacts automatically. Somewhere in his awareness is a hidden belief that generates all the physical symptoms of fear without his having to think about it. The flow of adrenaline that causes his pounding heart, sweaty palms, panting breath, and dizziness is triggered at a level deeper than the thinking mind.

People with phobias struggle desperately to use thoughts to thwart their fear, but to no avail. The habit of fear has sunk so deep that the body remembers to carry it out, even when the mind is resisting with all its might. The thoughts of a claustrophobic ("There's no reason to be afraid," "Small rooms aren't dangerous," "Everyone else looks perfectly normal, why can't I get over this?") are rational objections, but the body acts on commands that override thought.

Our beliefs in aging hold just this kind of power over us. Let me give an example. For the past twenty years, gerontologists have performed experiments to prove that remaining active throughout life, even up to one's late seventies, would halt the loss of muscle and skeletal tissue. The news spread among retired people that they should continue to walk, jog, swim, and keep up their housework; under the slogan "Use it or lose it," millions of people now expect to remain strong in old age. With this new belief in place, something once considered impossible happened.

Daring gerontologists at Tufts University visited a nursing home, selected a group of the frailest residents, and put them on a weight-training regimen. One might fear that a sudden introduction to exercise would exhaust or kill these fragile people, but in fact they thrived. Within eight weeks, wasted muscles had come back by 300 percent, coordination and balance improved, and overall a sense of active life returned. Some of the subjects who had not been able to walk unaided could now get up and go to the bathroom in the middle of the night by themselves, an act of reclaimed dignity that is by no means trivial. What makes this accomplishment truly wondrous, however, is that the youngest subject in the group was 87 and the oldest 96.

www.mentorsmagazine.com

These results were always possible; nothing new was added here to the capacity of the human body. All that happened was that a belief changed, and when that happened, aging changed. If you are 96 years old and afraid to move your body, it will waste away. To go into a weight-training room at that age, you have to believe that it will do your body good, you have to be free of fear, and you have to believe in yourself. When I say that aging is the result of a belief, I'm not implying that a person can simply think aging away. Exactly the opposite – the stronger the belief, the more rooted in the body it is and the more immune to conscious control.

According to the belief system you and I adhere to, Nature has trapped us in bodies that grow old against our will. The tradition of aging extends as far back as recorded history and even prehistory. Animals and plants grow old, fulfilling a universal law of Nature. It is hard to imagine that aging is the result of learned behavior, for biology cannot be denied.

Yet the core belief that aging is a fixed, mechanical process – something that just happens to us – is only a belief. As such, it blinds us to all kinds of facts that don't fit the belief system we cling to. How many of the following statements do you believe are facts?

a. Aging is natural – all organisms grow old and die.

b. Aging is inevitable – it can't be prevented.

c. Aging is normal – it affects everyone about the same.

d. Aging is genetic – I'll probably live about as long as my parents and grandparents did.

e. Aging is painful – it causes physical and mental suffering.

f. Aging is universal – the law of entropy makes all orderly systems run down and decay.

g. Aging is fatal – we're all growing old and dying.

If you take any or all of these to be statements of fact, you are under the influence of beliefs that do not match reality. Each statement contains a little objective truth, but each can be refuted, too.

a) Aging is natural, but there are organisms that never age, such as one-celled amoebas, algae, and protozoa. Parts of you also do not age – your emotions, ego, personality type, IQ, and other mental characteristics, for example, as well as vast portions of your DNA. Physically, it makes no sense to say that the water and minerals in your body are aging, for what is "old water" or "old salt?" These components alone make up 70 percent your body.

b. Aging is inevitable, but the honeybee at certain times of the year can shift its hormones and completely reverse its age. In the human body, shifts in hormones may not be as dramatic, but there is enough latitude so that on any given day your hormonal profile may be younger than the day, month, or year before.

c. Aging is normal; however, there is no normal curve of aging that applies to everyone. Some people entirely escape certain aging symptoms, while others are afflicted with them long before old age sets in.

d. Aging has a genetic component that affects everyone, but not to the degree usually supposed. Having two parents who survived into their eighties adds only about three years to a child's life expectancy; less than 5 percent of the population has such good or bad genes that their life span will turn out to be significantly longer or shorter. By comparison, by adopting a healthy lifestyle, you can delay symptoms of aging by as much as thirty years.

e. Aging is often painful, both physically and mentally, but this is the result not of aging itself but of the many diseases that afflict the elderly; much of that disease can be prevented.

f. Aging seems to be universal, because all orderly systems break down over time, but our bodies resist this decay extremely well. Without negative influences from within and without, our tissues and organs could easily last 115 to 130 years before sheer age caused them to stop functioning.

g. Finally, aging is fatal, because everyone has to die, but in the vast majority of cases, perhaps as much as 99 percent, the cause of death is not old age but cancer, heart attack, stroke, pneumonia, and other illnesses.

It is extremely difficult to ascertain what it would be like to watch the body age per se. Two cars left out in the rain will rust at about the same rate; the process of oxidation attacks them equally, turning their iron and steel into ferrous oxide according to one easily explained law of chemistry. The aging process obeys no such simple laws. For some of us, aging is steady, uniform, and slow, like a tortoise crawling toward its destination. For others, aging is like approaching an unseen cliff – there is a long, secure plateau of health, followed by a sharp decline in the last year or two of life. And for still others, most of the body will remain healthy except for a weak link, such as the heart, which fails much faster than do the other organs. You would have to follow a person for most of his adult life before you figured out how he was aging, and by then it would be too late.

The fact that aging is so personal has proved very frustrating for medicine, which finds it extremely difficult to predict and treat many of the major conditions associated with old age. Two young women can ingest the same amount of calcium, display equally healthy hormone levels, and yet one will develop crippling osteoporosis after menopause while the other won't. Twin brothers with identical genes will go through life with remarkably similar medical histories, yet only one will develop Alzheimer's or arthritis or cancer. Two of the most common conditions in old age, rising blood pressure and elevated cholesterol, are just as unpredictable. The aging body refuses to behave according to mechanical laws and rules.

After decades of intense investigation, there is no adequate theory of human aging. Even our attempts to explain how animals age have resulted in more than three hundred separate theories, many of them contradictory. Our notions of aging have been drastically modified over the last two decades. In the early 1970s, doctors began to notice patients in their sixties and seventies whose bodies still functioned with the rigor and health of middle age. These people ate sensibly and looked after their bodies. Most did not smoke, having given up the habit sometime after the Surgeon General's original warnings about lung cancer in the early 1960s. They had never suffered heart attacks. Although they exhibited some of the accepted signs of old age – higher blood pressure and cholesterol, and tendencies to put on body fat, to become farsighted, and to lose the top range of their hearing – there was nothing elderly about these people. The "new old age," as it came to be called, was born.

The "old old age" had been marked by irreversible declines on all fronts – physical, mental, and social. For untold centuries people expected to reach old age – if they reached it at all – feeble, senile, socially useless, sick, and poor. To reinforce this grim expectation there were grim facts: Only one out of ten people lived to the age of 65 before this century.

For centuries in the past, the human body was exposed to the killing influence of a harsh environment: inadequate nutrition, a lifetime spent in physical labor, and uncontrollable epidemics of disease created conditions that accelerated aging. Leaf through the accounts of immigrants passing through Ellis Island at the turn of the century; some of the photographs will horrify you. The faces of 40-year-old women look haggard and drawn, literally as if they were 70 – and an old 70 at that. Adolescent boys look like battered middle-aged men. Under the surgeon's scalpel their hearts, lungs, kidneys, and livers would have looked identical to those of a modern person twice their age. Aging is the body's response to conditions imposed upon it, both inner and outer. The sands of age shift under our feet, adapting to how we live and who we are.

The new old age arrived on the scene after more than half a century of improved living conditions and intensive medical progress. The average American life span of 49 years in 1900 jumped to 75 in 1990. To put this huge increase in perspective, the years of life we have gained in less than a century are equal to the total life span that individuals enjoyed for more than four thousand years; from prehistoric times to the dawn of the Industrial Revolution, the average life span remained below 45. Only 10 percent of the general population used to make it to 65, but today 80 percent of the population lives at least that long.

At any one time, your health is the sum total of all the impulses, positive and negative, emanating from your consciousness. You are what you think. If you are happy, this just means that you have happy thoughts most of the time. If you are depressed, it means that you have sad thoughts most of the time. Into this calculation enter all our other states of mind as well: our daily share of anger, fear, envy, greed, kindness, compassion, benevolence, and love. These are all simply thoughts. When one of them happens to predominate, it leads to a corresponding state of mind and, as we have seen, to a corresponding state of physiology.

In fact, we can restate the evidence for the psychophysiological connection in one sentence: For every state of consciousness, there is a corresponding state of physiology. If you are having hostile thoughts, for example, they will be reflected in your mood, your facial expression, your social behavior, and how you feel physically. You scowl, you are impatient and difficult to deal with, you churn up too much acid in your stomach and a lot of adrenaline in your bloodstream, and consequently you may develop peptic ulcers and hypertension. For an observant person, it is not at all difficult literally to read your thoughts. And the cells of your body are registering them far more accurately.

In most people, the psychophysiological connection operates more or less randomly. Thoughts arise from interactions with the world, these thoughts affect the body for better or worse, and they leave a lingering impression in the form of moods, tendencies toward disease, actual disease symptoms, and the process of wearing out the body over time, which we call aging. Very little of this is under our conscious control. However, it is obvious that some thoughts are under our control, and this simple fact leaves an opening for further growth in the proper direction, toward mastery of the self.

Mastery of the self has classically been called "enlightenment." Enlightenment simply means having control over the psychophysiological connection. The highly evolved mind is not a prey to random influences of ill health; it has mastery over what it thinks. Therefore, what it thinks is happy and healthy. Mastery of this kind is not something peculiar or "not normal." It is simply an extension of the normal ability to control some thoughts. This natural capacity, when given room to expand and evolve, goes in one direction, and that is toward more perfect health and greater happiness. That is what Dr. Salk meant by survival of the wisest.

Because it is in the nature of life to evolve, we do not have to do anything to evolve in the proper direction. Gaining mastery of the self, with all its benefits to health, means little more than stepping out of the way and allowing the infinite intelligence of the mind and body to cooperate more fully. That is what they want to do. When we stop interfering and are wise enough to let the psychophysiological connection work for us instead of against us, our minds rush as quickly as possible towards perfect health.

For more information on prograrms offered by **Deepak Chopra, M.D.,** please contact The Chopra Foundation.

The Chopra Center at La Costa Resort & Spa

2013 Costa Del Mar Road

Carlsbad, CA 92009

For more information or to contact us please email: foundation@chopra.com

234

Mindful Fitness

vs

Fitness Obsession

By Nordine G. Zouareg

Mr. World / Mr. Universe

Mindfulness is being aware of your present moment. You are not judging, reflecting or thinking. You are simply observing the moment in which you find yourself. Moments are like a breath. The next breath replaces each breath. You're there with no other purpose than being awake and aware of that moment. As my yoga master, Yogi Bhajan said: "If you don't go within, you go without!"

Why not practice the same approach to physical fitness? Use each repetition, each set of every exercise to its fullest potential as if it was the last time you were performing the exercise.

If you start by being aware of your breath and connect it to each repetition - breathe in when you come down breathe out when you come up - you know it comes and goes. It is like the end of one wave from among the endless ocean waves. They continue to come and disappear, to be followed by another and another and another. They come. They disappear. They come, they end, and they flow back to be covered by another incoming wave. You can hear the sound. Its rhythm puts the mind and the heart into a trance, and you go far away... but wherever you go, there you are.

My travels through this journey called life have taken me down many paths from which I now share some reflections on the "Holistic approach of fitness." The feeling good, looking good approach, rather than the looking good and then what? This is what I call the "connected" kind of attitude.

We are infatuated with fitness. We pay attention to our waistlines. We get liposuction. We get breast implants. We buy special cosmetic products. We try our best to look and feel our best. We tighten our skin, harden our bodies, increase our cardiovascular endurance and increase our lung capacities. We try to keep ourselves fit. But what about our spiritual fitness? There is no supplement for spirituality. There is no reduced calorie spirituality. There is no "Quick Fix" for seeking the goodness that is within us. The path is taken when you are on it.

My personal experience with the fitness obsession started the minute I lost control of my inner self. I wanted to please the world. I thought people were expecting me to be at a top level all the time, but in reality it was not so. People loved me then like they love now. They don't need to see me in a super shape. I just have to be me, love me and love them. Be in balance - that's all it takes. Love is the door to your spiritual, mental and physical fitness.

In other articles I will tell my many stories and how I went from Rickets to a Mr. Universe lifestyle, and from obsession to the manifestation of my inner-self over my outer self. The Holistic Fitness approach sees you as a gift. This doesn't change, regardless of whether you get outside validation or not. Know and remember that you are God's gift to the world in the form you are. You are an indispensable part of God's plan. If you don't fulfill your role joyously, even if it is unpopular, you will not have done God's work as fully and completely as you could. Assume the possibility that everybody's signed up in advance for the roles they play right now, with the cooperation of everyone being affected by those roles. Self-judgment and guilt will no longer have anyplace to stick. The dance that we do is one that encourages us to remember and directly connect with the source of all life here in this world.

Imagine feeling better than you ever have. Imagine looking better than you ever have.

Imagine the physical vitality spilling over into every aspect of your life. If all of your workouts, diets, and efforts have not gotten you to the fitness level you want to be at, there may be a missing connection. A connection of self, a connection into the spirit.

Nordine has won body building/fitness championships throughout the world by relying on training strategies he developed based on his extensive educational background and his 23 years experience in the fitness field. Nordine went on to claim the titles of Mr. France, Mr. Europe, Mr. International, Mr. World and ultimately Mr. Universe.

Now Nordine is offering his expertise in one of the most prestigious Health Spa Resorts: Miraval, Life in Balance. The "Miraval experience" is a diverse and exhilarating range of activities, pampering guest services, and innovative cuisine along with an internationally recognized spa, allowing one to experience the ultimate in a resort destination. It's a place where one can connect with life, health, meaning and purpose. More than a vacation, it is a place where you can appreciate the moment and bring life into balance. If you would like to work out with Nordine, you can find him at Miraval, Life in Balance Spa and Resort in Tucson, Arizona.

Website: www.miravalresort.com or call 1.800.232.3969.

You can also contact Nordine at www.totalbodywork.com.

Mention this book when making your reservation and you will receive a special rate.

Learn How to Live Longer
By Reducing Stress in Your Life
Promoting Health
in Your Body

By Grace J. Syn, D.C.

Health is

"…a condition of wholeness in which all of the organs are functioning 100% of the time."

~Webster's dictionary

"…. a state of optimal mental, physical and social well-being, not merely the absence of disease and infirmary".

~Dorland's medical dictionary

You have a choice in determining your quality of health

Health is something that most of us are given at birth and that should be maintained throughout our lifetime. Unfortunately, we are never taught what we need for health, or what specifically needs to be maintained.

We are born with a genetic health potential. If we understand what can interfere with that potential, we can avoid such interferences and keep it at the highest level. To understand how to obtain our highest optimum health potential, we first have to know that the essentials to sustain life are: FOOD, WATER, OXYGEN, and NERVE IMPULSE.

FOOD is the fuel and building block for growth and reproduction of all the cells and tissues. It is made up of proteins, fats and carbohydrates. Eating a balance of these three food groups is essential for your optimum health potential. Eating moderate size meals several times (4-6) a day is more beneficial than eating 2-3 bigger size meals a day. You are what you eat! In this day and age of processed foods, be sure to read labels before you ingest. As a general rule to determine the quality of food, if it has a long shelf life, you will not get much nutritional value from it. If you want your body to function like a brand new Ferrari you better fuel it like one. If you want your body to function like a 1976 Yugo, keep on feeding it junk food.

WATER is what makes up 75% of your body. It is used in every body reaction. If you stop fluid intake…you will die. A very common side effect of dehydration is

fatigue. If you find yourself tired and you know you've had sufficient sleep, chances are you haven't had enough hydration for that day. Unhealthy fluids (i.e., soft drinks, caffeine, alcohol, artificial sweeteners and preservatives) can deteriorate or decrease your body's health potential. So how much water should one take? The recommended amount of an ounce of water per pound of body weight should be sufficient.

OXYGEN is also used in every reaction of the body and is transported in our bodies by our lungs and blood (pulmonary and circulatory systems). Interference to these systems could stop oxygenation of our bodies and result in death. Research has shown that oxygen deprivation can cause almost any pathology (diseased cell), from something as common as fatigue to the extreme, such as cancer. Deep breathing regularly, particularly somato-reflex breathing (in through the nose and sinuses, out through the mouth using your diaphragm and abdominal muscles) stimulates your adrenal glands in releasing endorphins (epinephrine and nor-epinephrine, a.k.a. "happy hormones") into your system. Endorphins are also known as "natural pain killers." If you've heard of people being on a "runner's high" after a good cardio session, it's due to the endorphin release. Exercise and deep breathing increases oxygenation to all our cells. If oxygenation is not at its optimum, neither is your health potential.

NERVE IMPULSE is the most commonly overlooked and misunderstood essential for life, health, and well-being. Nerve impulse is an electrochemical charge transmitted by the brain through the nervous system to the body. It is the life force that keeps us alive and "charged." All body function is dependent upon this life force or brain impulse. If the brain stopped generating these electrical impulses, you would die. We are declared legally dead when brain impulses stop.

Your nervous system consists of:
1. *Brain*… the master controller
2. *Spinal Cord*… This is the circuit breaker board of the body; each "wire"(nerve) is surrounded by a moveable "circuit breaker"(24 moveable vertebrae) and sends information to "every room in the house," (every cell in the body).
3. *Nerves*… There are billions of nerves in the body. They are like the millions of telephone wires going to all the homes in a city. Every nerve has a body cell to which it sends communication from the brain.

Where exactly does the brain get its power?
• 90 % of the stimulation and nutrition to the brain is generated by movement of the spine.
• This would be analogous to a windmill generating electricity.

Source: Dr. Roger Sperry, Nobel Prize recipient for brain research.

What happens if there is interference to normal nerve transmission? Would the function of the organ or respective tissue be at its optimum potential?

One of the major causes for such nerve interference is misalignment of the spine, commonly termed by chiropractors as a *subluxation* (sub-luk-sation). Subluxations can interfere with the nerve, the spinal cord and reflex nerve pathways, resulting in abnormal function and lowered health potential. **If your spine is subluxated, you cannot be at your optimum health potential regardless of how good your food, water and oxygen is** because you are still having interference with one of the essentials of life and health…your nervous system.

"Every function of the human body is under control of the nervous system. Its function is to coordinate all the other organs and structures to relate the individual to his environment."   ~ Gray's Anatomy, 29th edition, p.4.

So what causes subluxations?

- Birth process
- Poor nutrition (legal and illegal drugs, poor diet, smoking, and alcohol)
- Trauma (physical stress from falls, accident, and not enough rest)
- Poor posture (sitting, standing, sleeping, and driving)
- Stress (emotional, chemical, physical) beyond what your body can adapt to

Q: Why is it so important to maintain your spine in good condition?

A: It surrounds and protects your nervous system. Subluxations are misalignment of the vertebrae, causing nerve interference. If left uncorrected, they eventually will lead to degenerative joint disease of the spine. This degenerative joint disease is also known as Osteoarthritis. The end stage of osteoarthritis is immobilization, joint fusion, and nerve atrophy.

When the spine is in healthy alignment, then there is no stress on the vertebrae. When there is no stress on the vertebrae there is no interference to the nervous system.

"Posture affects and moderates every physiological function from breathing to hormonal production."
~C. Norman Shealy, MD, Roger K. Dacy, MD, et al; APJM, 1994, vol.4p.36

When it comes to your health, the question to be asked is do you want to be proactive or reactive? Would you rather develop your health, or wait until you get sick and then do something? Do you want to find the cause of your health problem and correct it or just block the symptoms and allow the cause to persist? Ultimately whatever choice we make will produce a certain outcome.

www.mentorsmagazine.com

Drugs and Side Effects

Pharmaceutical drugs are a $49 billion a year business with over 2 billion prescriptions written per year. Each year, 119,000 deaths and 8.8 million hospitalizations are connected to prescription drugs, not to mention the 28% of hospitalizations for the medical treatment of side effects from these drugs. The death ratio of auto accidents is 75% less than that of prescription drug deaths.

~USA Today, 4/1/97. The Journal of American Medical Association 7/5/95

> *"I came to see Dr. Grace 14 months after having a heart attack at the age of 34. I was anxiety ridden, depressed, angry, and had daily headaches. I was prescribed acetaminophen with hydrocodone for my headaches and three different antidepressants to handle my anxiety. I was then diagnosed with high blood pressure and was prescribed three more medications to make a total of 10 pills a day. All the while I was regularly admitted at least twice a month to bring down my blood pressure and then found out that my blood pressure was staying elevated due to the side effects of all the medications I was on. Since I started chiropractic care with Dr. Grace, I have been getting the subluxations in my spine adjusted regularly. My body functions have become totally normal again and have had no need for the medications. Life seems a whole lot easier to live."*   *~Melissa C., happy patient*

The chiropractor's primary role is to locate and correct subluxations, thus removing nerve interference and allowing the body to restore its normal function. It is not a treatment for symptoms or a cure for disease, but merely a way of improving the body's optimum health potential, through proper nerve integrity. This is why everyone should see a chiropractor from the time they are born, and regularly throughout their lifetime. Maintenance of a healthy spine means optimum health potential.

Discover Chiropractic...

"The doctor of the future will give no medicine, but will interest his patients in the care of the Human Frame, in diet and in the cause and prevention of disease. *~ Thomas Edison*

Dr. Grace Syn is a speaker, progressive health coach, and author of the upcoming book *You've Got Some Nerve! – The Wellness Solution to an Overmedicated America*

For over a decade Dr. Grace has helped thousands of people achieve optimum health.

Visit **www.DrGrace.net.**
P.O. Box 7000-817, Redondo Beach, CA 90277

Thoughts:
A Fountain of Health & Well Being
By Alejandra Armas

Good health is not only the lack of disease and pain, but a complete state of physical, emotional, mental and spiritual wellbeing. Living in a world as fast, busy, polluted and stress-filled as ours, it may seem difficult to achieve and maintain health and inner peace. However, it is indeed possible!

Let's start with our thoughts. Everything that humankind has achieved was first a thought in someone's mind. Our thoughts and emotions shape all areas of our lives, mainly our health and wellbeing. We are repeatedly using our thoughts unfavorably, compromising our health as a result of it.

Creation is a process that starts in the mind, and health is definitely something great for us to create. YOU CAN – and YOU SHOULD – use the power of your thoughts to improve your life. In order to do it, you should be aware of the following Universal Laws & Principles:

Principle of self-recovery

The body has an innate ability to heal itself at a certain rate. Medicines, doctors, therapists and practitioners of the healing arts just assist in this process by accelerating this innate ability.

Principle of energy force

For life to exist, the body must have energy. Energy can be used in order to accelerate the healing process.
- Everything that exists is an energy
- Energy follows thoughts
- You become what you think of
- You magnify that which you think

Principle of thought forms

Thoughts exist as an energy
- Words are spoken thoughts, thoughts in action

Principle of cause and effect:

- Everything you do will come back to you magnified many times. You are responsible for what you create and thoughts are creations. Like attracts like. Negative thoughts, words and actions will attract negative outcomes and situations. Wholesome thoughts, words and actions will attract positive outcomes.

To take part in the creative process of our lives, we must become aware of our words and thought patterns. Based on the Universal Laws and Principles stated above, we should take responsibility and action in creating our own lives. This does not mean that we dishonor the inner development of events, or that we can get away with our past improper actions that may have produced illness or discomfort; neither does it mean that we dishonor a Divine Higher Power – for those of us who believe. It just means that we can participate in the process of creation, soften the penance and create new, positive karma which will help us in days to come. It means that we choose not to continue creating negativities, and we agree not to be part of that which is not wholesome!

Using constructive affirmations is a very powerful tool that will help us in shaping our health. Continuous positive thoughts become new "programs," which will create positive outcomes, becoming a fountain of well being.

As opposed to thinking "**I AM SICK,**" it is better to say the same in a more constructive way: "I am in the process of getting better." Not a lie, but a powerful creative, proactive affirmation! Think and affirm "I AM HEALTHY!" Why? Because by doing so you are actually identifying with the real YOU. Since you are not only your body, emotions or thoughts and, since you are a powerful being using these as vehicles, by saying "I AM HEALTHY" you are indeed identifying with that powerful being - with the soul, with the universe. By saying "I AM SICK" you are identifying instead with that which is not true – for the soul is never sick.

By saying "I HAVE A TERRIBLE HEADACHE," you are affirming that you, the one that controls and moves the head, has a headache! In reality, it is not you with a headache, it is indeed the body! Your body! Not YOU. You, the soul, do not have a headache. The soul can't have a headache! By saying "I AM SAD" you are actually declaring that you yourself are sadness, instead of your emotions experiencing sadness. You, the soul, are not sad, or sick, unlucky or terrible! By affirming what is not true your energy will decrease, compromising your body's ability to fight sickness or disease.

Think about how many times in one day you say things like "I can't do it," "I won't get better," "I feel terrible," or "I won't make it." You are giving your power away! You are actually helping the process of getting sicker and feeling worse! If you don't believe it, ponder on this :are you feeling any better? No? Then change the

content of the technique you are using! Because as a matter of fact, you are already using a powerful technique: affirmations! Same technique, same power, just different content. Give it a try - IT WILL WORK!!!

It doesn't matter whether you believe it or not! JUST REPEAT IT! Even if mechanical, you are creating an energy. The more you say it, the more effective it'll be, and by the law of cause and effect, the more you'll attract it, therefore, the more you'll start believing it! Regardless of our inability to see the air, it is there! Whether you believe it or not, the law of gravity exists... if you throw something, by the law of gravity, it will fall. Period. In the same way, you don't have to believe this: just try it. "You become what you think." It is a law!

Energy is like muscles. It has to be built. You must persevere and persist with your affirmations. Yet don't become fanatical. Keep living a normal life. No need to write down each affirmation 2000 times. No need to surround yourself with so many post-it notes. Just keep a simple yet consistent pace.

The power of YES

"Yes!" is much more than a powerful affirmation; it is a state of being. It means we are open and receptive to the blessings of life. Say YES to health, Yes to inner peace, Yes to love and Yes to all great things and all great people in life. Most of the time we are not receptive to what we most need or want, and we repeatedly say NO. An example is when someone offers help and the other answers, "No, it's OK, I'll deal with it," instead of saying "Yes, thank you, I appreciate it."

Also, get rid of all the "but's" and "what if's" that often come after a "YES," and just plainly say YES.

Repeatedly use this affirmation:

"I AM COMPLETELY OPEN AND RECEPTIVE TO HEALTH,
I WELCOME HEALTH AND INNER PEACE IN MY LIFE."

Imagine yourself healthy and repeatedly say YES to this vision.

Dealing with negative thoughts

At the beginning it may be difficult, for you have to fight the tremendous amount of negative thoughts coming from you and others. This is normal. As much as you create positive thoughts, you must also start clearing the way by getting rid of negative thought patterns coming from you or from others. By doing so, your negative thoughts and words will become less frequent and your mental and creative process will become clearer and sharper, which will result in a faster manifestation of your thoughts and words.

Every time you realize that you've said or thought something negative about your health and well being, you should stop and erase this form of energy. I'm sure you've heard people saying "cancel" or "erase" just right after they've said something negative. This is a good step towards dealing with our negative thoughts and words, but it is not enough. Canceling in this way does not deal with the energy created. Use your own energy and creative visualizations to disintegrate the thought-form created and then substitute with a positive thought. This works for all negative patterns of thoughts like fear, jealously, sadness, anger, even stress. For example, to clean fear, substitute with faith and trust.

Creative Visualizations are a very developed way of affirmation that, when properly done, involve energy. The following are a group of powerful visualizations for you to use when negative thoughts come your way. Do them as soon as you have the negative thought. The sooner you do it, the more effective it will be.

1. Be aware of your breathing. This will promote stillness and increase you energy level.

2. Do deep slow abdominal breathing and hold your breath before and after inhalation. Do this for several breathing cycles.

3. Remember you are not your body, emotions or thoughts. You are a being of light, love and power. You are the soul. Mentally affirm this.

4. While continuing to be aware of your breathing, imagine, visualize or have the intention of one of the following:

   a. White Board: Imagine the negative thought, fear or pattern on a white board. Then imagine and have the intention that you have an eraser made of light in your hands. Erase. Then imagine on the same whiteboard the contrary or positive thought. i.e., if you are stressed, see yourself stressed on the white board, with as much detail as possible. Erase it, then see yourself enjoying life, happy and relaxed.

   b. Ocean of Light: Imagine that you are swimming within an ocean of light, and the waves of light wash the fears, negative thoughts of patterns from you. You can also imagine the negative thoughts in the sand. As the waves come, these thoughts are washed away, leaving behind the positive ones.

   c. Waterfall of Light: Imagine you are under a waterfall of white light. Have the intention that all fear, negative thoughts or patterns are flushed away by it.

   d. Small Fire: Imagine there is a small fire in front of you; use your breathing to exhale the negative thoughts to the flames. While you inhale be aware of the inner stillness and the positive thoughts.

5. Think of the positive outcome you want to achieve. In this case, think of your health and wellbeing. Think of it as if it was an energy, or a scent. Intentionally inhale this healthy energy into your system while mentally or verbally affirming: "I AM HEALTHY, I AM STRONG, I AM HAPPY. I AM FULL OF LOVE AND LIGHT." You may continue letting go of negative thoughts or patterns by exhaling them after each of these inhalations. Always end the exercise by inhaling the positive energy.

6. Give thanks.

Other tools to assist you

Aside from your thoughts, you could also use other tools that are very powerful and of which you can take advantage:

- Practice a form of meditation to achieve inner peace and manage stress.

- Prayer – It has been scientifically proven that those who pray or are prayed for heal faster. Faith plays an important role. It increases the amount of divine energy within and around you, therefore highly accelerating the process of recovering. As you tune in and pray, give thanks for what you want, as if you have it already. Imagine it happening and offer this to The Divine.

- Breathing Exercise. There is a series of breathing exercises that could help you increase your ability to fight sickness. Proper breathing increases your energy level, cleanses and energizes your energy body and boosts your immune system. Start by becoming aware of your breathing. Breathe slowly and deeply. Hold between inhalation and exhalations. For better results, use breathing in combination with creative visualizations.

- Tune in with the pain and ponder the reasons why you could possibly have it and what could you learn from the experience. Once learned, the pain will start dissipating.

- Create positive karma through tithing and service – extreme cases may require extreme measures. When confronted by a major sickness, remember the law: "It is in giving that you receive." Tithe to a good cause and have the intention that it will come back to you in the form of health.

- Create a positive healthy environment, surround yourself with positive, happy and supportive people, and let go of bad habits. Remember, your attitudes shape you.

- Smile... smiling opens up your heart energy center. Your heart energy center controls the thymus gland, which is in charge of the immune system. No wonder happy people tend to be healthy! SMILE!

Finally, let me try to inspire you...

BELIEVE and GO BACK TO LIVING! There are plenty of people that don't believe, plenty of people that don't have faith and have lost hope. We live in such a fast world that we've almost forgotten the basics, the foundations. Don't be part of it. Don't be just one more. BELIEVE! Develop your inner powers and sense of inner peace. Start living again!

SLOW DOWN: How sad we've become as a race, walking almost as machines, doing without stopping, getting stressed out and always on the run. How did we learn this? When did we forget? Are you enjoying the path? No project is truly important if the price to pay is your inner and outer wellbeing. It's too high of a price. Never compromise your inner peace and inner beauty. Never sacrifice your true being. At the end, it is not going to be about how many miles you ran, how many people you defeated, how much you stressed out, or how much money you accumulated. None of that matters. That last moment, when you are just in front of the soul, what will matter is only whether you learned the lessons and enjoyed the ride.

Start now using your powerful affirmations and welcome to a new healthier YOU!

These principles are not intended to replace orthodox medicine, but to complement it.

Alejandra is a Personal Coach, Mentor, and bi-lingual International Speaker and Writer. She is also a Senior Certified Energy Healer and Senior Instructor of Grand Master Choa Kok Sui's teachings – who's principles she uses and personifies. Alejandra is currently based in Los Angeles, CA. For more information please go to www.manifestingsuccess.com or call 310-995-9039.

The Minerals of Your Life

By Ann Louise Gittleman, Ph.D., C.N.S.

Here's the best-kept secret in nutrition: minerals are the spark of life and are even more important than vitamins. You see, plants manufacture vitamins but minerals must be obtained from the soil – and minerals are NOT in the soil anymore. This is why EVERYBODY needs to know about minerals.

The secret – that minerals are more important than vitamins – has been under wraps for nearly 65 years. According to an overlooked document issued by the U.S. Senate in 1936, "Our physical well being is more directly dependent upon minerals we take into our systems than upon calories or vitamins, or upon the precise proportion of starch, protein or carbohydrate we consume." U.S. Senate, Document No. 264, published, 1936.

Many of us are aware we can live for a prolonged period without food – but NOT without water. This is because water provides us with the minerals of life. Let me take you on an abbreviated Magical Mystery Tour of what minerals can do for you.

Besides their role in promoting blood formation, fluid regulation, protein metabolism and energy production, minerals are also co-factors for enzyme catalysts for every biochemical response in the body. Can you guess which mineral is involved in over 350 biochemical processes like muscle contraction, nerve conduction, and the prevention of anxiety, irritability, asthma and panic attacks? It's widely considered the most important mineral in the body. All of the other major minerals (like calcium, potassium and sodium) are dependent upon its presence in order to function.

It's magnesium

Even sleep can be affected by the lack of magnesium. People who are magnesium deficient tend to fall asleep readily but wake up periodically. They toss and turn and wake up exhausted. I recommend keeping a bottle of magnesium right on your bed stand. Magnesium is designed to support nighttime rest or occasional sleeplessness.

Now try this one: which mineral is involved in over 100 biochemical processes like the stimulation of taste, smell, wound healing, immunity and the maintenance of thick hair (without split ends) and enhancement of healthy blood sugar levels? If you guessed zinc, you're right on.

247

Minerals also maintain strong bones and teeth. But not just with calcium, also with magnesium. In fact, the research of Dr. Mildred Seelig – widely recognized as the most distinguished magnesium expert in the U.S. – suggests that a 1:1 ratio of both calcium and magnesium is essential for bones, teeth and the prevention of hypertension and hardening of the arteries.

Excess calcium – without equal amounts of magnesium – can result in calcified arteries and heart valves, migraines, cataracts, gallstones, kidney stones and irritability. Some researchers even suggest that a 2:1 ratio in favor of magnesium to calcium is even better for overall health, including bone density.

Magnesium gives your bones the flexibility and strength of ivory. Ivory is a combination of 50 percent magnesium and about 50 percent calcium. Chalk, on the other hand, is 100 percent calcium and looks dense on the outside but is very porous and weak and easily breakable.

The moral of the story is calcium should not be taken on its own. If it is, it will pull magnesium out of body parts in order to assimilate it, creating a further magnesium deficiency.

Minerals maintain organ and glandular strength. The liver's key minerals – the body's head honchos for detoxification of all wastes – are potassium and sulfur. The liver contains twice as much potassium as sodium. Sulfur is an important nutrient because it's needed to make glutathione, the liver's most important antioxidant for neutralizing those nasty free radicals associated with every degenerative disease from cancer to heart disease.

The thyroid gland needs both iodine and selenium to make thyroid hormones while the adrenals need zinc for the production of adrenal cortical hormones.

Minerals can support mood and relieve stress and frustration. The copper-zinc ratio is the most important ratio when it comes to behavior. Elevated copper and deficient zinc have been associated with hyperactivity, Attention Deficit Disorder, violence and depression. The Pfeiffer Treatment Center in Naperville, Illinois has found that 80 percent of hyperactive patients and 68 percent of behavior disordered patients have elevated blood copper levels.

Many high copper depressives experience severe post-menopausal syndrome, are intolerant to estrogen and have a family history of post partum depression. This group also has a high incidence of acne, eczema, sensitive skin, sunburn, headaches and white spots on their fingernails. The ideal ratio of zinc to copper in the blood stream is 8:1.

Think zinc!

Minerals are your body's batteries and spark plugs. There are over 70 trillion cells in the body and each is like a biological battery – a mini dynamo that generates life. Minerals are the catalysts to keep the battery going and to hold a charge. Without minerals in the proper ratio, your cellular membranes can't maintain the proper liquid pressure between the inside and outside cell walls. Without this balance, the cells become weak and eventually die. Your immune system depends upon this mineral balancing act right down to the cellular level.

Remember that without the battery and spark plugs, even the most expensive automobile won't run. The minerals of life recharge us on a minute by minute, daily basis empowering every cell, organ and tissue of the body.

So, where did all the minerals go?

We need to get our minerals from the water we drink and the food we eat. The problem is as a result of past and present farming methods, there are virtually NO nutritional minerals in our farm and range soils today. As a result, the crops that are grown are mineral deficient and the animals and people who eat these mineral deficient crops get sick. Many of today's long term degenerative diseases like arthritis, heart disease, hypertension and arteriosclerosis are caused by nutritional deficiencies. Now you can add asthma, irritability and anxiety to the mix.

A fascinating study at the Earth Summit in Rio De Janeiro in June 1992 compared the mineral content of soils today with soils 100 years ago. Researchers found that in African soils there were 74 percent less minerals present in the soil today then there were 100 years ago. Asian soils had 76 percent less, European soils 72 percent less, and South American soils 76 percent less. Soils in the U.S. and Canada contained 85 percent less minerals than they did 100 years ago.

Additional data compiled by Paul Bergner of Boulder, Colorado shows the disappearance of minerals from our soil graphically. Bergner compared data from 1914, 1948 and 1992. Besides soil depletion, minerals get axed due to other factors like stress, drug interactions, coffee, alcohol, sugar, excessive grains and heavy metals. Let's take a look at these:

- Stress – Hans Selye, M.D., a pioneer in stress research found that stress – whether from lack of sleep, injury, pollution, or from stimulants like coffee, sugar and drugs – will cause the body to lose minerals even more than vitamins. The key minerals most affected by stress are magnesium, calcium, zinc, potassium, sodium and copper.

- Drug Interactions – Many drugs can severely restrict the percentage of minerals we get from the foods we eat. In fact, some drugs reduce mineral absorption as much as tenfold. The birth control pill interferes with both zinc and selenium absorption, which can lead to memory loss, muscle weakness and weakened immunity. Hormone replacement therapy, like Premarin, can leave you short of magnesium. No wonder women report side effects like depression and muscle cramps. Antacids that contain aluminum disturb both calcium and magnesium metabolism. Diuretics, as well as antibiotics, are notorious for flushing potassium out of the body, leaving your muscles tight and tense. Cortisone, Tagamet and Zantac impair zinc absorption, making you susceptible to viruses and anxiety. In fact, in many holistic circles, zinc is known as the "good-mood" mineral.

- Coffee, Alcohol, Sugar, Excess Grains – These popular food and beverage robbers are major mineral thieves. Calcium, as well as other important minerals like magnesium, are lost in the urine when you drink coffee and/or alcohol. Caffeine is so diuretic it alone doubles the rate of calcium excretion. A mere three cups of black coffee can result in a 45 mg loss of calcium – and women between the ages of 35 and 50 drink more coffee than any other age group. Sugar robs us more because in the process of being metabolized, refined sugar uses our magnesium, manganese, chromium, zinc and vanadium. Grains contain phytic acid – a phosphorus-like compound that combines with calcium in the intestine and blocks its absorption. Grains can also provide too much insoluble fiber, which binds with and sweeps out minerals like manganese and zinc from the body.

- Heavy Metals – When it comes to heavy metals, minerals can really save the day. Toxic metals – those unbound, electro-magnetically active ions – are everywhere. Space does not permit to discuss all the heavy metals, but here are two of the most insidious and ubiquitous – mercury and aluminum – which researchers have suggested are at the root of a myriad of disorders.

- Mercury – Found in large fish like tuna and swordfish, silver amalgam fillings, water supplies, seeds treated with mercurial fungicides, vaccines including both infant and adult vaccines, eyedrops and contact lense solutions (thimerosal), nasal sprays, eardrops and hemorrhoid creams. Classified as a poison because it is a neurotoxin and irreversibly blocks protein synthesis. The main target organs and glands for mercury are the kidneys, thyroid and pituitary. The most threatening mercury compound organic methylmercury. The minerals selenium and zinc are both antagonists to mercury toxicity. Metabolic dysfunctions associated with mercury toxicity include:

    1. Alopecia (hair loss) – causes impairment of copper Metabolism
    2. Excessive salivation
    3. Vision loss
    4. Ataxia – failure of muscular coordination, muscle weakness, numbness and tingling, tremors

5. Birth defects – higher incidence of cerebral palsy, mental retardation and neurological deficits
6. Infertility
7. Hearing Loss – mercury has an affinity for the acoustic nerve
8. Depression – accumulation in the thyroid and pituitary glands causing a slowing of the metabolic rate
9. Memory loss – migraine headaches, mood swings, nervousness
10. Dermatitis – caused by a mercury-induced zinc depletion
11. Blushing – rashes
12. Hyperactivity
13. Immune system dysfunction resulting in multiple sclerosis

- Aluminum – Found in antacids like Maalox, Mylanta and Gelusil, buffered aspirins, aluminum cookware, cans, antiperspirants and deodorants, cosmetics, water supplies, baking powders, salt and various brands of colloidal minerals. Penetrates the blood-brain barrier accumulating in brain cells, impedes the body's utilization of calcium, phosphorus and magnesium, and neutralizes the protein-digesting enzyme pepsin in the stomach. Magnesium and selenium are aluminum's mineral antagonists. Calcium is another healing mineral that counteracts metal toxicity – the mineral antagonist to lead and excess iron. Metabolic dysfunctions potentially associated with aluminum toxicity include:

1. Alzheimer's disease – dementia
2 Kidney and liver dysfunction
3. Neuromuscular disorders – possible link with Parkinson's disease
4. Amyotrophic lateral sclerosis
5. Anemia – due to the interference of aluminum with iron metabolism
6 Colic – affects bowel activity and can cause digestive disturbances
7. Dental carries – impairs bone calcification and competes with natural fluoride
8. Fibromyalgia

New horizons in mineral research – the mind, body, spirit connection

By far, the most exciting research today is being conducted at the Pfeiffer Institute where they are exploring the origins of behavior. Pfeiffer researchers feel that violent behavior may not be just a matter of genes or upbringing, but may be more related to nutritional imbalances.

In a study published in the journal Physiology and Behavior, Dr. William Walsh of the Pfeiffer Institute compared results of blood tests given to 135 assaultive men to those of 18 controls with no history of violence. It turned out the violent young men had lower zinc and higher copper levels than the control group.

The more imbalanced the ratio, the more severe the frequency of aggression. When the young men were given extra zinc in the form of supplementation, their violent episodes substantially declined.

I guess you could say, "A Deficiency Made Me Do It" – and zinc is probably one of the three most deficient minerals in our diet today, a shame because zinc plays a significant role in brain function and well being. It is a mood-supporting nutrient.

The Pfeiffer Institute also made headlines when Dr. Walsh released the results of his heavy metal evaluation of Beethoven's hair. Walsh discovered more than 100 times the amount of lead in the famed composer's locks. The lead toxicity is now believed to be the underlying cause of Beethoven's deafness and irrational behavior. Today we know lead binds to phospholipids of the nervous membrane. Toxic amounts of lead in children have been associated with a reduced IQ, hyperactivity, inability to concentrate and learning difficulties. Other minerals you will be hearing about in the years ahead include:

- Sulfur for pain management, and as an anti-arthritic agent

- Vanadium, chromium and zinc as insulin – co-factors and potent nutritional therapy for diabetes, low blood sugar and Syndrome X. The mysterious sounding Syndrome X, a term coined by Stanford University's Dr. Gerald Reaven, refers to a group of health problems including insulin resistance (the inability to properly metabolize sugars), elevated cholesterol and triglycerides, weight problems and high blood pressure.

Tomorrow's health today

The right mineral balance will provide you with tomorrow's health remedies today! One of the very best, non-invasive ways to assess your personal mineral needs is through mineral tissue analysis via a tablespoon or two of your hair. Uni Key, the official distributor of all of my products, books and services, offers hair analysis through an FDA approved and regulated laboratory (800-888-4353 OR www.unikeyhealth.com). In closing, I believe that health is God's greatest gift to us. Health is that which we use up for the first 60 years of life in order to obtain wealth, after which we use up our wealth to try and recapture our lost health! Minerals can lead the way.

Ann Louise Gittleman, Ph.D., C.N.S., is continually breaking new ground in health and healing – from natural hormone replacement to effective, safe and cleansing weight loss. An award-winning author of 20 books with over 3.5 million copies in print, her latest New York Times bestsellers are *Before the Change* and *The Fat Flush Plan.* For more, visit www.fatflush.com.

Being Your Best
at Any Age

By *Dr. Marcus Laux*

Having the best of health can be achieved, but it is not a given. I believe that for most of us, good health before the age of 35 is what we inherited through our genes while our health thereafter comes more from how we choose to live. Yet, with all of today's complexities, demanding schedules, fake fast foods and technological trappings, it is challenging to make the time for our first priority, our greatest of wealths – our health.

All aspects considered, your strongest health insurance comes from pulling the plug on stress, eating less and moving more. The healthiest people in the world all have this in common: they lead more simple lives. Regardless of personal income and social status, they've made a choice to live a life that is arguably more deeply rewarding and personally satisfying. A life filled with realizing hopes and dreams, as opposed to a life chasing questionable ones. A quality of life and health earned each day, not borrowed heavily against for a promised payoff some day to come.

Strong genes help less than we thought

Genes factor into our health equation far less than was previously thought. While great genes are a plus, it is our internal environment that dictates how and what gets produced from our genes. They can be turned on and off by our diet and lifestyle. Genes have the ability – in fact, a DNA mandate – to make a variety of proteins, depending on the signals and environment they are immersed in. It is our day-to-day living that mostly determines this, and it's our habits and practices, far more than any other factors, that create our health, our predisposition to disease or ageless longevity. There is no magic potion or new product that will ever replace the power of your daily decisions, actions and habits to engender health. You alone have the awesome power to change your health experience in the world.

Mind and body are equally important

The mind and body are inextricably linked – it is impossible and indeed futile to determine where the one ends and the other begins. They are both irreplaceable parts of a larger whole. We are simultaneously both a body of energy, with thousands of electrical firings per second in the neurons of our brains and spinal cord, and a sophisticated, adaptive, biological organism pre-programmed to survive. We are a

253

spectacular blend of electrical, magnetic and biochemical biology that interplays, interacts and self-adjusts, if given the opportunity. All healing modalities, from meditation to surgery, strive to create the right environment, the right opportunity, for us to self-adjust to a higher vibration of health.

Just as our external environment affects our health – our thoughts and feelings – conscious and unconscious, play significant roles in our unfolding health every moment. They impact us as powerfully as our physical and environmental encounters do.

You can change your mind anytime

Our needs and desires, our emotions and thoughts, equally influence our health. Our relationship with ourselves is delicate and needs nourishing and balance, so critical in a speeding world much out of balance. Slow down, unplug the noise and get in touch with what you know you want and need to do for you. We all know what we need to do, but we have excuses, reasons, expectations or blind spots.

So, when is it time for you to declare your needs? I say now. You decide, but don't wait too long. Being selfish can be a very good thing. Saying 'no' can be the best response given when it respects you. Taking a second, a day, a week off, to get back on track can rekindle your spirit.

It's never too late to change

Good intentions followed by changes are paramount to ensuring health. It is the commitment to your plans, your beliefs and consistent action to that end that delivers your desires, and promotes and protects your health at every age. It is never too late to start right now, right where you are, to create the health you want. We are all programmed to respond and adapt. The notion of old age meaning advanced decrepitude is outdated, based on lack of knowledge. Aches and pains and loss of function are not inevitable – in fact, they are flat-out avoidable. I've worked with a man who at 55 years old had diabetes, heart disease, hypertension, arthritis and obesity. He drank, smoked, worked a high stress job and ate poorly. He needed to take charge of his health, or he was going to die sooner rather than later. He did take charge, and last I knew, at 68 years of age he was cycling across America, and was off all medication. He created a new vision, set new goals and, with God's grace, made himself into a completely renewed person. What's your vision?

Eat real food

What you eat, and how much, is the foundation to bulletproof health. From studying healthy long-lived peoples around the globe, as well as from animal studies on longevity, it is clear that eating high quality foods, rich in nutrients, yet lower in calories, creates the optimal setting for achieving lasting health, greater life spans and less disease. And it is possible to be fully functional, intact and sharp-witted with keen eyesight for your entire life-trip. Recent evidence now puts our potential life-span at around 150 years old. Some animals may live to be 1,000 years old. Better genes, maybe, but superb food, no junk, regular movement and lower stress – you bet.

Yes, you are what you eat

You are what you are from the food that is consumed. Life feeds life. There is no way around this simple, yet profound, fact. Eat bad fats, and every cell is set up to falter. Eat sugar, and you imbalance your hormones and dull your immunity. Eat junk, and you create a paler, weaker version of what you are meant to be.

Eat organic fresh foods, some cooked, some raw, seasonally and locally when possible, and watch yourself rejuvenate, replenish and renew. The killer diseases of today are chronic and degenerative. 'Chronic' simply means that it is ongoing, in large part due to our everyday diets and environmental exposure. 'Degenerative' means we are slowly falling apart because we are not maintaining, replenishing and renewing by providing what our bodies need to thrive. The missing ingredients are from the farm, not the pharmacy.

Take time to smell the roses

Stress is a fact of life. Let it be a friend in your health, and not a factor in your disease. Stress can motivate your behavior, and even improve your performance. Choose your stresses, and deal with them as tasks to be handled and accounts to be settled. You control stress by using it as an opportunity, a challenge and a priority. We all must learn what we have control over and what we don't. Stress has no control over us, unless we so empower it. This also means you can neuter it. Stress is not your boss, but a masquerading wannabe. Choose instead to make it an ally.

Accept limitations

You can only do so much in a day. Let the rest go. Work smarter, work better and then stop. Make technology work for you. Use your phones, pagers and computers to free your time for living. They can be a leash of limitations or a new lease on freedom.

Go spend time with your friends, family and yourself. Play fun and fully. Rest well and deeply. Leave the stress behind – don't carry it from one to the other. Just put it on your list at work, and when ready, take it up and make your best efforts. At the end of your day, leave it on your desk. Do what you can, and leave the rest. Really – release it for now. It will improve your mind, metabolism and your fun factor. When you are living in the moment now, worry has no home.

Check in on yourself

It is not only what you eat that counts, but what is eating you that takes a bite out of your health, mood and energy. How do you know what's in the back of your mind? Here are a few clues. What do you think about when driving? What pops into your

255

head as you are falling asleep, or as you wake? What's on your mind when you are taking a shower? Or looking in the mirror? Anything less than love, respect and acceptance of yourself is a red flag. It is so interesting that we can see every part of our body, except our face, the part to which we all attach our identity, and often so much more. We need something that is not us, to tell us about the 'face' we put out to the world – a mirror, a friend, a parent, a teacher, coach, a passer-by. Examining yourself by yourself can reveal many places to start to grow healthier than ever before. Get to know yourself.

Find what moves you and do it

Just look at your body. A most obvious fact is, pound for pound, we are mostly muscle and bone. We were given amazing joints, ligaments, tendons and a spine for one thing – to move. We are designed to move, walk, run, jump, dance, swim and stretch. This action is mandatory for our best of health. Moving our bodies does everything good for recovering balance and mood, building all levels of mental and physical health and helping remove the wastes while managing our metabolism. Everything good, nothing bad.

Exercise should not be torture, but movement enjoyed, at your pace and pleasure. It is not about no pain, no gain. Our bodies really appreciate regularity of all kinds, exercise included. Exercise is the celebration of life itself. 'Use it' or 'lose it' should ring a bell here for you. The journey of good health starts with the first step. Exercise can be anything. Discover, uncover or recover exercise that you enjoy, and do it! Stay with it and health will follow as day follows night. Results are measured by the month, not by the numbers on your scale.

Everyday things matter

Change your mind about your mind. All lasting improvement and health starts here. Change your mind about disease, as it is really dis-ease. Put your body at ease, on the regenerative road to health, and naturally experience one of life's greatest gifts and miracles – healing. In the end, all healing is self-healing. The doctor stitches, the physician prescribes, the bandages protect, but you, the person, heal. The power of your life force, the energy that flows through you like breath through a flute, is strengthened, purified and powered by the vital messages from nature (the nutrients from our diet and clean air) and by your actions (the result of fully vested thoughts and beliefs).

The combination of eating real foods, regular physical exercise performed as part of your daily activities, social involvement and cooperation within a network of friends and associates, with a good share of humor, appears to be the tried and true recipe for healthy living. Being truly connected to yourself, family and friends helps insure good health. Life begets life. Life is given through intimate expression, and thrives a lifetime from drinking deeply from the well of personal bonds. Communication expands our heart and soothes our soul. Let it save your life and

others as you flower as a friend. Build bridges, not barriers.

Life is not about being perfect, but it is about being purposeful. Do you have a philosophy, a belief system, a game plan for your daily life? Do your actions reflect your beliefs and help you get what you want? This is your litmus test. Physician, heal thyself.

Know yourself. Know where you want to go. Love yourself. Live by your principles. Act your truth. Realize your dreams. Walk with the wise.

Dr. Marcus Laux is a licensed naturopathic physician with a Doctorate from the National College of Naturopathic Medicine in Portland, Oregon. He is an Affiliate Faculty Member of Bastyr University in Kenmore, Washington and editor of Naturally Well Today, a monthly newsletter. Learn more about Dr. Laux at www.drmarcuslaux.com.

Notes

Remember Your Family and Realize Prosperity!

© 2004 Kim Muslusky

Stupid Breakups

By Dr. Laura Schlessinger

A listener wrote to me about having asked her husband why, after twelve years and two children, he left her for another woman.

"He said he had to think about it. Two days later he called back to tell me his answer. He said, and I quote, 'I always wanted you to go to my mom's house and learn how to make jam, but you never did.' I was dumbfounded. All of this because I never learned how to can fruit? I said to him, 'Oh, okay. . . well, thanks.' I hung up the phone and sat there for a few minutes. Then it hit me. All of this was not because of the me that I was. It was because of the him that he was. It gave me a great tool in getting the closure I needed. There was no abuse in the marriage, no arguments. . . just not enough 'jam.'"

We'll never know if he meant that figuratively or literally; probably a bit 'o both.

Fortunately, I don't get many such calls, e-mails or letters from folks whose reasons for breaking up sound quite that stupid, but I am deeply concerned by the growing number of unnecessary and unwarranted relationship breakups based on "modern" notions of rights and happiness.

About two-thirds of divorces currently are sought by women, and my male callers tell me that their wives left because of "growing apart," "not happy," "feeling underappreciated," "needs not being met," "differences in changing goals or lifestyle," "boredom," and the old favorite, "find myself."

It is important to note that violence, drug and alcohol abuse, neglect and abandonment, and promiscuous infidelity, which used to be the areas of complaint that women had about their husbands, are rarely the motivation for the wife to call it quits. In fact, it is usually the opposite. Some women seem willing to be more patient with these behaviors, than to sustain themselves through the growth and effort needed for the maintenance and nurturance of a marriage when the only issue is moon spots or boredom.

I *dis*-credit feminism for this sad and sorry, embarrassing development in gender relations. Remember Gloria Steinem's proclamation that, "A woman without a man is like a fish without a bicycle?" What the heck was that about? Feminists have emphasized men as the "evil empire," oppressing their women with sex (one other prominent feminist called all sex "rape"), child-bearing and child-rearing (that's being remedied by abortions, day care, and surrogate mothering), and marriage itself (subservient, second-class citizenry). When women become "enlightened," they leave. To what?

One listener, a grandmother and recovered feminist wrote to me:

"Back in the seventies, I read The Feminine Mystique, *about the housewife's 'problem with no name.' I promptly left my husband and all three beautiful daughters and went back to college looking for that elusive 'something' that would make me whole.*

"Raised in the 'Birthplace of Women's Rights,' I quickly became a vocal feminist. It took me years to figure out what a sham the women's rights movement really is. The horrific results are all around us. The goal of feminists was, and is, destruction of the family. To that end, they have been very successful.

"I'm a grandmother now, and I try every day to correct the wrongs I've committed on my children."

Every so often I find myself going on a tear on my radio program about this very issue. I rant about the obvious negative impact on women, not to mention men, children, and society, by the warped notions of what feminists support. How does aborting babies from their bodies for reasons no more important than timing elevate a woman's consciousness? How does shacking-up with some guy(s), becoming sexually intimate in a noncommitted relationship, elevate a woman's spirituality? How does having babies out-of-wedlock, with the concomitant problems with poverty, child care, and isolation elevate a woman's status? Obviously, it doesn't. And, as I've asked time and again on my radio program, "How have you women allowed such a stupid philosophy to destroy your lives, and that of your children and society?"

Another listener wrote in with her complaint about the warnings she got from her liberal, feminist, college friends about what kind of a man she should avoid. She now believes that by listening to that, she jumped right into Stupid Breakups:

"When I was a senior in college I decided to break off my relationship with my boyfriend of two years. He was an intelligent, affectionate, religious man, who had a promising career as an attorney ahead of him and a deep, loving relationship with his parents and five siblings. He expressed to me a desire to marry and assured me that when we had children, I would not have to work and would be able to raise our children at home.

"I was mortified! Appalled! He thinks women should stay home and raise their kids! 'What a jerk!' I explained to my equally liberal, feminist friends. Of course, they agreed. 'What year does he think this is! It's men like that who keep us down!' one friend said.

"Well, I broke it off with him and made a 'better choice,' according to my friend. A twenty-nine-year-old college senior, with a drinking problem, who smoked, covered in shall-we-say body art, and a shaved head. He lived at home and, of course, had no job and no money."

According to her letter, her father went out and bought her my first book, *Ten Stupid Things Women Do to Mess Up Their Lives*, and is happy to report that her eyes are now open, and she is married to a wonderful man (with a job and no body art). One of the main issues of that book was my restating the obvious, which is that women want love, attachment, family, and children. Though choosing to have a major career instead is a reasonable, personal choice for some women, diminishing the value of motherhood and marriage by outright denial and attack or by relegating them to the edge of a woman's more important worker existence is cruel, because it denies the basic psychological and biological truth of women to bond and nurture; and that of men to provide and protect.

Be wary!

Young women, brought up on all this feminist propaganda, are wary about marriage. Young men, brought up on all this feminist propaganda, are wary about women. Try being a young man in college these days, exposed to the feminist dominated reeducation process going on under the guise of neutral academics in courses in psychology, sociology, and even history! I have had innumerable men write to me about their growing fears in being able to find a nice girl who will get married and not soon after walk away with his kids and his home.

Men and women are being programmed to be wary and careful about not getting used. Unfortunately, for too many folks, having to provide for his family, or having to raise children is now being viewed as in that category of "being used."

In addition to the destructiveness of feminism has been the overall shifting of a society from the nobility of obligations and commitments to an emphasis on the rights without a balanced emphasis on "responsibilities." Without a firm sense of responsibility to others and their needs.and rights, we are a group of neurotic ants, each with our own selfish mission – and you can pretty well visualize that state of chaos!

This listener certainly could:

"There was a time I let the word divorce into my vocabulary, and once you say

it, it becomes a part of you and suddenly consumes you. I was very close to divorce, and I was sure I no longer loved my husband. All I could think of was ME, and what I deserved, and everything I gave to him was attached to the condition that I get something in return. I am not sure that is the reason it wasn't returned – no one likes to receive with expectations. Every moment at home, all I did was complain of not having enough. I spent so much time wondering what was in it for me, that I didn't see just how much I already had! Lose yourself in SERVICE, and it is then that you will find yourself."

Bow to the all-important MEEE!

Face it, it's a fact, you cannot have in life, or from another person, all that you imagine you should, could, or would. Real life simply has more texture than that. Additionally, can you really imagine being all of what another person imagines they should, could, or would have? No, of course not. Spending one's time in coveting is to lose the moment of appreciation of what you do have-which generally includes many blessings and advantages. For example, though my husband can't dance to save his life (something I've always loved to do), he would give his life to save mine or our son's. Somehow, I think that's a pretty good trade-off. And, I'll bet, you could look at your relationship in the same way, once you threw away the notion that G-d put you here to gratify every desire or fantasy that plunked into your awareness.

It's that ugly movement toward self-fulfillment, with its protection of the self against the "destructive" needs of another, be it spouse or children, that has caused the largest number of Stupid Breakups.

"I believe in thinking about yourself before others – but only to an extent. If you are in a relationship it is your right to take care of yourself and put yourself before the relationship. . . but not selfishly."

Oh yeah? How do you figure that?

"For example," she continued, *" I am a college student and I will always put my education before my relationship, because it is the education that I will have forever, the guy might not be there forever."*

Now, why might the guy not be there forever? Death in the service of his country? Death by natural causes? Probably not what she is thinking. She's probably thinking about how many of her closest friends and relatives have been in and out, in and out, in and out, of various pseudo-commitments and she is worried.

As another listener wrote:

"I have talked to many of my friends whose parents are divorced. They tell me they feel personally flawed because the legacy of their parents' divorce scars them in

some way that says they are part of a lineage of people who can't follow through, are capable of making huge mistakes, and who walk out when things get tough. They all doubt their ability to spot and maintain love, because they see that their parents thought they were in love, and it didn't 'work out' for them."

Interestingly, this letter was written by a young woman who says that she is part of an unusual and unfortunately small segment of the public in which her parents are still married – yet, by today's reckoning, should have been divorced.

"Did the fighting, yelling, un-child centered living make me a little neurotic and make it hard for me to become a well-adjusted adult? Yes! But one thing I could always hold on to was that my parents never divorced. I had to work through a lot of bad habits and personality flaws, but I never doubted that I would be able to be committed to someone, that I could carry though with a promise, or that I would ever marry until I was completely ready. I know my parents were not in love for most of their married life, and yet they still stayed in it. Did I see my mom as a wimp? No way. She is the strongest person I know, and I admire her greatly. My dad has had my respect from day one."

The argument is often made, in cases like this listener, that all she has learned is how to have a bad relationship. Wrong. She doesn't want the same marriage her parents had in terms of how they behaved toward each other, but she does want the same marriage, in terms of the ultimate commitment they had to family and to vows. Ideally, they would have used their determination to commitment to improve their behavior, or become more compassionate about each other's shortcomings. Though that is not the ultimate point of commitment, it is the ultimate opportunity within commitment.

People need to work harder at marriage

One of the reasons I keep reminding people that "love is not enough" for a quality marriage is that emotions are liable, vulnerable, situational, unpredictable, and without an IQ. Commitment and respect for vows, promises, obligations, and tradition are much more worthy and predictable building blocks for a good relationship. You may get your "jollies" fantasizing about some movie star or neighbor, but nothing fills your heart with deeper affection (and perhaps passion) than watching the tenderness of your spouse with the children, having your spouse be compassionate and non-combative when you're in a mood, or having your spouse be solicitous when you feel (and look) like garbage.

If you really think there is anyone who can sustain a happy, fulfilled state all the time, you're wrong. You're also wrong if you think there is some one person out there with whom you certainly would sustain a perpetual happy, fulfilled state. You're also wrong if you think that the best of relationships don't go through stages, and phases, and problems, some seemingly insurmountable:

"My Stupid Breakup was from my second marriage. I was 'unhappy.' I've been married three times. My Priest finally explained the five Stages of Marriage to me. Stage 1: Falling in love. Stage 2: Discovering the foibles, faults, etc. Stage 3: Deciding what to do about this new knowledge. Stage 4: (If you reach it) Is the hard work involved in getting through the realities of Stage 2. Stage 5: Is the glorious falling in love at a whole new level of intimacy and commitment.

"A light went on! Now I know that when the going got tough, I got going. WOW! What a revelation. The stupid comes in when I consider the harm to my children and the pain I caused my ex-spouse. If we had known that relationships go through these stages, I think we would have been able to work through the problems."

I believe that millions of people would be able to work through their problems if they had that knowledge and support from their families, friends, and society at large. Unfortunately, there have been studies showing that even the so-called Marriage Education courses at high schools and colleges, according to current research, are negative and hostile to the institution. Ironically, those who are married are happier, healthier, and wealthier. Go figure.

In most cases, couples don't try hard enough to stay together. They don't talk about the problems, try to identify the issues, or work them out. And they don't take the time to remember what made them fall in love with each other. One listener added:

"I believe that most divorces are caused by materialism. In a way, our society is becoming corrupted by materialism. There is competition about having the best car, the biggest house, the nicest clothes – but no one seems to care about having the closest family, the most dinners together as a family, and ongoing friendships with family members."

I have written in many of my books, and reminded people on my radio program, that though divorce has been used as the easy way out of the challenges of marriage and family, the three A's – addiction, adultery, and abuse – justify divorce as a valid consideration. Nonetheless, that doesn't mean that there is never a way back from even these travesties and tragedies.

One listener wrote to me of her alcoholism and her loss of faith in marriage, G-d, and herself. She spent a year in AA, with a growing realization that she might lose her daughter.

"I knew that I did not have feelings of love for my husband, so it was a big struggle, and I knew the only way to get the feelings back, was to have faith, pray, go to church, and get help. It was not easy, and there were times where I wanted to give up, because it is very hard living with someone you do not love, but I knew G-d wanted us to make it work. If I could just keep the faith in G-d, I knew he would give

me my feelings back for my husband, and He did, indeed. We now have a five-month-old son, and we are very happy."

She went on to say that she is disgusted with what she put her daughter through and believes that parents should think more about their children than themselves and the world would be a better place. That means making your marriage work – and it does take work!

When there are terrible problems, like the three A's, it becomes a major challenge to consider whether or not to stay. When there is repentance (responsibility taken, true remorse, behaviors to repair and not repeat), there is hope. When there is no repentance, the hope is just postponed disappointment.

One listener wrote that he was still hopeful in spite of his wife's continued shack-up affair and her abandonment of the children, whom he raises alone.

"I think that people give up too easily on marriage when love, understanding, and forgiveness can help your partner remember what it was that caused them to commit to you in the first place. . . .Giving up on a marriage without attempting to prove your love and worth is a stupid reason for a breakup."

I wish him well, although reuniting with a woman who would abandon her children is nothing I can get too excited about.

I'm finding myself

I'm always amused by this expression, "I have to find myself." First, there is the notion of being somewhere other than where you are (some kind of cosmic lost-and-found). Then there is the idea that you can't find yourself under the present circumstances of marriage and children, and finally there is the epiphany that you can't simply find yourself in the bed of someone new.

Truly, you find yourself in your commitments; you find yourself in the eyes of people who depend on you; you find yourself in your noble responses to life's challenges; you find yourself in your actions and decisions; you find yourself right where you are now.

This notion of "finding oneself" is an intellectually dishonest approach to frustration, a pouty reaction to obligations and routine, and a bratty manipulation of another's compassion and understanding.

"I dated a guy for two and a half years in college and found my true love in him. He was and is everything that I could ever want from a man. I knew in my heart that he would be a decent husband and father. A few weeks after I returned from a study-abroad trip through our school, I called off the relationship, because I felt I needed

to find myself as an individual. That was the worst decision of my life. I will forever regret that breakup," writes a listener.

Why does finding oneself as an individual seem to imply that you must unload significant people from your life like your spouse, boy/girl friend, and/or parents? The answer is that the most immature part of yourself has reverted back to infanthood – wanting to be the center of the universe without obligations: You get to have, you don't have to give.

With that attitude, you will either end up alone, or with superficial escapades, and regrets for a Stupid Breakup.

Don't lie to yourself or anyone else. When you feel like it's time to get going, stay put and face whatever it is that worries or frightens you.

Welcome to fantasy land

What must you be thinking when you put a fantasy aside your reality and believe that the fantasy will have more depth, longevity, satisfaction, respect, promise, and meaning? The answer is that you don't think – you just imagine.

One of the newest and most destructive forces on marriage today is the Internet. Cyber-affairs are costing too many children and innocent spouses the warmth and comfort of an intact home. Both men and women are carrying on in chat-rooms and develop "feelings" sufficient to propel them out of their homes and families to be with someone they "know will be everything that's missing in their lives." Everything, of course, other than a brain!

"My wife and I have been married for twenty-seven years. I thought we had a good relationship. We have had our problems, but we always seemed to work them out. To make a long story short, I bought my wife a computer two years ago, and it seemed to make her happy, because she always said she was bored. She had fun in the chat-rooms, flirting and having a good time. I thought it was harmless. But, as time went on she spent more and more time on the computer. Well, seven months ago I found out that she is in love with a man that lives eleven hours away from her, whom she's never met. She lies in her bed and cries for him. She still talks to him every day and tells him she really loves him and is going to marry him.

"I love this lady with all my heart. I really don't know what to do. I know in my heart she still loves him – she tells him all the things she once told me."

I mean, really, how insensitive and cruel can one be to someone she once thought she couldn't live without? And why is anyone bored? The answer is, only because he or she is boring. Bored people rarely think of anything or anyone besides themselves and being entertained, thrilled, titillated, excited, distracted, or being the center of attention.

When people call and tell me that they're bored in their lives, or bored in their marriage, I jump on them to admit that they don't do anything to add to the well-being of themselves or their family – they just want to feel a certain feeling and, in that laziness, think that there is just some other guy or gal who'll just make it happen. Good luck.

The grass is greener

"I left my husband of five years for a much younger man, hoping that the spice would reenter my life. WRONG!!! I thought I could find happiness in someone else. WRONG!!! I left my husband and hurt my three children very badly. Nine months later I realized that a lot of things were wrong. . . but with ME. I had just turned thirty, went back to work full-time, exhausted from the kids, and wanted out, yet realizing that what I was feeling was totally normal, and by leaving my husband the stress was still there because it was me!!!

"I strongly urge people to get help for themselves first and take some accountability for their actions and stay AWAY from temptation because now I realize I may have lost the best husband and father in the world all because of my self-centeredness."

This listener hit the main point of my argument, which is that when you imagine improving your life by simple demolition is to miss the truth. The truth is that you are largely the architect of the quality of your life. Therefore, begin first with renovation – of yourself, your attitudes, your reactions, your expectations, and your actions. Only then can you hope to have any credibility or power in your determination to make improvements in your relationship, marriage, and family.

Another important issue brought up by this listener is the idea of avoiding temptation. Unfortunately, between the Internet and the workplace, a lot of temptation presents itself.

"I thought I had to go to work to get a life and get away from the kids. The money was nice, but it only caused me to feel I didn't need my husband anymore. I divorced my husband."

Well, nothing but bad things followed. At work she got lots of attention from men, and liked it. As she started to become more aware, she began to appreciate that her husband was faithful and considerate. She ended up marrying some guy who molested two of her three children. After two decades of therapy for her children and herself, she reports that they are doing better. Based on her experiences she had this closing message:

"Stay home with your kids. It keeps away so many problems. So much temptation. Stay married because, believe me, no matter how nice a guy he is or how

much he loves your kids, it is never the same as their real dad."

The temptation issue is one that is too often, and inappropriately, scoffed at. It is not fashionable to say that people should not be alone with members of the opposite sex. It is not fashionable to say that married folks should not carry on solo "friendships" with members of the opposite sex. It is not popular to suggest that people avoid even the appearance of wrongdoing so as not to cause pain to their spouse. Yet, sensitivity to these behaviors strongly adds to the value of your relationship and your partner. All actions taken to preserve and protect your commitment – do just that!

There shalt be no gods before me say, Mommy and Daddy

"We were married for eleven years with three small children. Our marriage was wrought with in-law problems from the beginning. We both saw how his mother despised me from the onset of our engagement. We loved each other deeply, and thought that our love would conquer all of life's adversities. My husband saw what was ongoing (insults, snubs, slams) yet was torn over his loyalties. . . his wife, should he defend her? . . . or his family, should he support them?"

I am flabbergasted by how many people are absolutely tyrannized by a clearly disturbed parent – to the extent that they will jeopardize, disrupt, or abandon their healthy, happy relationships. When they call me, they ask if they can dishonor their parents by not listening to their choice in a spouse, reprimand a destructive parent, or disconnect with a parent who is blatantly attempting to destroy their marriage. There are parents who are so insecure, mentally ill, or downright evil, that they will even sink to undermining their children's lives to feel alive, in control, powerful, and important.

Sometimes these parents will operate indirectly: offering money with conditions, pleading desperation (illness or upset) for visits and support, virtually turning their adult, married children into their own parents, or by being punitive when their child even plants the lawn with grass that isn't the parent's preference.

I've heard it all. Recently, a male caller told me that his mother-in-law-to-be offered to give his fiancee a quarter of a million dollars if she would make him sign a prenup specifying that his name would be on nothing (like their own home). I told him not to sign and not to comment to his girlfriend about the money and to wait to see if she takes the money. I told him that if she took the money, she was not a candidate for marriage because he'd be marrying her mother. Several days later, he called back. She had, on her own, decided not to take her mother's money. Wonderful. Because if she had broken up with him because she catered to her mother's neurotic need to control and her hatred of men, that would have been a Stupid Breakup.

Since young people today seem to be more geared to "have it" than to "earn it," they find themselves obligated to their parents in the most unhealthy ways. If they live in their parents' homes, or on parental property, or in a house paid for by their parents, or live on income supplied by their parents, they seem to revert to their child-parent behaviors as though they had to be careful not to lose an allowance this week.

As I tell folks, "If you can't afford the wedding, and your own place to live, or the clothes on your back – you're not ready to get married. If you can't afford the car you'd like to have, or the neighborhood you'd like to live in, or the toys and jewelry you fantasize about, earn them. If you stay attached to your parents in an infantile manner, it will probably destroy your adult relationship."

Unresolved personal psychological and emotional issues...

- *"I came from a broken home, my mom married a man who beat and molested me, and the only consistent support I got was from this guy who was very nice. I suggested that we see other people because I was bored and confused. I know I let a good man go and broke a heart that didn't deserve it just for novelty and insecurity."*

- *"My self-esteem used to be so low, that when I would be in a great relationship, and the guy started to really care, I would do anything to make things bad so that he would break up with me."*

- *"I broke up with her that night for no better reason than for not wanting her to ever break up with me. The saddest part was that she had no intention of doing that. I had dated a [girlfriend of mine] who cheated on me, and it broke my heart really bad since she was my first love. I guess I just didn't want to get dumped again, so I took the initiative and broke it off first. To this day I miss that girl. I guess you could say that in not wanting to be hurt by her, I hurt myself."*

- *"I grew up in a very dysfunctional home where my father molested me in front of my entire family, so I did not know what true love was – that is, until Ronnie and I came together. I was able to be myself and still have his love. When we became engaged my parents sat me down at the kitchen table and told me that Ronnie was controlling and brainwashing me. They told me that my mom was so upset about our relationship that it would make her lose the baby she was carrying, and if she did, it would be my fault. So, I broke off a relationship with a man whom I was crazy about and was perfect for me. My parents abused my trust in them, so they could keep me in the house to care for their kids. It was stupid to ignore my own instincts. I take responsibility for my actions by continuing to attend therapy. But, there will always be that part of me asking how I could be so stupid."*

These are a few of the thousands of letters, faxes, and emails I've gotten from

folks suffering from real and serious problems, stemming anywhere from simple immaturity, to painful reactions to the abuse and insanity of their original homes, to mental illness. When I talk to some of these folks on the air I remind them that everybody is capable of loving, and worthy of being loved. How we all differ is in our ability to come out of ourselves to sacrifice for another, and our willingness to become vulnerable and open to somebody else.

Those qualities are sometimes not easy to come by, and for some people, quite damaged and frightened by their upbringing, it becomes a serious challenge. This is the area of searching for oneself that does have merit: *becoming* the kind of human being who can be of open heart with wisdom, not cynicism. For those of you for whom this is a challenge, promiscuity, substance abuse, and workaholism are not the solutions. Soul-searching, therapy, spiritual development, and risking are the solutions.

All these considerations are why I beg clergy to refuse to marry people who are unwilling to undergo at least six months of premarital counseling. This is the most wonderful opportunity for you to do something scary (face truths about yourself) and wonderful (become a more loving, open person).

Consider yourself an artist. As talented and creative as you are, without good tools, your best work will never be expressed. As a human being in a loving relationship, wishing to create a happy home, you are your tools; therefore, you are your own limitations. Please put aside your ego and face-saving notions to get the kind of education or therapeutic assistance you need to become the best tool you can be.

Stupid Breakups are caused by your not wanting to see the worst in yourself – and if you choose to stay blind, you will never have the love you want:

"One mistake was never taking responsibility for my own shortcomings. When I got in trouble I always expected someone to bail me out – including God. And most of the time that is what happened. I was a dreamer who never had the intestinal fortitude to stick it out until my dreams came true.

"I married two times, and did the same stupid things again, and then something happened. I was flying mining equipment into old Mexico and crashed a plane into a mountain. It should have killed me, but by the grace of God, it didn't. Two days later, I was sitting by myself on the side of the mountain, my life devastated, and said to myself that I know someone else who can do a better job with my life than I have. I had no idea why I was saying that or to whom I was talking, but I strangely felt that 2000 lbs. was lifted from my shoulders and peace and joy came upon me and everything was okay, even though I had gone broke in business, lost my second marriage, and just crashed a plane.

"With a relationship with God, and the teachings of the Bible, I got married for

271

the third time. This marriage will work because I finally realized that love is a decision, not a feeling (commitment, covenant), and that feelings come later. We fuss and argue, but never let it interfere with our marriage covenant."

From all the correspondence I receive, it would seem true that the single most impressive tome for helping people get focused on a purposeful life and a satisfying relationship is Scripture. I believe that's because people who open themselves up to G-d are already in the mode of thinking beyond themselves, more charitable of heart and action, more resolute in their intent to "work it out," and more savvy about the deeper levels of satisfaction.

So, in conclusion, to avoid Stupid Breakups, now that you've read this book, open up the Bible.

Dr. Laura Schlessinger is an internationally syndicated radio host and author of six *New York Times* bestsellers. She lives in southern California with her husband and son.

Preserving a Legacy of Love and Wisdom for Generations to Come

By Gerard Smith

From the time I was a teenager, I wanted to be successful. Always seeking achievement—as far back as I can remember—I felt the need to discover and understand the success secrets of those I admired the most in order to duplicate them in my own life. The more I grew, and the more I achieved, the more I wanted to learn. As an adult, simple questions still piqued my curiosity: "What is success?" "Is it the same for everyone, or is success a very individual thing?" "What does "success" mean to those who are already successful?"

These questions, I learned, are not so simple. The fascination led me to ask over one hundred successful people — world leaders, celebrities, business people, scientists — for their personalized definitions. Their poignant and colorful responses were so eloquent I compiled their personal letters into the book, *Celebrating Success: Inspiring Personal Letters on the Meaning of Success.*

Two letters in particular really caught my attention. Erma Bombeck, a wonderful humorist who explored the laughter and wisdom in everyday life, wrote:

Success is usually measured in terms of what we're remembered for. I thought my kids would remember me as a woman who wrote twelve books, received sixteen honorary degrees, and wrote for thirty-one million newspaper readers a week. My daughter told me that she would always remember me for caving in and buying her a stupid leather coat she thought she'd die if she didn't have ... and ended up wearing once. So you see, success isn't necessarily a monument to achievement, but small acts of love.

The second letter came from game show host Monty Hall. While he is most vividly remembered as the host of "Let's Make A Deal," you may not know that he has devoted countless hours to charitable work throughout the U.S. and Canada. Monty Hall wrote that he measured success by evaluating his life, his contributions to society, his family and friends. He concluded:

www.mentorsmagazine.com

My father defined my success thusly: "Do not talk to me of my son the TV star— talk to me of my son the humanitarian." When your father defines your life in that manner, that is success!

The words of Erma Bombeck and Monty Hall made me contemplate the importance of the connection from one generation to the next—how we are shaped by the example and the expectations of the generations that came before us, and how our children are shaped by the way we have lived. I came to understand that how we live our lives—what we think, feel, and believe—has an impact far beyond the tangible details of our existence.

As we have been shaped by the events, beliefs, values, and experiences of our parents and grandparents, so we will shape the lives of our children in ways we can only imagine. Our beloved 40th President, the late Ronald Reagan, once said, "Live a life of love and legacy." Our lives are a legacy of love and wisdom that we leave for those around us. And the most significant thing we can do is to capture this legacy before it is too late.

My two most important mentors

As I became an avid student of others' achievements—spending hundreds of days gleaning the definitions of success from famous people all over the world—I suddenly realized I had completely neglected two of the most important mentors I would ever know…my own parents. I knew a little about the rich history of their lives—my mother telling stories of delivering nearly a hundred Zulu and Indian babies in the bush country of Africa, and my father recounting tales of his work on the sugar plantations of Indonesia. But the essence of my parents' lives was unspoken, simply because I had never asked the right questions. What made them fall in love? What were their spiritual beliefs? What did they remember of their own parents? What was the smartest financial move they ever made? What was their funniest memory of my childhood? How would they define a successful life? And what advice would they give their as-yet-unborn grandchildren?

Driven with the desire to capture my parents' legacy, I launched the daunting task of creating a list of thought-provoking questions in chronological order. It was to serve as a road map that would guide them to recall their childhood, parents, grandparents, education, courtship, marriage, early family years, travel, and profession – memories most likely long tucked away. The questions were designed not just to capture facts, but also to reveal the core of my parents' hearts and minds, to preserve who they are, what they believe, and the emotions they have experienced—to capture the love and wisdom of their remarkable lives. I planned to ask them for handwritten responses, but soon realized that it was already too late. Strokes and blindness had compromised their health and both could no longer write. The slow, steady march of time had stolen part of their legacy. The lessons learned were a stark awakening.

Inspired by the urging of friends who applauded my efforts and were eager to do the same for their own parents, grandparents and children, I finished my journal called Generation to Generation: A Legacy of Love and Wisdom. While it prompts for handwritten stories and recollections, I also created an audiotape version so that those who are incapacitated or uneasy with written response can record their life journeys in their own voice for their children and the children of future generations. It is my hope that this book will guide people to seek inspiration in the lives of those they love—the richest and most important sources of wisdom available to us—and preserve that legacy for all time.

The most powerful legacy of all

In our quest to maximize our capacity for greatness, we spend an enormous amount of time looking for examples of success among teachers, business people, scientists, celebrities, and world leaders. Far too often, we neglect to benefit from the wisdom of those closest to us. We may know that Grandpa started from nothing and became a successful businessman during the Great Depression, but how did he do it? We may know that Mom had to raise three kids on her own, but what could she teach us about being a parent and holding a full-time job at the same time? The experiences, beliefs, and convictions of our parents and grandparents can teach us far more than the books and tapes of the most successful people in the world, because it is our own personal history.

Each of us should contemplate the importance of the connection from one generation to the next—how we are shaped by the example and the expectations of the generations that came before us, and how our children are shaped by the way we have lived. How we live our lives—what we think, feel, and believe—has an impact far beyond the tangible details of our existence. The mothers and fathers, grandparents and children of this world need to take the first step—to understand that the most significant thing we can do is to capture this legacy before it is too late. The incredible journey of relaying what each of us holds most dear in our hearts and souls will ensure that our children and their children will have more than just fading memories to remember when loved ones are no longer near.

To capture a legacy, start by taking the time—making the time—to be with your parent or grandparent. Present the Generation to Generation journal as a gift and set a date to go through the journal with them. The experience of sharing memories becomes a treasured memory in itself. Wisdom is rarely contained in the events of a life, but is found in what was learned from the events. Ask the right questions—reveal the essence of their life by triggering memories, beliefs, thoughts and feelings of times gone by. Ask what they learned. Ask for the advice they would give on the topics of love, money, happiness and family. Ask them to explain their spiritual beliefs and why they believe as they do. Most important of all, however, savor their feelings. Did Dad like working at his job? How did Mom feel about bringing up children? Finding the right questions will help you reveal the inner souls of the people you love.

Dr. Dennis Waitley has inspired people all over the world to pursue their dreams. His answer to my question, "What is your personal definition of success?" was both simple and profound. He wrote, "Success is looking in the mirror and seeing a worthy role model for the children of the world to emulate." Remember that you are a role model for those who will come after you. You, too, are leaving a legacy, and the best legacy you can leave is to capture your own love and wisdom today, and every day to come. Ask yourself the important questions: What do you believe? What do you think? What have you learned from the events of your life? And what feelings do you wish to share with those in your life today as well as those who will come after you? Preserving your love and wisdom for future generations is the essence of mentorship. It is the most important gift we can leave for those to come.

Southern California author and speaker **Gerard Smith's** interactive journal, *Generation to Generation: A Legacy of Love and Wisdom,* is the ultimate road map of thought-provoking questions designed to capture a legacy forever.

Visit www.LightTheFire.com to buy one for each person you love.

Youth Sports:

How to Create an Extraordinary Environment for Your Child

By Steven Buonaugurio, MEd

What is the world teaching our kids today?

Kids today are growing up in a world that is sending mixed messages. They hear it is right to share, yet they see with their own eyes that some people have three homes and others have none. They are taught that it is wrong to use drugs, then observe adults spending hundreds of dollars to cheer on athletes who do. They are told to tell the truth, yet see little repercussion for politicians and entertainers who do not.

The value of youth sports

Youth sports can be a place for our children and teenagers to escape the confusion. It's a powerful vehicle through which they can learn and grow in a safe environment that is set up for their success. Through youth sports, we offer values and build character in an environment that is child-focused, outcome-driven and where everything is on purpose.

Difficult times in youth sports

For the past several years we have been experiencing some difficulty in youth sports. Referees are being physically threatened by disgruntled parents. Antagonistic fathers have fought, even to the death. Youth sports is at risk – and so is the well being of our kids.

Consider this:

• Young athletes constantly hear **"It doesn't matter if you win or lose,"** but they see the expensive championship trophies handed to the winners.

• Coaches say, **"What's most important is to learn from mistakes and grow,"** yet young athletes have parents who have never seen a practice…but attend every competitive game.

• We call it Youth Sports, but teenagers and children often see the adults having more fun than they are, as their coaches play with their professional clipboards and sport shiny team jackets with their names embroidered.

These kind of mixed messages are confusing to our young athletes. It creates a window of opportunity for children and teenagers to lose faith in the adults around them. When the well being of a child is not the primary driving force in an environment, they know it, and a message is sent that they might be unsafe.

I once had a child tell me, *"Coach, it matters to me if I win or lose. When I win my father is happy and he takes Mom and me out for pizza. When I lose he hardly talks to me on the drive home."* Is this a message that we want to send our children?

What I did that can work for you

A few years ago I asked myself if I was sending any mixed messages to the 7th graders that I coached in basketball. I wanted to make sure that I was congruent with the environment I was creating for my young athletes. Committed to this outcome I asked myself, **"What can I be doing even better?"** This question changed the way I coached forever.

I knew I had to get clear with my team. On the first day of practice my 12-year-old boys were outside the gym, anxiously waiting to get started on their jump shots and fast breaks. Since I always practice with my kids, they were surprised and disappointed when I showed up for practice in a shirt and tie and with no basketballs.

"What's up, coach?" they asked with total confusion. "Aren't we going to practice today?" I told them that what we were going to do would be better than any practice. Instead of going into the gym, I escorted my team to a classroom down the hall. Since youth sports are about growth and learning, I decided to start our season in the classroom. I asked my team of fifteen 12-year-olds one simple question, **"What is your outcome this season?"**

"To win!" most of them shouted. "Are you sure?" I asked. They were curious as to where I was headed with my questioning. Eventually, a discussion began. The kids started to get that I was asking them to dig deeper. Two hours of the most interesting and philosophical conversation then took place. To this day I wish I had captured it on video tape. It was the best practice I ever coached. The thoughts and ideas my players were tossing around were brilliant, sophisticated and filled with emotion. Many different ideas surfaced about what the team's outcomes were for the season, but in the end it was the following list that we all agreed to:

Outcomes (in order of importance):

1. To become better basketball players so we can move on to play in high school.
2. To have fun and create great memories.
3. To build friendship, camaraderie and team spirit.
4. To grow as individuals and become better people, sons and citizens.
5. To win.

www.mentorsmagazine.com

Listing our outcomes paid off in an abundance of ways throughout the course of the season, but my proudest moment as a coach came at the end of our season. It was our final test as a team. I was approached by the coach of a local 8th grade team. He offered us the opportunity to play his boys as our season ending game. His team was older, much bigger, and had more experience. A win was not in our statistical favor, and a loss would give us a losing record for the season. I was uncertain what to do. I wanted to offer my team the challenge of playing an older and more experienced team, but I did not want to taint their season by ending it with a loss and a losing record.

Several of my players expressed to me that they didn't want to play the older team because they didn't want to get embarrassed. I even had a few parents call me and say it was not in the best interest of their child. Feeling pressure to do what was best for my team, I remembered what my focus for the season was. I needed to make sure that I was not sending mixed messages to my players. I called a team meeting to make sure we stayed aligned with our outcomes for the season.

It was an easier decision than I thought. As I wrote our outcomes on the chalkboard, it became clear to all of us. The team's #1 outcome was to become better basketball players, the #4 outcome was to grow as individuals, and winning was our least important outcome. The choice was made by the team to play the game.

Impressively, we almost won the game. The intense battle boosted my players' confidence. The lessons they learned on the court that day were invaluable and would not have come if we had not re-aligned and acted with our outcomes in mind. It was the most fun we had all season.

When you know your intended outcome, you get tremendous results.

The "Top 10" Things you can do

The strategies I used as a coach, along with actions you can take as a parent, will greatly improve the quality of experience your child has with youth sports and will ensure your child gets the best results. Here are the "Top 10" things you can do:

1. Know your outcome

Before making any decisions for your children about the sport they take part in, first decide on what outcomes you want for your child. What is the outcome you are expecting to accomplish by having your child participate in this sport? If you want your child to learn teamwork, you probably shouldn't sign them up for tennis.

2. Let your child pick their sport

It is great that you have an idea of what you think is best for your child. Now make sure that your child is picking a sport that they want. Often times, kids will go along with what their friends are doing. Explore this and be sure you know why your child is picking a particular sport.

3. Help your child create their outcomes

Sit down with your child and create a list, in order of importance, of what their outcomes are for their participation in a particular sport. Like with my team of 7th graders, this can be one of the most impacting processes for your child.

4. Create a list of values with your child

This will help guide the kind of person and athlete your child desires to be. These values will provide a focus for your child and a sense of personal development goals.

5. Create a list of your child's expectations of you

What can your child expect from you? What do they want from you? How many games will you attend, how many practices? Will you cheer loudly? Ask your child, "What can I do to best support you?"

6. Define with your child what it means to win and lose

Have your child write down exactly what their rules are for whether they win or lose. The teams I coach usually come up with something similar to this: We are winners when we play our hardest, grow as a team and as individuals, and risk failure. This allows them to feel like winners even when the score says they did not win.

7. Celebrate growth – not wins.

Take interest in your child's practices as well as their games. Celebrate when they learn a new strategy for their sport, improve a specific skill they have been focusing on, or when they apply something they learned from their sport to life.

8. Talk to your children's coaches

Ask them questions about their values in how they coach and what they expect from their team. Get them thinking about their outcomes.

9. Show this article to your child's coach

If someone has chosen to work with your child, it is likely they enjoy it and would love to become even better at what they do. Share with them the knowledge you come across, and expect those who work with your children to continue their professional development.

10. Ask the right questions

Questions elicit the brain to think and then draw conclusions. It was the power of the one question, "What is your outcome this season?" that shaped the changes I made as a coach with my players. Through the use of questions, you can help guide your son or daughter through extraordinary experiences with their sports.

Asking the right questions

Asking your child the following questions consistently will guide their focus to positive thinking and will greatly improve the quality of their experience and what they learn. **Explore these specific and empowering questions. Ask them to your child in everyday conversation, before and after their games and practices.**

Pre-Season

- What is your outcome? What do you expect to get out of this season?
- How will you know that you got these results?
- What can I do to support you this season?

Pre-Game/Practice

- What specifically about today's game or practice are you excited about?
- What are you going to focus on today?
- What ways do you hope to grow or learn during today's game or practice?
- What characteristics are you going to focus on during today's practice or game?

Post-Game/Practice

- What was great about today's game or practice?
- What did you learn today?
- What did you do that was great?
- What can you do even better next time?
- In what way did you become even greater today?
- What were some specific efforts you put forth today that you are proud of?

Empowering questions to ask yourself:

- What is the outcome and purpose of my child's participation in this sport?
- Is my child getting the results they deserve?
- What are the values my child is learning through this sport?
- How can I make this even more empowering for my child?
- How does my child need me to show up?

Now Take Action!

If you take action on any of these "Top 10" things you can do, and begin to use any variety of the empowering questions, you will be helping create an extraordinary

www.mentorsmagazine.com

environment for your child. You will increase the benefits your child gets from youth sports and you will see results that you and your family deserve.

Youth is a time to learn and grow, experience failure and success, and have fun. You have already taken the time to learn more about how to maximize your son or daughter's childhood experiences. Now take the next step by following through. You – and your kids – will be glad you did!

Steven Buonaugurio is a character educator whose dynamic presentations influence kids, teachers, parents, youth coaches and organizations across the country. For more strategies and guidance on empowering kids visit: www.StevenBuonaugurio.com.

Organization:

Rising to Higher Ground and Creating Peace

By Jane-Marie Sandberg

Physical organization has always been easy for me to see and has become easier to accomplish over time. Somewhere in the middle part of my life, I forgot this for a while. My husband and nine children, who were not willing to accept what I offered to them, became the resistance that made me stronger and the springboard for the lessons I have learned. Because of this; strength and empowerment have transferred into all of the areas of my life.

I have realized that physical organization principles work as effectively in emotional and social situations and in fact, in the intellect and culture of a person's life as well. As I learned these things from experience and inspiration from God, I also realized that there was a great need for spiritual organization. The need for organization on six levels (spiritual, physical, intellectual, cultural, emotional and social) was understood and developed. Thus, the S.P.I.C.E.S. program was born...

Though it has always been difficult to organize my family, who have not wanted to be organized, I learned skills that I teach to others who...
- know a great deal about organizing but are presently deluged with life,
- want to get organized but have no idea how to progress in this area of living from where they are right now and
- don't want to improve but know they must.

Those who become organized after years of chaos are propelled forward into success and peace, experiencing what they have never felt before and feeling renewed in the process.

My personal journey

I was born into a family with one brother and one sister already ahead of me. At the age of five, I found myself in the position of an emotional adult. My parents had separated prior to their divorce, and as a single mother my mom had to do things she probably never would have chosen to do otherwise. She returned to school to become a nurse. My brother had long since left home and my sister was going through her own struggles.

My mom did what she had to do to get her degree to better care for her children. As a six-year-old, I spent the mornings home alone, got myself ready for kindergarten and left when the paper clock matched the real clock to walk the seven blocks to school. I never missed school and I was never late.

This experience and others shaped my life. I learned that I was capable of succeeding in anything I wanted to do. I learned that emotionally, I was stronger than some adults. I learned that I could be myself and it was okay. What I hadn't learned to deal with was abuse from my father and others, and the debilitating words continually directed at me. This lowered my self-esteem and my expectations of how I should be treated.

S.P.I.C.E.S. – Six levels of organization

• Spiritual

This is the most important type of organization. When you know who you really are, self-worth increases substantially. Knowing who you are and what you value, and then lining this up with your actions and your beliefs, boosts your capability of knowing what you can really do and acquiring the strength to "leap tall buildings with a single bound."

• Physical organization

Being physically organized is one area which most of us are aware of because it's so easy to see. We can tell when we're living or working in a mess. It's all around us, occupying our minds, draining our energy and wasting our limited, irreplaceable time.

• Intellectual organization

Often we find ourselves overwhelmed with thoughts that swirl around in our minds, centered on what we have learned, what we have to do, and what we have to think. The avalanche is more than we are prepared to deal with. I ask the questions that cause sorting, filing and elimination in the minds of my clients, allowing them room to deal with everything pressing down upon them. In answering these questions my clients sort the situations and events that have caused them anxiety, and then they know what to do about them.

• Cultural and social organization

Sometimes we go along in life, weighed down by stress caused by the perception of our relationships and the groups we associate with. Social organization deals with individuals and cultural organization deals with groups, but the principles are the same in dealing with difficult people.

• Emotional organization

While sorting through my own relationships, I realized that my marriage, which I had been trying to hold together, was not worth the effort I had been expending. I totally believe in the sanctity of marriage, but I couldn't fix all the difficulties by myself. The abuse intensified. It could go from 0 to 6 on the Richter Scale in less than 15 minutes. I never knew when the ground would shake beneath our feet.

One day, I left. I walked out with my four youngest children after deciding that no one deserved to live like we had. I didn't have a completely detailed plan, but I did have a plan. Through the help of God and people placed in my path, I succeeded a day at a time.

We have organized as individuals and as a family this past year in all six of the areas of need. It was hard, but I appreciated the peace that came with deciding and have never regretted that choice to step forward and protect myself and my children. It was hard to make such a far-reaching decision. Some wonder why I took so long. I think it's the same way with everything. You can only do what you can do. You can't do it before you're ready. It takes time to get ready and force doesn't help.

Organization in all of its forms is important and valuable. Recently, a client hired me to develop a program to assist their investors in organizing their retirement. The program helps individuals and couples make the best plan to address their wants and needs for their futures in each of the S.P.I.C.E.S. areas. Those who took the program enjoyed themselves, did a lot of thinking, created a retirement plan and made new friendships. My client was able to build a closer association with his clients as well. It was a win/win/win situation.

This program is currently being offered for sale as a 4-cd set with companion workbook. It is recommended that all individuals who are retired or will be retiring think through the program so that there is a organized plan for spiritual, physical, intellectual, cultural, emotional and social enjoyment, consistent with their expectations and dreams for the "best years of their lives." It is especially important for couples to make the plan together so retirement will be just right for both partners.

Learning the hard way

There are many varied and powerful life lessons that I have experienced, mostly the hard way. These lessons have taken me in the specific and wonderful direction I am headed now, that of helping people exchange chaos and confusion for peace and order.

For example, years ago I had difficulty thinking what to say to people. On a good day, I could fill about ten minutes with small talk and then it was time to leave. I made myself take a job with a survey company, asking product and habit questions of the public. It was one of the hardest things I ever did, but this one lesson translated into my life today looks very different.

Now I love talking with people. I know how to word the questions that bring out the best solutions from inside my clients in order to solve their own problems, whether the disorganization is physical, social, emotional or whatever. I love to interview and am easily able to assist others in feeling comfortable, making our encounters enjoyable for both of us. In this way I have taken a painful situation of my past and transformed it into something fun and rewarding.

Here are some of the favorite lessons I have learned in my life:
- Organization has great value.
- Life is hard.
- Life is even harder than I thought.
- I'm actually smart which I didn't understand as a child.
- I can do anything I put my mind to.
- I have many talents.
- Increased spirituality makes a huge difference, as does increased faith and trust in God.
- I can be kind even if I'm hurting.
- Controlling my tongue is hard, but worth it.
- I can't change anyone else, but I can improve myself.
- I will not tolerate any further abuse from anyone.
- There are so many things I don't know how to do yet.
- Freedom is sweet.
- I am no longer a victim. (This is possibly my most valuable lesson to date.)

Organizing by setting boundaries

I've considered my life a "Work in Progress." As I continually progress I have gained much, but nothing as profound as the lessons I've learned on setting boundaries (joancasey.com). I mistakenly understood that if I loved someone unconditionally then I shouldn't have boundaries .... big mistake!

It's important to mention here that though I was raised to be a victim it was by my actions that I taught others to continue to treat me as a victim. Once I changed the way I valued myself, all my relationships had to be redefined. Years of progress, discovery and failures brought me to the realization that I am a valuable person, with great capabilities and with no need to accept abuse, of any kind, from anyone.

By setting firm boundaries, I found that I had the courage and strength to organize my relationships. You can too, through simple organizational strategies used in all six of the most important areas of your life.

These things which I have learned and experienced have become the basis for the work I do with my clients, either on an individual basis or through seminars, workshops, e-classes, and teleconference calls. I either consult with my clients until they are clear about what steps they will take next on their own, work with them personally to overcome their difficult situations, or in cases where it's appropriate, I do the organization work on their behalf.

Five of my children still remain at home. Each is now more willing to learn the life skills I have been teaching them for years. Progression is imminent. I have so much to be thankful for. I have the peace inside necessary to succeed, once again, because of organizing the S.P.I.C.E.S. of my life. You can too, whatever your situation and needs! I have the unique qualities necessary to zero in on what organizational difficulties are holding you back from achieving your greatest potential and to encourage you to move off your plateau. Although it's very simple to do, it is sometimes not easy…but still very, very worthwhile.

The greatest thing is that my lessons aren't over. I can't even imagine the new and wonderful things I will learn this year in my next "work in progress" experience!

Jane-Marie, *Queen of Organization* and mother of 9 children, increases effectiveness with those striving to make a difference in the world in their own fields of expertise. By improving personal organization, she helps improve productivity in the lives and businesses of her clients. Her S.P.I.C.E.S. method produces order, plans, processes, and systems to help people become more effective in what they do.

Visit her at QueenofOrganization.com.

Email her at jane-*marie@queenoforganization.com.*

How To
Own a Business Together
& Stay Happily Married

7 Salvation Factors for all Business Owners

By Marcie Hanhart

"Oh, I could never work with my husband (wife) It would just be too hard. I can't imagine how you do it!"

For almost 12 years, when my husband and I told people we owned and ran a company together, we heard that … and in many ways, their reaction was correct. Working with your spouse is one of the most challenging experiences imaginable for most people. My husband and I have compatible skill sets, personality types, and working styles that, on paper, are different enough to create perfect symmetry for the company.

We would have benefited greatly, however, from a business coach to help us with the tricky waters I call the "Salvation Factors." But first, a little background.

Business by default – not by design

In 1992, I was lured away from my consulting practice in New York City to build the market for a new high tech company in New Jersey. I took this position to have more time with my 3-year-old son, and so that my husband, who'd recently decided to leave the stress of Wall Street, could "start something new." Within weeks, my "employer" was taken over by venture capitalists who pulled the plug, and I was jobless. It was then that my husband asked me to join him in his newly emerging software venture. I had every reason to say yes. Since the early 1980s I had been instrumental in starting new businesses and bringing products to market for Fortune 500s. I operated a consulting firm and had owned another company with a partner. All the ingredients were there.

What we didn't figure into the mix was that we were two very strong individuals, who had worked successfully and independently for many years…and we each had strong opinions and viewpoints which, as it turned out, were frequently in opposition!

The ideal versus the real

Ideally the marriage bond should enhance the working relationship, and working together should enable husband and wife to have a greater understanding and tolerance.

"The ability to grow together and achieve together has strengthened our bond, but we work hard at it every single day."- G & J, financial planners

How do they work hard at it? Why does business and marriage combined work well for a few and not for others? How can the situation be made positive? The Ideal is: one dream, one focus, one harmony. The Real is often: competition, disagreement and sometimes being so closely in focus as to not see the forest for the trees!

"Seven Salvation Factors" for any business, but crucial to a Marriage Business Partnership.

1) Separate and clearly defined roles

Often "best business practices" that would naturally be put in place are skipped in a husband/wife run business. Perhaps this is due to the assumption that "formalization" of responsibilities is not necessary since "we are in this together." Wrong! Defined roles, responsibilities and accountability are essential to the morale of any team member and to the effective operation of any business. This is even more so in a Marriage Business Partnership because the dissatisfaction and lack of resolution of issues travels from office to home and back again. It is never escaped! Pick roles based on expertise and fulfill them.

"Having two diametrically opposed areas of expertise works for us...one of us is the creative visionary and the other is the business realist. This may seem like a head to head conflict, but it helps us to ground our business in a realistic manner" – W K, Owner, Architectural Firm

- **Define and write down job descriptions** and then – except for standard management review meetings, or when asked – stay out of your partner's domain!

2) Have a plan and agree on it

In any business you need to have a plan and work that plan. As the adage goes: "If you don't know where you're going, how will you know when you get there?" I add, "How will you know <u>how</u> to get there?" In a Marriage Business Partnership, agreement on what you are aiming for and how you plan to get there is crucially important because it enables you to agree on strategies to get there. You have a basis to provide mutual support and avoid the inevitable conflicts that result from "assuming the obvious." The obvious is rarely the same to two, as it is to one.

- **Develop a specific purpose statement.** Discuss it. What is it you are in business to do? (Hint: it's not just putting food on the table!) Write it down with 3-5 strategies to achieve your stated purpose. Agree on it.

3) Act with mutual respect – "Inside" and "Outside"

"Having my married partner in the business reduces my effectiveness because I can't hold her as accountable as I would if she were just another employee"- D B, Employment Agency Owner.

Clear definition of roles works ONLY when each partner respects the position of the other. It is no good to assign roles and titles, only to have them undermined, contradicted or ignored by the partner. This disrespectful behavior eats away at the operational effectiveness, as well as your emotional bond...AND, others see it, too.

"The different management styles between myself and my husband used to lead the staff to try to play us off against each other. We now work consciously to show a united position and mutual respect in front of the Team. –N L, Restaurant Owner

- **Treat your partner with the same respect and responsiveness** with which you would treat any other employee. You've mutually decided on roles for a reason, so be accountable to one another. Follow through, and the staff will follow also.

4) Communication and listening

Effective communication is the key to understanding and harmony. At Action International, we say, "Communication is the response you get." We might speak a lot, expressing all that's on our mind, or we may say very few words. In the end, if we're not getting the result we seek, something is wrong – either in the saying or in the listening, or both. Two major obstacles to effective communication are competition (the overriding desire to be right) and the inability to listen (understand) what the other person is saying – often because we're too caught up in our own position. Both of these are killers...but the converse are saviors.

"We don't really have disagreements. When we have a differing of opinion, we discuss it; we consider all the different ideas and try to make the best decision – i.e. what's best overall and in the long run. What has the most positives and least negatives. When we jointly come to a decision, we implement it. When we're exhausted, tempers can be short...but with a little bit of venting by one and a lot of listening by the other and a few hours sleep, all is well." - G & M, Financial Advisors

- **Practice communication.** Set the target of understanding the other's viewpoint and stick with it. "Be direct, productive, and results-oriented." You may not always agree, but by keeping your end goal in mind and acknowledging that your partner is driven to achieve the same, you will move forward in greater harmony.

5) Picture why you're doing this ... and keep it in your mind's eye.

When you can visualize the "Why" – why you are in business, why together, why it's important to you – the daily decisions, disagreements, and disappointments fall into perspective and find resolution more easily. Remind yourself that you are doing this because of the VISION you have of your life together, your goals, and your future!

- **Write out your VISION and see it in the present.** Share it, discuss it and remind yourself of it daily. Each time you express your common dream out loud or use it to drive your decisions, your business will move in that direction and your bond will grow stronger.

6) All work, no play, breeds unhappiness at the end of the day!

When I decided to write this article, I asked my dermatologist, who practices with her husband, "What is the most difficult aspect of working together?" She did not hesitate.

"Being together all the time. We could never get away from it; we could never get away from each other. There seemed to be no personal or alone time. That's why I've cut back to part-time and now we do totally separate things."

Immediately, an image flashed through my mind of my own son, some years back, defiantly assailing us at the dinner table with, "Can't you guys talk about anything but work?" He didn't like it…and who could blame him? We were letting the business take over our lives.

- **Set a schedule for work time and non-work time and stick to it diligently!** You both need down time – to breathe, to enjoy personal and family time together. That's when renewal comes – both personally and for the business. Be the "gatekeeper" for each other and don't let business sneak in when it shouldn't.

7) Use a Business Coach to help you.

The steps above are easy to understand. But understanding is different from doing. We may "know" what it takes to be in harmony with our mate – yet, 50% of first time marriages end in divorce. "I know what I need to do to improve my business" is stated by most owners, yet estimates indicate only 20-30% of businesses make it past the first 5 years. Knowing what to do and actually implementing the knowledge are not the same.

Let's take a moment to look at another situation. We all know and accept that to become a great athlete, you need a coach. Why not, then, embrace the same opportunity as a business owner? Athletes don't become good by just reading a book, or talking with other athletes. They must put the knowledge into practice, and they must do so consistently. Coaches provide an objective, knowledgeable eye, give feedback, guidance and encouragement, discipline and provide perspective as the "coachees" practice the actions that will define them. No different for a business person, but the "stakes" are doubled (business and home) when partnered with a spouse.

Over 20 years, Gina and her husband have built a massive financial business. Her advice:

"...have discussions rather than arguments and use your mentor to resolve differences...Never change a winning game, but always change a losing one. AND when you decide to change, seek guidance from your mentor."

- **Hire a qualified business coach to help you.** Your results will come faster and more harmoniously...and that will be the reward.

"If you are successfully growing the business and truly love each other, the respect that comes from building the business together truly enhances the marriage. All the petty stuff no longer matters." – N L, Restaurant Owner (and coachee).

Marcie Hanhart is a former television news producer, advisor to Fortune 100s including IBM, Pioneer, Grolier, and GTE, the creator of award-winning applications in fields from banking to avionics, and owner of several businesses. Marcie now coaches other business owners in order to help them maximize their potential.

Contact Marcie at *ActionCoach@digitus-associates.com* or 908.696.9500.

Family ... One of Our Most Important "Why's"

By Nicholas W. Kontras

"As important as your obligations as a doctor, lawyer, or business leader will be, you are a human being first, and those human connections – with spouses, with children, with friends – are the most important investments you will ever make. At the end of your life, you will never regret not having passed one more test, not winning one more verdict, or not closing one more deal. You will regret time not spent with a husband, a child, a friend, or a parent ... Our success as a society depends not on what happens in the White House but on what happens inside your house."

– Barbara Bush, Wellesley College, 1990

Before I agree to coach a businessperson, to assist them in improving their profitability and reducing the time they spend in their business, I carefully assess their goals and vision for the future. I have found that I am most effective in teaching someone "how" when their "why" is already well developed.

By their "why," I am referring to what motivates them at the core of their being. To use a French expression, I want to discover their "raison d'etre," or reason for being.

In some cases, that can be as simple as the accumulation of material wealth. Many individuals still believe that money can buy happiness. If they are successful in accumulating the money they set out to acquire, they eventually realize the futility of that quest. Many rightly conclude that family, or faith, or "giving back" is a far more powerful long-term motivator than wealth accumulation.

My father and mother are in their 80's, both still vigorous and energetic. Soon their time will come, and the Good Lord will take them from this earth. My prayer is that I will be with them when the end comes. I know that they want to be surrounded by family at that time.

And so it is with most of us. We dream of gazing into the eyes of our children and loved ones in those final moments before death. Those who remain will grieve the loss, but celebrate the happy times together throughout their lifetime. The happiest times were those when we were together with family and

friends…celebrating weddings, births, vacations together…connecting with one another…catching up on each other's lives.

Family has always been an important part of my life. It was part of my upbringing…always there. But as I have aged and assumed the leadership role in the family along with cousins in my age bracket, I have come to realize that "family," however you define it, must be nurtured and be a matter of constant focus. Like so many other things of great value, it does not come into existence of its own accord.

YES…You do have a family

Many of us do not have a traditional family – husband, wife, children. But all of us have a "family" of one sort or another. Whether single or married, we have a significant other. We have biological parents, or defacto parents, those who have chosen to commit themselves to loving us and nurturing us through life. If we have no "family" at all, hopefully someone of faith has reached out to us, and somehow shared God's love with us.

When I married my wife, Agni, she had two children, Jason and Dawn, seven and five at the time. I could not have been more proud of my new family. When I look at pictures of Jay and Dawn walking down the aisle with Aggie and me in 1985, tears come to my eyes.

Later, we had two children of our own, Alex and Kristi. During their teenage years, Jay and Dawn chose to live with their biological father. It was difficult for Aggie and me to accept their need to make this choice, but over time we did. Since their departure, both have returned to live again under our roof.

So my family was anything but traditional…blended is the term often used. With patience, prayer, and trust that each person must take his or her own path through life, we have adjusted to our circumstances, and have made a "family" out of what God blessed us with.

Family vision

Now that we have determined that we all have a family, how do we nurture that family to achieve that enviable state where the family becomes a significant and meaningful part of our lives…our "why?"

Having goals in business is a no-brainer. You are forced to if you are in sales, and most employees are given some semblance of a goal, either directly or indirectly. But we rarely tend to think of a goal in terms of our family.

I have found it very beneficial to have a concrete vision / mission statement of what I want my "family" to be. More specifically, we need to clarify what the "family" wants itself to be. It is not about me, but about "us."

In the past, this goal has been written by me during quiet times of reflection. Soon, it will be drafted by my family, in a cooperative effort over time, and will be completed this summer before Alex leaves for college. Love, understanding, support, involvement, patience, and acceptance are all descriptors we have discussed individually. "Special" times together will be a part of the goal too.

By being concrete and written, this family mission / vision statement can serve to remind us of our values, principles, family goals, and obligations to one another. It will encourage us to support and "live" these throughout our lives. While different from a monthly sales goal, it is far more important, and will have a much more significant impact on us as individuals over a lifetime.

Nurturing the vision: Walking the talk

This vision must be nurtured, discussed, and become a part of the priorities and daily choices we make. As the primary stewards of this vision, my wife and I will strive to regularly revisit the vision / mission statement, and to live it by nurturing and supporting the principles, values, attitudes, practices, and traditions set forth therein. As Harry Truman once said, "the buck stops here!"

This means regularly setting aside our selfish agendas and deferring to the family, in order to allocate the time, effort, and resources necessary to nurture the family. Is it painful to give up that round of golf in order to prepare for a family outing? Yes. Is it worth it? You bet!

Nurturing the vision: Communication

Regular contact with each other is paramount. This has never been easier. Between cell phones, cell-phone text mail, e-mail, and land lines, distance is no longer a hurdle. The issue is whether we have decided to make it a priority to stay in touch in a meaningful way.

Currently, we all live in Cincinnati, Ohio, in America's heartland. But over time, we will separate. Alex will be off to college in Grand Rapids, MI this fall. Dawn will leave the home and may someday leave the city. But we are all committed to regularly engaging each other in a meaningful way, and thereby nurturing the "family."

Nurturing the vision: Acceptance

During the past 18 years of marriage, and with each of four children, my wife and I have gone through many stages spiritually, mentally, and "parentally." Both of us grew up in traditional Greek families, with clear rules and expectations, and rather dominant parents. Bearing the brunt of such a gushing, smothering love has at times been a challenge. Through it all, we have learned the value of acceptance.

By acceptance, I mean an understanding that we are all fearfully and wonderfully made, by an invisible God, and we each are as He chose us to be. We will all take a different path through life. What is important are the values and principles by which we live, and not how they are expressed in the individual choices we make.

Let me illustrate. My wife and I are committed Christians, and also believe in the importance of good health – eating a balanced diet and getting regular exercise. We make a practice of worshiping together on Sunday mornings. Our children are at various stages of spiritual growth, as well as at various stages of acknowledging the importance of certain practices in maintaining health. As our children have grown to adulthood, lived away from the home, and chosen their individual lifestyles, we have necessarily had to be patient and come to accept the choices they have made. Constant reminders to them about what they are not doing are unproductive as a motivator. Setting a good example has, over time, had a tangible influence on all four children. In the end, they are responsible for how they choose to live their lives. We must accept their choices, and find common ground where it lies. We must not compromise our values in our own lives, but must respect how others in our family have chosen to live theirs.

Nurturing the vision: Tradition

My wife and I have found that family traditions are a great part of the closeness and togetherness we feel as a family. Both of us have made every effort to incorporate special times together into our "family" life together.

We strive daily to celebrate the evening meal together. Yes, it is difficult to do so with everyone going in different directions. But if we make it a priority, the laughing, the connections, the surfacing of problems, and schedule coordination all seems to knit us together in a way that would not otherwise be possible.

Weekend meals together as a family, have become an important part of our lives. Whether they occur on Friday night, Saturday morning, after church on Sunday, or late Sunday afternoon over pizza or leftovers, they are precious times. Gone are the days of believing that everything has to be just so…the house clean, a formal meal prepared, or all preparations for the next work day completed. We come together in a relaxed way and "chill," as the expression goes, connecting with each other in a way that seemed to elude us before. The kids were always receptive to this…it was my wife and I who put up the roadblocks early on. Now we know better, and put first things first!

Sunday worship continues to be a special time several times a quarter, when we manage to get the entire family to church. There is something about hearing the word of God together, as a family, that makes it special.

On Thanksgiving morning, we have recently begun volunteering at a soup kitchen or similar venue to prepare meals for those less fortunate. Service as a family has been a special experience. It is humbling, helps us count our blessings, and keeps our good fortune in perspective. And it truly does remind us that it is better to give than to receive.

Other traditions include our Christmas Eve gift exchange, opening the "stockings" my wife has faithfully stuffed for over a decade, as well as looking at family photo albums and videos on New Year's day. We have begun taking special vacations together, and have traveled to Australia and Hawaii in recent years as a family.

Never underestimate the value of a tradition of special times together. The memories of those times will forever serve to knit the family together in ways that are truly meaningful.

Never give up ...

It was 1972. I was a Lieutenant in the US Navy JAG Corps, sitting on a three-hundred foot rock off the coast of California at Pfeiffer State Beach, in the Big Sur area south of San Francisco. It was a cold, crisp, sunny day in June. The surf was pounding away at the large black rocks, and the white spray was soaring into the air. I looked out over the Pacific Ocean, knowing that my next duty station, Subic Bay, Republic of the Philippines, was somewhere out there. I remember praying to God that if He chose to spare my life, bring me back home to Ohio safely, and bless me with a family some day, that I would bring them back to this same rock.

Twenty years later, almost to a day, I was there again with my family – on that same rock, with my wife and four children. Never give up on your family, and on your efforts to make them a significant and meaningful part of your life.

Remember the "why" and the ability to persevere in your daily effort to execute the "how" truly will become an easier task.

Nicholas W. Kontras, J.D., is a professional Business Coach affiliated with Action International, practicing in the Greater Cincinnati, Ohio area. He is a graduate of Ohio State University School of Law, served as a JAGC Officer in the US Navy during Viet Nam, and spent over two decades as a Sales Executive and Sales Manager for Digital Equipment Corp., Compaq Computer Corp., and Hewlett-Packard Corp. He has owned five profitable small businesses over the past 3 decades, and is currently residing with his wife and 4 children in West Chester, OH, north of Cincinnati. He can be reached at 513.874.6399, or via e-mail at *Nick@CoachNick.biz.* His website is www.CoachNick.biz

Teaching Children Moral Living

By Dr. James Dobson

My friend and colleague, attorney Gary Bauer, served for eight years in the Reagan administration, ultimately being appointed Senior Domestic Policy Advisor to the President. During his latter years in the White House, Bauer also headed an historic Commission on the Family that revealed surprising findings about the nation's adolescents.

After two years of investigation, Bauer's commission learned that Americans in every age category were better-off at the time of the study than they had been ten years earlier. Both adults and younger children were found to be more healthy, better fed, and better educated than before. More tax money was being spent on children and more programs and bureaucrats were in place to address their needs. There was, however, a striking exception to this conclusion.

Teenagers were found to be considerably worse off than in the prior decade. Their many problems could not be blamed on government, on educators or on the medical community. Rather, Bauer and his co-workers found that young people were busily killing themselves at an alarming rate. It is shocking to see just how hostile the world of the young has become and how poorly they are coping with their difficulties.

Suppose the parents of yesterday could visit our time to observe the conditions that prevail among our children. They would be appalled by the problems which have become widespread (and are spreading wider) in our homes, schools and neighborhoods.

Gang violence and one-on-one crime among the young is an indescribable shame. Wandering droves of children and teens are shooting, knifing and bludgeoning each other at an unprecedented rate. Commonly, now, innocent bystanders and little children are caught in the crossfire, as bullets from automatic weapons spray once peaceful neighborhoods. It is not unusual in the large cities for ten or fifteen young people to die in a single violent weekend. Emergency units of virtually every inner city hospital are taxed to the limit trying to deal with the casualties of gang warfare now being waged. They call it "battlefield medicine." The killings are so common that many don't even get reported in the news. Only when the body count reaches record proportions do people seem alarmed by what is happening. Who would have believed in 1970 when *Dare to Discipline* was first written that this would have occurred?

Isaac Fulwood, Chief of Police in Washington, D.C., blamed the city's "love of drugs," when the homicide rate there set another record for the third straight year. He could have just as easily pointed his finger at City Hall. At that same time, Mayor Marion Barry was making headlines around the country (and a mockery of law enforcement) for his conviction of cocaine possession.

"The United States is breeding a lost generation of children," proclaimed one authority, citing teen violence statistics compiled by U.S. Justice Department. These figures showed that since 1983, robberies committed by juveniles under eighteen have increased five times, murders have tripled, and rapes have doubled. The leading killer of black males aged fifteen to twenty-four is now homicide; only car accidents kill more white youths.

"During every one hundred hours on our streets we lose more young men than were killed in one hundred hours of ground war in the Persian Gulf," lamented Dr. Louis Sullivan, secretary of the Department of Health and Human Services during the first Bush administration. "Where are the yellow ribbons of hope and remembrance for our youth dying in the streets?"

No longer is extreme violence something that happens only on television. It is a reality of daily life for many of our youth. In 1987, gifted students in a Washington, D.C., public school science class were asked how many knew somebody who'd been killed. Of the nineteen students, fourteen raised their hands. How were they killed? "Shot," said one student. "Stabbed," said another. "Shot." "Shot." "Drugs." "Shot." All of this from thirteen-year-old children.

Similar findings were compiled in a study of 168 teenagers by researchers at the University of Maryland School of Medicine. When asked about their exposure to violent crime, an amazing 24 percent of these Baltimore teens had witnessed a murder; 72 percent knew someone who had been shot.

Wherever one chooses to look within adolescent society, trouble is evident. A root cause for much of the unrest, of course, is the continued prevalence of alcohol and substance abuse by the young. A recent Gallup Report indicated that before graduating from high school, a staggering percentage of teenagers are hooked on mind-altering drugs of some type. 85 percent experiment with alcohol. 57 percent try an illicit drug, and 35 percent get drunk at least once a month. And lest those of us with Christian homes get complacent, there is not much difference between churched and unchurched families in the evidence of teen substance abuse. It's enough to make a grown man or woman sick! Indeed, there is an ache deep within my spirit over what we have allowed to happen to our kids. What is it going to take to alarm the mass of humanity that sits on the sidelines watching our kids struggle for survival? It is time for every God-fearing adult to get on our faces in repentance before the Almighty.

www.mentorsmagazine.com

We have permitted this mess to occur! *We* allowed immoral television and movie producers to make their fortunes by exploiting our kids. *We* allowed their filth and their horribly violent productions to come into our homes via cable, video, CDs, and network trash. *We* stood by passively while Planned Parenthood taught our teenagers to be sexually promiscuous. *We* allowed them to invade our schools and promote an alien value system that contradicted everything we believed and loved. *We* granted profit-motivated abortionists unsupervised and unreported access to our minor daughters, while we were thinking about something else. *We*, as parents, are guilty of abandoning our children to those who would use them for their own purposes. Where in God's name have we been? How bad does it have to get before we say, enough is enough?!

At the core of these individual tragedies is a moral catastrophe that has rocked our families to their foundation. We have forgotten God and disregarded His Holy ordinances. But it is our children who have suffered and will continue to pay for our lack of stewardship and diligence.

Of all the dimensions wherein we have mishandled this younger generation, none is more disgraceful than the sexual immorality that has permeated the world in which they live. There is no more effective way to destroy the institution of the family than to undermine the sexual exclusivity on which it is based. Yet that has been accomplished, deliberately and thoughtfully by those who despised the Christian system of values. Today's "safe-sex" advocates are advancing that campaign with devastating effectiveness.

Why is there so much resistance to abstinence-based programs?

Well, some educators honestly believe that "kids will be kids," so we should show them how to play the game right. I don't agree with them, but I can respect their honest difference of opinion. There are others, however, particularly those Planned Parenthood and SIECUS types who are in the business of promoting promiscuity and abortion, whom I believe have other motives. For them, something else is going on. The subject is not merely an intellectual debate about children and what is their best interest. No, the topic is highly inflammatory. They become incensed when the word abstinence is even mentioned. Have you ever wondered why?

Dr. James Dobson is a licensed psychologist and the president of Focus on the Family. In addition, he is heard regularly on more than 4,000 radio stations worldwide. Dr. Dobson holds a Ph.D. in child development and 12 honorary doctorates. He has two grown children and resides in Colorado Springs with his wife of thirty-seven years, Shirley.

Rare Exclusive Interview
with
Brad Sugars

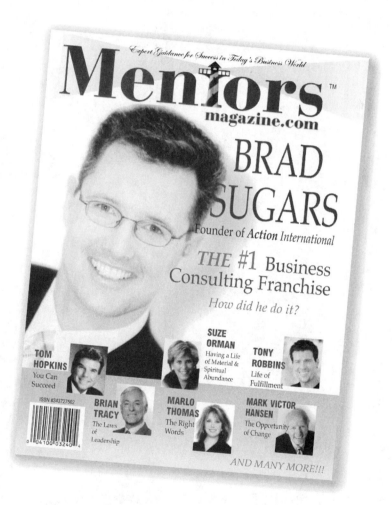

BRAD SUGARS

BRAD 28
QLD

Brad Sugars

Founder & Chairman of Action International

Interviewed by Linda Forsythe

I'm delighted to bring to you a transcript of my wide-open conversation with Brad Sugars – LIVE from Australia!!!! Brad has devoted his life to helping people discover the potential within themselves through business ownership and wealth creation. In fact he is considered so good at it...he has been pronounced a world leader in the field of entrepreneurial business! Brad Sugars is the founder and chairman of Action International. This dynamic company is THE #1 business consulting franchise in the United States and the 39th top global franchise. This honor was bestowed upon Action International by Entrepreneur Magazine's rankings in the Franchise 500 issue of January 2004.

Drawing from the genius of Brad's wisdom and flair, Action International is committed to assisting small business people to achieve personal and professional mastery. In other words...a fabulously successful business!!! Brad Sugars' special passion is to re-educate the world through "edu-tainment." He uses business and wealth creation techniques that individuals use to capture their destiny. This may mean fostering relationships with colleagues, family and associates or directing focus to achieve business and personal goals. It also means mentoring them in business-proven techniques. The final goal is to create an environment which will give the business owner the ability to create the lifestyle of their dreams. What is even more incredible...the business owner receives this with proven systems already in place!!!

Linda: Thank you, Brad, for taking the time to share with all of us in this interview many of the great lessons you have learned in your life! By the way...I love your Aussie accent!

Brad Sugars: Well, it's great to be here.

Linda: To start off, I know you started in business at a very early age. Tell us, how DID you get started in business?

Brad Sugars: I'm sure my Dad would tell a slightly different story than my version. My Dad says I started in business when I was seven. He caught me selling my Christmas presents to my brothers. I then realized by accident (and the hard way), that you should never sell anything that you can rent. If I had rented to my brothers, I would have gotten the presents back plus the money.

Linda: (Laughs) Well, that definitely showed an entrepreneurial spirit at a young age! What is your version?

Brad Sugars: I personally say I started when I was fifteen. I lived in a town called Adelaide, a city of about a million people. I got a job as the paper delivery boy. Delivering papers in Adelaide, in the freezing cold in the winter time was not a fun job. So, I employed several of my friends to do it. I realized at that point and time: you don't have to do the work. You can employ other people and then make a profit along the way. So, I was kind of different I suppose. My first real businesses, though, started when I attended University. I was pursuing an accounting degree towards a Bachelor's of Business. Studying for my degree really didn't take up many hours. I decided to start several other businesses. Everything from direct-from-the-manufacturer to wholesale, ladies retail fashion, and (probably the one that got me fired up the most) a photocopy shop. The photocopy shop was like a Kinko's for you guys, but one of the first of its kind. This was about ten years ago here in Australia.

Linda: Do you think being an Australian has helped or hindered you in your growth?

Brad Sugars: I think it helped. We live in a country geographically the size of the United States, but with a population basically the size of New York City. So, when you consider that, doing business here is far more difficult. We have a lot higher cost structure. Our tax structure is also higher than that of the United States. We have a much more difficult environment to succeed in.

Unfortunately, for me, I started my business (or maybe fortunately when you look at it), when Australia was in the middle of a recession. That was really the only economic times I knew. If I could prosper in a recession, I could also prosper when we hit the good times. (I now like to think we are always in good times because the businesses that I run have grown, whether they are down times or up times). I believe if you have the fundamentals of business correct, then it doesn't really matter what the economy is doing as long as you are focusing on doing what you need to do.

Linda: That's a great point. Many of the people in the States, where I live, have the mindset that while the economy is down, their sales are going to be down. Yet, the sales superstars I know... generally succeed in any environment.

Brad Sugars: It's true that there's more money made in down economies than in up economies. We have to remember that in life the seasons are always there. There is Summer, and after Summer, what happens...there's Fall. So you have to prepare yourself. One of the great things about Australia is we are very much a farming people. Our people understand that when they plant, they are getting ready for the Summer and the harvest. They then naturally store something for the Winters. I think that many business people, (mainly the younger ones), have grown up in such good economic times – they have only been in business maybe ten years. All they have seen is good times, so when the bad times come, they forget. "Hang on! We were supposed to put away a little bit for this time."

Linda: Brad, talk about some of the mentors you have had in your life.

Brad Sugars: Mentors are very important. I found that some of the greatest mentors I ever had were my parents. My mom is a real book-smart lady and she gave me a lot of that book – or – educational intelligence. My dad on the hand, is a real street-smart type of guy. He has the common sense. I learned a lot from him about philosophy of life, and how to think through things. The most important concept he taught me was to back myself. So, if you get into a situation where you have to make a decision, go with your own instincts. Go with your own feeling on it. Because nine times out of ten, you will make it work if it is your own decision. Whereas, if you go with someone else's decision, you will probably let it fly.

Also, when I was sixteen years of age, the Rotary Foundation, a worldwide organization, sponsored me in the "Rotary Youth Leadership Awards." They took me away for a week and taught me all about leadership. It really sparked me; I got into that whole learning thing. I also went to a Jim Rohn seminar. I know many people know of Jim Rohn, but I was just sixteen – and it was a $400 seminar. That was a lot of money for a sixteen-year-old kid, and I had to make it myself. My parents didn't give me the money. There was one thing that Jim said to me that really stood out. "If you work harder on yourself than you do on your job; if you build a library and every single day of your life you read another book, you will become a much better person, and life will get easier." I think the Rotary Youth Leadership and the Jim Rohn seminar were probably a couple of turning points for me.

Linda: Brad, I am sure you would agree that "the right mindset" is one of the things that the create highly successful people. You had the mindset at sixteen to invest $400 in a seminar. It was your own money. What was your thought process? Why did you chose to invest that money and go to the program?

Brad Sugars: I think to be totally honest, my assumption at sixteen was that I had no idea what I was doing so I better go and learn. Unfortunately, many people get to be much older and they are not naive enough to succeed. What I mean is that when you get to the age of thirty, forty, fifty, sixty, you're supposed to know what to do. You get it in your head that, "I'm an older guy, or an older gal, and I should know what I am doing." Well, I was lucky enough that I started when I was sixteen. I was naive enough to realize that I didn't know anything, so I better go and learn from the masters. That's where a lot of people fall down. They get this whole "I know" philosophy. The fastest way to kill yourself in learning and growing is to say you know anything. Teenagers get it, but parents seem to hold onto it for some silly reason.

Linda: So, when people in high school and college are in that learning phase – they graduate from high school, they graduate from college – they get out of that learning mindset. This becomes a weakness for people. Is that what you are saying?

Brad Sugars: I would take it one step further. I think when people went through the college or university system, they were not actually learning, they were being schooled. And what they were being schooled in was – to get good jobs, to work the rest of your life, to pay taxes, to be good – and do as you're told. Yet, some of the better schools teach you how to be entrepreneurial and to think for yourself.

I still remember my Dad telling me when he attended University, they went to logic and ethic classes. Today, where has that gone? I think we need to come back to a simple point: "That to succeed in life, the number one key facet is you need to be able to think for yourself." And yet, the majority of us look to others for solutions.

Part of being a mentor, part of mentoring others, and one of the things that I absolutely drum into my coaching team, "Your job is not to do the thinking for your team, your job is to get them thinking." If it isn't our own idea, we are not as empowered or not as passionate about making what we do work. Give your team passion by letting them think up their own ideas.

Linda: Good point! Action International is about coaching business owners. What do you see as the three biggest lessons that businesses need to succeed today?

Brad Sugars: First of all, you are not a carpenter. You are not a hair dresser. You are NOT the person that does the work. You are the owner of the business. You must keep that one thought in the top of your head for the rest of your life...I always told people when I worked with business owners, "When someone comes up to you at a party or a networking function and asks you, "What do you do?" If you answer, ''I am a carpenter," or whatever your professional business is, then you have limited your ability. I always answer with, "I am an entrepreneur. Currently I am building an X, Y, Z business." It might be a carpentry business, or an insurance agency, or currently I am building a real estate business. Always keep that mindset. This comes back to what I call your identity. The two most powerful words in the English language when combined together are "I am."

Many times I have heard people speak who give themselves negative identities, such as "I am poor." So, I think the most important idea would be to get it straight in your head what your new identity is. "I am a business owner, therefore I am building something that runs without me."

My definition of a business is a commercial, profitable enterprise that works without me. If I have to be there, I've built myself a job. So my entire aim is to build it so it can work without me. That doesn't mean I don't do anything. You have to love what you do. I love business coaching, so I still do it. But it can work without me, so I have choices in my life. I don't feel trapped.

The second biggest thing business owners have to learn is team building. A number of business owners I meet have the whole "I can't get good people attitude." When I was twenty one, I said to my Dad, "You know Dad, I can't get any good people in my company." He turned to me and said, "You know Brad, you get the people you deserve." My Dad is a very dry, very blunt man. Sometimes that works with me, other times, it doesn't. But this time it hit me right between the eyes. I realized that if I am an atrocious leader then I get really bad people. So I have to learn to be a great leader and then I will attract top people. I have to build an awesome company that attracts awesome people. Have a vision. If I run a poor business, I will attract poor people to my business. So that whole leadership and team-building aspect is vital to running a business and being successful.

And a third major point a business owner must learn is how to bring in new business. Whether that means bringing in new clients, or bringing them back to buy more, or to have better sales strategies, it is fundamental. Anybody can cost-cut. But you cannot cost-cut your way to riches, it's as simple as that. If you want a wealthier business, you have to either bring in more business, or get more profitability from your team. You may even hire better people who can get more profitability for you. It's really that growth aspect of a business that our coaches focus on for business owners.

Linda: Brad, what do you see as some of the reasons for business failing? Some succeed and some fail. They may be in the same market, sell the same exact product. One fails and one succeeds. What do you see as some of the main differences?

Brad Sugars: We can spend weeks on this one subject alone. When I can sit down and compare two businesses in the same market, I look at attitudinal things. I start by looking at the mindset stuff. The reason I do that is how your mind works will determine where you start. I teach a very simple formula. It's "We Do Have." You are not a human having or a human doing, you are a human being. So who you are is vital to what you do and what you will have. One aspect that could determine the success or failure is your attitude.

The second aspect, and most probable of the two, is the knowledge of the person running the business. If a business owner is having trouble in sales, he'd better learn more about sales. If he is having problems in finance, he better learn about finance. If he is having problems in team-building, he'd better learn more team-building. See, when I talk to business owners, unfortunately, they have been taught to be specialists. You may be the best brain transplant surgeon in the world. While that's a great advantage to you, it is also a double-edged sword, as are most things in life. So your biggest advantage also can be your biggest disadvantage. That advantage might get that doctor a whole bunch of new business, it also means that doctor has to go to work every day to make money. What I look at is the knowledge base.

I believe that our job as business owners is not to be a specialist but to be a generalist. To be good enough in all areas of business so that you can ask the right questions of the people you employ to run that segment of your business. You need to understand that one simple principle. (I'll teach it to you in a very scientific methodology.) There is a law called the "Second Law of Thermonuclear Dynamics." The simple explanation: if you look at a tree that is outside your office right now (if you are sitting inside, just imagine your potted plant or tree in your office), that tree can not stop growing. Yes, that tree can stop growing, but then it will be dying.

The same is true for human beings in businesses, and life. It is a law, it is a scientific fact. If it is not growing, it is dying. My martial arts instructor used to say to me "The best form of defense is offense." Ever seen a football team go out after half-time to protect their lead? They always lose. So a business owner who is not looking to grow, is going to die. That's what differentiates two businesses in the market place. One is trying to hold it steady, one is trying to grow.

Linda: When it comes to marketing, what can companies do right now to get more customers?

Brad Sugars: Getting more customers is one of the common fallacies of business. The reality of it is, we don't focus on more customers first, we focus on the fundamentals. What are the average dollar sales to the customers you are getting right now? Are you selling enough to people who are walking through the door? Number two (this is what I call my "five ways to build a business)", is from my book *Instant Cash Flow*. How many times does a current customer come back to buy from you? Now if you say to me, "I only sell one thing, one at a time, or I'm a real estate agent, and my clients don't buy a house more than once every seven years." Well, then, wait a minute, you need to rethink what business you are in and how you can start to build that business from a point of view where you can bring that customer back time, after time, after time.

The next area that we look at is the profitability of the company. You know, most of our customers, most business owners – the biggest challenge they have is not charging enough for what they do. Their profitability is so low, there is very little chance of them making a profit. If you are reading this today, and you have a business, I want you to do one favor for yourself. Nine times out of ten, one of the first strategies to implement is to increase your prices ten percent across the board except on your top one or two lines. Do your realize that ninety percent of your customers will never notice? If you think they are going to notice, you need to learn more about marketing.

But, the reality of it is, you can get that profitability up (that's area number three by the way, not area number one.) We look at the average dollar sale, the number of transactions, then the profitability. Then gang, we go back to the first area: bringing in more leads. And before we get you more leads, we look at how can we convert the leads to clients.

You can run a $10,000 advertising campaign, bring in one hundred new leads, but if you don't sell to any of them, then it is a complete waste. You must measure these things. Let me tell you two simple secrets of marketing. Marketing is math: if the numbers work, it is good marketing. I don't believe in all this creativity around marketing. I am an accountant by training, so I am an accountant in marketing. If the numbers don't work, it is bad marketing.

The number two secret I want to tell: test and measure everything you do! For example, my wife owns a beauty salon. One of the things we just did is devise a new marketing campaign. But instead of running only one advertisement, we ran six different advertisements; and we tested the results of each one. One of them got twelve times, or twelve hundred percent more than the others. Guess which one we are still running? If you test and measure, you can get more results.

There are seventy-eight different strategies for lead generation for a business. The challenge is most business owners are only using two or three of them. The top strategy I would recommend is referrals. It is one of the fastest ways to grow a business. It has been called everything from a host parasite to a host beneficiary relationship. I just call it a mass referral from the clients you are dealing with.

Linda: Brad, can you give us one example of that?

Brad Sugars: I'll give you a real simple one on that. I had a ladies fashion store. We sold high-end ladies' fashion. We found out by doing a survey of our customers that more than sixty percent of the ladies who shopped in our store drove either BMW's or Mercedes automobiles. So guess whose database I wanted to have? It ended up we did a deal with the BMW dealership where I gave away a beautiful silk kimono gown to every lady who ever bought a car from them. We gave away over six hundred silk kimono gowns. When I say gave away, I bought them in Hong Kong for $16 a piece. What you need to understand in marketing; it is all about the acquisition cost of obtaining a client. What I mean by that is – if I spend $100 on an ad and I got one client – that client cost me $100. The math just works out like that. In the instance when I just give away something I know for every client I get through the door, it will cost me $16. That is one of the fundamentals of marketing. If you can control what it will cost to obtain a client, you can absolutely, every single time, plan your marketing from that cost basis, so that it will always be profitable.

We gave away over six hundred free silk kimono gowns. The average lady who came into the shop to collect the free silk kimono spent $450 in the store while she

www.mentorsmagazine.com

was there. Anyone quick with math will know that was an extremely profitable campaign for us.

I'll give you another example. A jewelry store gave away a voucher for a free hair cut at a local beauty salon to all of their past customers. Consequently, the beauty salon got all these new customers who bought high-end jewelry. Then the beauty salon gave out vouchers for free jewelry cleaning at the same jewelry store. So the jewelry store was introduced to the hair salon's top clientele. It's about businesses getting together who have similar target audiences; sharing their databases, and sharing the relationship they have built with those customers.

Linda: Brad, are there some simple keys to getting and keeping good people in the current market?

Brad Sugars: Yes, they're the same keys you use in any market. I have six keys for building a winning team and I will run through them for you.

1. Strong Leadership. No company ever succeeded with a weak leader at the helm. That's not strong management. You manage resources, you lead people.

2. A Common Goal. I've been lucky enough in my life to meet General Norman Schwarzkopf twice. He taught me one extremely valuable lesson. He said when he was in Vietnam, he was given a three by five card that he kept in his top pocket. On it were the seventeen politically correct reasons he was in Vietnam. But, when he went to the Gulf, he told all of his soldiers – whether they were Australian, British or French – one common goal: "To kick Saddam out of Kuwait." He said by having that one common goal, the team succeeded much faster. In business or any team you are building, strong leadership, and a common goal.

3. You've got to have set rules of the game. What are your rules of playing? If you want to understand the rules of the game, take a look on Action International's website, www.action-international.com. We have Twelve Points of Culture that are our rules of the game for playing our business. They are important because when most people join a company, all the rules are unwritten. What happens is you only learn the rules after you make a mistake – people don't enjoy being in that environment. For an example: say I dropped you from a helicopter...and when we landed, you were blindfolded. You didn't have any idea where you were. I put you in the middle of a massive ten-acre field.

Would you start running? No, because you are blindfolded, you don't know where the boundaries are, so you don't run. Whereas, in my companies, when people join, they know the boundaries. Therefore they start running from day one.

4. You must have an Action Plan. Who is doing what by when? If we don't know what we are doing, who is doing it, and who is responsible... we are dead meat.

5. Support Risk-Taking. Most business owners and most teams don't support risk-taking. I have watched a football team try a new concept in a game. The coach supports them taking a risk because he knows that is the only way the team can grow. The same is true in business. If you are not making mistakes in business, then you are failing. Because if you're not making mistakes – you are not trying anything new.

6. There must be one hundred percent involvement and one hundred percent inclusion. It is up to each team member to be responsible to involve themselves. But it is up to the team leader to include those not involved up to that point in time. I have a simple analogy for that. Here in Australia, we have the Rugby World Cup happening right now. A rugby team is fifteen players who run on the field. What happens if five of those people are really there just to make up the numbers? They are not really contributing anything. What's the total score of that team for how many are playing? Well, you have to remember, you are either growing or dying. You are a positive or a negative. You can't be a zero. What we're saying is that there are ten running out there trying their best. There's five not doing the best they can: really doing nothing. They're just there to make up numbers. Most business owners would describe those employees as they are "doing just enough to get by." The reality is those five employees are a negative score. You have plus ten, minus five. Your total team score is only five playing. There is no synergy, and therefore that team cannot create massive results.

Linda: Do you have some tips for time management?

Brad Sugars: Yes, change the wording of it to self-management. You cannot stop that clock from going around. You can manage yourself much better; do the things that are most important and urgent. Stephen Covey said in his book Seven Habits, put a very simple balance in there. "The urgency versus the important. If you are doing a task because it is urgent but it is not important, then you are wasting your time." Most business owners I meet lack the discipline to do what they should be doing.

Let's say I am playing baseball and I am the third-base guy. My job is to stay on third base. If I go out and try to catch a ball in the outfield because the outfielder doesn't seem to be performing well that day, then who is on third base? Nobody? So you have to do the role assigned to you. That comes back to the action plan I was talking about. If you know who is doing what, then it is okay. You can do your job and you won't have to do others.

Most business owners don't have enough trust in their team because they haven't set up the systems for their employees to do a good job. Therefore, business owners end up running around in circles – a managerial approach – where they are putting out fires. They're lacking in time, not because they don't have enough time, but because they are doing everyone else's job. Look, if the employees are not good enough to do their jobs, get rid of them. Hire someone that is good enough to do their job.

www.mentorsmagazine.com

Try to keep a time log for one or two weeks. What did I do this week? What were the top five things that chewed up hours from my week? Because you have to keep a balance. If you sum it up: you get about four thousand weeks in life. That's about eight years of age, at about fifty weeks a year. I know some of you are sitting there saying, "That is not very motivating." Well, it's not. Some of you have already done two thousand and five hundred weeks. It's going to be a challenge for you. But look at this from a simple viewpoint. If you are doing tasks that are unleveraged, or that you should be paying someone else to do: then you are wasting your life.

A prime example of that: people who I meet that wash their own car, or mow their own lawn, or wash their own clothes. They do this stuff and say, "Well, Brad, I do this because I like it." Well, what is your time worth? I'll give a simple scenario. Say your time is worth $50 an hour. That's all. Then from now on, for the rest of your life, you are not allowed to do a task that you can pay someone else less than $50 per hour to do. It frees up a minimum ten to fifteen hours a week of your life. You can either invest that time in your kids, or your spouse, or your business. Do the things you should be doing. We never, ever, ever succeed by doing it all on our own. Many business owners I meet have this mindset, "No one can do it as well as I." You're right, no one can, no one ever will. But what would you rather have? One hundred percent of your own results, or the results of one hundred people doing it at eighty percent of what you can do? To give you the Math, that's one times one hundred or eighty times one hundred. Eighty percent of one hundred people is still better than one person at one hundred percent. You have got to be sure that you have employees doing jobs for you that really aren't worth your time to do. There's a balance you have to keep there. I always say that the moment I can afford half of an employee's salary, or half of his wage – I employ him. Because I know that the employee coming on-board will generate the other half.

Linda: What do you think is the secret between business success and life success?

Brad Sugars: Number one, there is no such thing as secrets to business or life success. Everything is written in a book somewhere or recorded on a tape. From the days when Vic Nightingale started recording and from the days of all of this stuff, there's no such thing as a secret to success anymore. George S. Clason wrote *The Richest Man in Babylon* for us all to read decades ago. The challenge is, "Will you read it?" So, if I take a look at the principles of success, that would be more my philosophy. The principles are:

1. There's only one reason to be in business, to create a profit. Yes, you have to create outcomes. Yes, you can add value to the world. Yes, you can do all that. But, if you are not running at a profit, you cannot do any of the other things. You cannot employ people. You cannot change lives; you cannot add a value in a product or service. You cannot innovate. You cannot create new products: you cannot, cannot, cannot. So first and foremost in business, run at a profit.

2. Start digging for gold and start filling pans. Let me explain, when the gold miners first started hurrying out to the gold rush; everyone ran out and started looking for pans. Levi Strauss sat on the sidelines and said, "Hey, you know, if I sell a pair of jeans to every person digging for gold here, I am going to make a fortune." Likewise with the Internet gold mine that came in. The people on the sidelines are the ones that made all the money from it. When everyone hurries out to dig for gold: you should be selling them the pan. All these different analogies that we draw from teach the same principle.

3. Your knowledge is key. If you're not building knowledge, it is a complete waste of your time. Your business only grows as far as you do. The old saying "You grow to your level of incompetence," really brings that one to the forefront.

Life success... I think the key is: define what success is for you.

Success for me is spending an hour on the beach with my two-year-old daughter. Digging a sand castle with her – that's success for me. However, to define success overall, I have to add all the other categories in my life. Life is not just family, it is not just business. It is also about health, it's also about community, it is also about prosperity. It is about ALL of these different areas we have in life. To define success as just one of those irresponsible to yourself, and to those close to you. One of the major keys for me: I am an "AND" person, not an "OR" person. I meet many people who think you can have love or success, spirituality or money. Well, hang on a second...I live in an abundant world! That's why the vision of Action International is: A company of world abundance through business re-education. Abundance to me is the mindset that we are allowed to have all this other stuff, and we add value to the world. That's what it comes down to. Define your success. Define what it is.

I use a simple analogy. It is this: If you and I were to go down to the water's edge and we dove on in... Then if I grabbed you by the throat, and pulled you under the water until you were almost drowning... Do you want to get above the water, or do you absolutely have to? Do you need to? The answer is simple. You NEED to get above it. My question to everyone is, "Do you want to be successful, do you want to be wealthy?" Or, "Do you need to be successful, do you need to be wealthy? If you do need to, who do you need to be successful for? Just for yourself? What about for others? Who else do you need to be successful for? Why else do you need to be that person or need to be successful? The moment you determine a strong enough "WHY?" All of the "HOWS" will show up.

Linda: What drives you to continue to go out and do what you do?

Brad Sugars: Probably three things.

1. I love what I do. The old saying, "If you can do what you love, your vocation will be a vacation." I love seeing the results we achieve with business owners. When we go to a business owner who is struggling – and twelve months later their business is flying... I love what I do! Now they are working only twenty hours a week. I get a letter saying, "Hey Brad, you've never met me. I am working with one of your coaches in Wisconsin. But I just wanted to say thanks." That for me is one of the major incentives for why I do what I do.

2. I think it is in your **blood. As a human being you know if you are designed to** be someone who succeeds and leads. If that's who you believe you are, then those of you reading this today, I know that's in your blood as well, because you are reading this article. If it wasn't you, then you wouldn't be interested in all the concepts above. When it is in your blood to do it, it's in your blood to do it. It is an integral part of who you are. It is an important part of who I am.

3. I tried retirement once and it was awful. It is not fun. I was twenty six years of age. I had promised myself when I was seventeen that I would set a goal to retire at twenty-five. The day before my twenty-sixth birthday, my team came into my office, packed me, locked my door, changed the clocks, put all my stuff in a box, left it out at the front office. They said, "You are no longer allowed back into this office. You said you are going to retire. You can. You're financially able to retire; the company runs without you. Get out." So I left. I started playing golf. My handicap got down to nine: so I was in the single digits. I was playing three rounds of golf a day. I was playing with seventy-five-year-old guys. They were all standing around, waiting to fall off the perch. I was thinking to myself: "Man, this is not what it's cracked up to be." So, I did what any sane man would do. I rehired myself! I'm no longer retired. I'm rehired. But...I'm financially retired. I don't ever have to work again.

I love what I do so much: I enjoy it. You cannot retire if you are a successful person. You can't stop, you have to keep the brain active. I work a lot less now because I have two beautiful daughters. I spend a lot more time with them and my wife now than I did previously. I couldn't give this "family time" up for the world.

Linda: Brad, there are hundreds of people reading this interview all over the world. If there are business owners reading this article right now, and they want to ask your company to help them, what do they need to do to get started?

Brad Sugars: Getting our company to help them is really easy. Make a phone call, or jump on the Internet, or send a fax. If you are in business right now, and you want to start succeeding, then you must start to focus. Write down the twenty things you know you should be doing, you know you're not doing, and begin. The challenge is though, to get yourself the discipline necessary to succeed. Where and who does it come from? My coaches have coaches. I have coaches. We all need a mentor. The challenge in business is finding a coach suitable to mentor you. That's why we started Action International. We are in forty eight countries, with over five hundred business coaches doing this day-in-and-day-out, keeping business owners on track.

Linda: What type of business owner is a good client for you? Who is a good fit?

Brad Sugars: A good fit is an owner/operator. We find that it is more their attitude that makes a good fit, rather than a specific business type or size. We work with everything from a micro-business doing $100,000 or less a year – up to a $100 million company. We try to stay clear of the multinationals. The owner/operators are really who we get the best results with, because they don't have to go to a committee to get permission to utilize the ideas they conceptualize. We can get quicker results in that way. That's why we specialize in that market.

Linda: What about Industry?

Brad Sugars: With five hundred coaches around the world, you name the industry and we have a coach who has either owned it, worked in it, ran it, coached it, or dealt with it for ten years. The strangest business we have ever dealt with was one that does glamour trekking. I don't think anyone has worked with a weirder business than that. If you know of one, give us a call, we'd have to take on a good challenge.

So, when people want to get started, I think Tony Robbins said it best, "When is now a good time?" It's very easy to say, "I'll start tomorrow." It's very difficult to say I will start NOW! It's also very difficult to stay disciplined to what you need to do. We all know what we need to do. By having a coach, you will do what you need to, and also, you will gain the knowledge you need. I think success for a business owner (and for those choosing to start their own business) is getting off on the right foot with a coach. That is far better than wasting two to three years of your life struggling, by yourself, to accomplish these ideas. I would say to all business owners, if you want to succeed, whether you can't a coach or not; read my books, watch all the DVDs, learn the concepts. I'm not trying to promote myself. I just want people to understand that to succeed you have to be pushed on the right paths, and you have to grow.

For me, it come down to a gentleman named Ilene Pritagean who won the Nobel Science Prize for his study on a concept called perturbation. Perturbation is a simple process that says for anyone to grow, pressure must be applied. It follows, that for anything to grow, pressure must be applied. For example, to turn coal into a diamond, the pressure applied is massive. In order for a business owner to grow, you cannot just have the pressure of the bank manager, your team members, your husband, or wife. You have to get positive pressure. Someone who will pull you along with them, and you will improve with their help. It is a key to growth. If there is no pressure, there is no growth.

Linda: Any final thoughts you'd like to share with the group?

Brad Sugars: Yes. I have to do a little plug for Action International and our coaches. I have been helping businesses grow now for ten years. I've watched our coaches work with business owners. We have CDs full of testimonials from our clients and books full of examples of our clients' successes. If anyone reading this article does not have a mentor for your business, I want you to be certain to get one. If you are contemplating becoming a coach or are currently a mentor, wanting more structure and more profits from this: go the website and have a chat with my team. We run this business in such a way that every person that come to it adds value to it, and also learns from it. Please, make sure that you check it out. At the very least, you can order all my books from www.BradSugars.com. Do yourself a favor and do some research.

Now, some last points to learn. Three things:

1. To add to a point I brought up earlier... Jim Rohn said, "Never wish life were easier. Wish you were better." That is the essence of how we grow and succeed in life.

2. Business truly is a simple thing. That doesn't mean it is easy. If you are struggling with business, it is because you are lacking knowledge in some arena. There may be many arenas in which you are lacking knowledge. What my business coaches do is make business simple. I even have a board game named "Leverage." It teaches you how to make sure you succeed in business, how to build a business that runs without you. But, that doesn't mean it is always easy.

3. If success were easy, then everyone would be doing it. If you are struggling at times, that is a good sign you are on your way. Most people that go out there to do these concepts see a problem. But, I call it an opportunity. It really is! A problem is just an opportunity disguised as a learning situation. It will be either a stepping stone or a rock in your shoe. Either way, you go after it! Really keep in mind that life is not a one-year plan.

What I mean by that is too many of us overestimate what we can achieve in one year; but underestimate what we can do in ten. For example, some people say they want to dominate in industry. Well, dominating an industry is a ten-year plan, not a one-year plan. The concept is it will be a lot easier to follow the plan of someone who has already done it than trying to redesign the plan yourself. Learn, grow and master so you can help others on your team so that life will be your oyster!

Linda: Those of you reading this interview who want more information from Brad or his company, can go to www.Action-International.com.

Brad Sugars: For those business people in the North American market, you can go to a site that lists our coaches, you can go to www.action-international.com. It is the fastest way to find them. To find and order my books, go to www.bradsugars.com.

Thanks from Australia and I say, "Good Day."

INVEST IN
YOUR SUCCESS...

Tapes, Books, Boot Camps, Seminars,
Newsletters and Coaching from our
WALKING WITH THE WISE II
contributors are available at:
www.mentorsmagazine.com

Move Forward with Boldness
on Your Quest
and Mighty Forces
Will Come to Your Aid

© 2004 Kim Muslusky

MENTORS Magazine Motto